TONY CANZONERI

TONY CANZONERI

The Boxing Life of a Five-Time World Champion

Mark Allen Baker

McFarland & Company, Inc., Publishers
Jefferson, North Carolina

LIBRARY OF CONGRESS CATALOGUING-IN-PUBLICATION DATA

Names: Baker, Mark Allen, author.
Title: Tony Canzoneri : the boxing life of a five-time world champion / Mark Allen Baker.
Description: Jefferson, North Carolina : McFarland & Company, Inc., Publishers, 2023 |
Includes bibliographical references and index.
Identifiers: LCCN 2023013563 | ISBN 9781476689630 (paperback : acid free paper) ∞
ISBN 9781476649702 (ebook)
Subjects: LCSH: Canzoneri, Tony, 1908-1959. | Boxers (Sports)—United States—Biography.
Classification: LCC GV1132.C36 B35 2023 | DDC 796.83092 [B]—dc23/eng/20230407
LC record available at https://lccn.loc.gov/2023013563

BRITISH LIBRARY CATALOGUING DATA ARE AVAILABLE

ISBN (print) 978-1-4766-8963-0
ISBN (ebook) 978-1-4766-4970-2

Front cover image: promotional photograph
of Tony Canzoneri (author collection)

Printed in the United States of America

*McFarland & Company, Inc., Publishers
Box 611, Jefferson, North Carolina 28640
www.mcfarlandpub.com*

For Matthew Robert Baker (1970–2021)
The glass I thought was half full is now empty,
The heart I thought was strong is now broken,
The brother I thought I have I now had,
I will miss you the rest of my life.

Table of Contents

Acknowledgments

Voltaire once quipped, "Appreciation is a wonderful thing. It makes what is excellent in others belong to us as well." My gratitude to everyone associated with this title at McFarland.

Those who know me understand my proud association with the International Boxing Hall of Fame in Canastota, New York. My service has been rewarding because of so many wonderful individuals associated with the museum, especially Edward P. Brophy, executive director. I would also like to acknowledge Jeffrey S. Brophy for his outstanding research and ongoing friendship.

This book would not have been possible without the assistance of the Library of Congress. Chronicling America, a website providing access to select digitized newspaper pages and produced by the National Digital Newspaper Program, was another outstanding source. Adding to my periodical research was newspapers.com by Ancestry, which filled the gaps left behind by other sources.

The International Boxing Research Organization (IBRO) was organized in May 1982 for the express purpose of establishing an accurate history of boxing; compiling complete and precise boxing records; and facilitating the dissemination of boxing research information and cooperating in safeguarding the individual research efforts of its members by application of the rules of scholarly research. As an organization, it has been successful because when needed, its people and data are there. Thank you to my fellow IBRO members.

Living in the state of Connecticut, I am fortunate to have a great support system. My gratitude to all the independent bookstores in Connecticut for supporting local authors, especially Bank Square Books in Mystic. Larry Dasilva (Nutmeg TV), Wayne Norman (WILI–AM), Roger Zotti (*The Resident*, IBRO), the Authors Guild, IBRO, *Journal Inquirer*, and *USA Boxing New* (Alex and John Rinaldi), thank you for your inspiration and advocacy of my work.

There are many talented individuals, in and around the sport of boxing, who don't get the credit they deserve. Recognizing this, the state of Connecticut created its own Boxing Hall of Fame located inside Mohegan Sun Resort & Casino in Uncasville. I wish to express my appreciation to everyone associated with the organization for their support.

Strength and inspiration were drawn from my friends and family. My thanks to friends Dana Beck and Brian Brinkman, Mary DeSimone, Steve Ike, Rick Kaletsky, Ann and Mark Lepkowski, and Jim Risley.

To my family, Marilyn Allen Baker, Aaron, Sharon, Elliott and Tyler Baker, Elizabeth, Mark, Paisley and Monroe Taylor, and Rebecca Baker: thank you for your love and support. To Richard Long, my wonderful father-in-law, who has always been a second in my corner: I am grateful for your support.

In loving memory of Ford William Baker, James Buford Bird, Flavil Q. Van Dyke III, Deborah Jean Long, David Arthur Mumper, Nancy L. Allen, Richard Alan Long, Thomas P. Allen, and Matthew Robert Baker.

To my wife Alison, I will modify a quote from Jane Austen: "Dare not say that man forgets sooner than woman, that his love has an earlier death, or any death at all."

Preface

I'll say it for you: It's about time somebody wrote a biography of Tony Canzoneri. Honestly speaking, I hope there are many more. As an elite fighter and multiple division champion, he deserves it.

Confident, energetic, and indefatigable, this compact and stylish fighter would constantly pressure his opponent. His intimidating, low-held, lethal left was like a land mine waiting for the slightest bit of pressure to detonate. His majesty atop a canvas was so impressive that many of those who followed him into the ring mimicked his style, including Lou Ambers and the incomparable Willie Pep. Cocky? You bet, as losses were a rarity.

This is my 27th book, fifth biography, and 10th boxing title. As with my biographies of Oscar "Battling" Nelson, Abe Attell, Lou Ambers, and Willie Pep, I was dismayed by the lack of recognition given to the subject. Utilizing the Library of Congress's Chronicling America newspaper database in an informal search, I determined that from the apex of his career in 1936 to his final bout in 1939, Tony Canzoneri's appearance in newspapers (popularity/searches) had only dropped about 17 percent. He remained a very favored and noteworthy individual. But by his death in 1959 at the age of 51, his appearances had fallen to 9 percent of what they were in 1936. From this point forward it plunged—in 1970, it was less than 1 percent of what it was back in 1936. Tony Canzoneri had essentially disappeared from the media's radar screen.[1] With this publication, I hope to change that.

Waxing poetic only about Canzoneri's championship battles wasn't an option. An elite boxing career demands a comprehensive appraisal, though I hasten to add that out of respect for the subject and his family, this work focuses on Canzoneri's public life and professional career, relying primarily on contemporaneous accounts of both.

Since early fight films are often incomplete and newspaper accounts can vary, I utilized all available resources to provide an accurate round-by-round assessment of some significant contests.

Introduction

The Ring Prowess of Anthony Canzoneri

For more than six decades, the illustrious ring career of Anthony Canzoneri has been neglected. Reduced to retrospective newspaper columns, periodic magazine rankings, and occasional history books about the sweet science, one of the most colorful and talented figures of the 20th century has faded into obscurity.

Yet when *The Ring* celebrated its centenary by ranking the 100 greatest fighters by performance, there was Anthony Canzoneri, with that trademark smile, at number four. His position yielded only to Sugar Ray Robinson, Joe Louis, and Muhammad Ali.

Author and historian Bert Randolph Sugar, in *Boxing's Greatest Fighters*, ranks Tony Canzoneri number 12. Ahead of him are the likes of Sugar Ray Robinson, Henry Armstrong, Willie Pep, Joe Louis, Harry Greb, Benny Leonard, Muhammad Ali, Roberto Duran, Jack Dempsey, Jack Johnson, and Mickey Walker.

Think about that for a second. The average fight fan can recall the accomplishments of Robinson, Louis, or Ali with little difficulty. Yet few could tell you why Tony Canzoneri, a compact fighting machine, was considered for any list, let alone what weight class he fought in or whom he fought.

A product of superior genetics, this son of Italian immigrants appeared destined to be a meat cutter or cartoonist rather than a boxer. Since his father oversaw a small grocery store in a comfortable New Orleans neighborhood, Tony Canzoneri was guaranteed both a trade and a hot meal (assuming he was faster with the serving spoon than his five siblings).

Giorgio Canzoneri, the family patriarch, enjoyed the sport of boxing. When Tony's older brother, Joseph, tested his skills in the ring, he was given the support and encouragement of his father. With the door to the sweet science open, Tony also walked through. Heroes of the day were boxers, athletes such as Pete Herman, world bantam champion, who as fate had it lived only a few blocks away. Proximity to opportunity, as everyone understood, was a key to success.

Instruction, from his brother or a trainer in the gym, pacified the observant youngster. If an opportunity arose to be in the company of Herman, he took it. Not yet a teenager, he forged his skills at the local club before embarking on a noteworthy amateur career.

The first major disruption in Tony Canzoneri's boxing world, or so it was perceived by the youngster, was his parents' decision to move to New York City. Heartbroken at the thought of starting over, Tony didn't know what to do. That's when Pete

Herman—convinced Canzoneri was a future standout—came to his rescue by penning a letter of introduction to Sammy Goldman, his former manager.

Seeking out Sammy Goldman, the compact teenager lied about his age, but certainly not about his skills. Convinced that Pete Herman was correct, the veteran boxing manager mentored the youth. By the summer of 1925, Tony Canzoneri held three amateur titles—New York State, metropolitan and junior national. Fighting at 112 pounds, he was unmatched in his division. He wisely worked to Goldman's timeline and not his own, and an opening-round knockout at the Rockaway Club marked his professional debut on July 24, 1925. Tony Canzoneri's pugilistic journey to immortality had begun.

Defeating boxing legend Johnny Dundee and Bud Taylor (in the pair's rubber match) gave Canzoneri claim to the featherweight title in 1927, even though there was one more mountain to climb. With a record of more than 45 victories against three losses and seven draws, Tony Canzoneri defeated the hard-hitting Benny Bass in a close split decision to capture the undisputed world featherweight championship.

Although no boxer under age 21 was permitted to fight for the title in New York State, Tony Canzoneri kept his crown. And wore it proudly. In his first defense of the title, he took a split decision loss to Frenchman André Routis on September 28, 1928. He had won and lost a major title before the rules even permitted.

Flat-nosed and exuberant, Tony Canzoneri, whose appearance yielded comparisons to a miniature Babe Ruth, watched as his popularity soared. With his trademark smile and handsome countenance, he melted more hearts of the opposite sex than Rudolph Valentino. Admiring teenagers cut out his photographs from newspapers and magazines and pinned them to their bulletin boards. He had Frank Sinatra's look seven years before the Hoboken crooner was born.

Setting his sights next on the lightweight division, Canzoneri knew things wouldn't be easy. Still, that was the title he most sought. A split decision loss to Sammy Mandell on August 2, 1929, for the world lightweight title was a setback, as was a non-title loss to Jack Kid Berg five months later. Nonetheless, Canzoneri rebounded and put together a string of 10 consecutive victories before losing to Billy Petrolle on September 11, 1930. Unruffled by defeat, the boxer pressed onward. In his next bout, on November 14, 1930, Canzoneri knocked out Al Singer at the 1:06 mark of the opening round. The breathtaking victory garnered the world lightweight championship. He was making it look easy.

On April 24, 1931, Tony Canzoneri knocked out Jack Kid Berg to pick up the NBA world lightweight title along with the NBA world junior welterweight title. In a rematch with Berg, he successfully defended both titles on September 10, 1931. He did the same against Kid Chocolate on November 20, 1931. Often forgotten regarding the latter: Had Canzoneri made 130 pounds for this bout, he would have been awarded Kid Chocolate's junior lightweight title as well and would have become the first four-division champion in history.

A loss to Johnny Jadick on January 18, 1932, cost Canzoneri the world junior welterweight crown. Thankfully, his prized lightweight crown remained intact. In a magnificent performance (perhaps his best), Tony Canzoneri successfully defended his lightweight title against slugger Billy Petrolle on November 4, 1932. Regaining the world junior welterweight crown by defeating Battling Shaw, he once again held multiple titles.

It was time to fill his pockets in 1933. Sammy Goldman booked his champion for back-to-back stadium bouts against Barney Ross. Two decision losses cost him his title but in retrospect little else. He quickly got back on track, and when Ross vacated the lightweight title in 1935, Canzoneri was there. Taking a 15-round unanimous decision over Lou Ambers, his former sparring partner, he became the first to regain the world lightweight championship.

The lightweight champion was on his game and compiled 11 consecutive victories—over contenders such as Frankie Klick, Joe Ghnouly, Johnny Jadick, and Jimmy McLarnin—before his first title defense. Lou Ambers took Canzoneri's title, then confirmed the verdict in a 1937 rematch. Big losses always derailed "Canzy," but he quickly got back on track. He won 10 consecutive victories before taking a tough loss to Eddie Brink in the spring of 1939. That year, he experienced five consecutive bouts without a victory (0–3–2). Having never undergone such a disappointment, the elite pugilist was concerned.

Washed up? Canzoneri didn't think so. To bury the comments, he wanted one more big opportunity. And he got it. Six consecutive victories landed him at Madison Square Garden for the final time. The venue had always been a proving ground for his ring prowess, so why not now? A victory over Al "Bummy" Davis, the "hottest" fighter in boxing, would either bury his critics or bury him. It would be the latter. At the conclusion of the fight, there was only silence as the damaged and defeated figure of Anthony Canzoneri, one of the most popular fighters ever, walked to his dressing room for the final time. The man who fought 18 world champions, multiple Hall of Fame members, and a plethora of rated contenders had left nothing on the table.

Having won the lightweight championship, junior welterweight championship, and featherweight championship, Tony Canzoneri had few peers: *The Ring* magazine named Canzoneri, along with Barney Ross, fighter of the year for 1934; Jimmy Cannon, the popular syndicated columnist, believed there wasn't a boxer alive in 1953 who could give Tony Canzoneri a decent fight; in 1954, boxing historian Oscar "Fearless" Fraley compiled his list of the best 10 fighters in the last 35 years: Jack Dempsey, Henry Armstrong, Benny Leonard, Sugar Ray Robinson, Joe Louis, Harry Greb, Mickey Walker, Gene Tunney, Rocky Marciano, and Tony Canzoneri; in 1956, Barney Ross, no introduction needed, ranked Tony Canzoneri the top lightweight fighter of the past 30 years; in 1959, Nat Fleischer named Tony Canzoneri the seventh-greatest lightweight ever—ahead of him were Joe Gans, Benny Leonard, Owen Moran, Freddy Welsh, Battling Nelson, and George Kid Lavigne; in 1999, the Associated Press ranked Tony Canzoneri as the fourth-best featherweight, the third-best lightweight, and the third-best junior welterweight of the 20th century; Tony Canzoneri was inducted into *The Ring* magazine's Boxing Hall of Fame in 1956 and the International Boxing Hall of Fame in 1990; and the September 2001 issue of *The Ring* magazine ranked Tony Canzoneri as the eighth-greatest lightweight of all time.

After his prestigious boxing career, the colorful gladiator wanted more. The thought of two elite careers in a lifetime was an impossibility to most, but not to Tony Canzoneri. From conducting dance bands to acting, he established himself as a respected entertainer. As a staple in gossip columns, Tony Canzoneri was noted in the company of everyone from Frank Sinatra to Mae West. He partnered up with

Joey Adams and Mark Plant, and the trio packed theaters, clubs, and comedy houses. While his marriage to show girl Rita Roy didn't last, it resulted in Canzoneri's only child, a daughter. Asked days before his death if he had any regrets, he stated that he did not. The past was the past; it was the present he was concerned about. A mere two decades, one month and eight days after his last professional fight, Tony Canzoneri died.

ONE

Birth of a Champion

"The two most important days in your life are the day you are born
and the day you find out why."—Mark Twain

On a crisp autumn morning in 1957, four male college graduates from Binghamton, New York, boarded a train bound for New York City. It was the week before Thanksgiving, and the bustling streets of Manhattan were something they had never experienced. As all four friends had been to the Bronx, and the city skyline was familiar, even if the reality of being there wasn't. The Bronx wasn't Manhattan, but for that matter, what was?

The holiday season filled the air as crowds poured in and out of department stores, jammed sidewalks, and made it nearly impossible for the group to view even a seasonal window display, let alone determine what street they were on. After devouring an overpriced pizza, the group hit the streets in search of the popular haunts frequented by sports celebrities.

As diehard sports fans, they had been to the Polo Grounds and Yankee Stadium, but never had the time, or money, to penetrate Manhattan. Their first destination: Jack Dempsey's Broadway Bar and Restaurant in the Brill Building on Broadway between 49th and 50th streets. They were mesmerized by the sight of the crowded venue. The group managed to find a small space at the racetrack-shaped bar. Ordering drinks, they did their best to blend in with the crowd. But it was hopeless; they had "tourist" written across their foreheads. Gawking at the patrons, they scanned the crowd, looking for a familiar face. Naturally, like everyone else there, they were looking for "The Manassa Mauler." But they didn't see him. The only boxing person they recognized was Robert K. Christenberry. Having recently made an unsuccessful run for mayor, the former NYSAC commissioner was with a group of people waiting for a table. Nevertheless, it excited the quartet. Finishing up their drinks, the group paid their tab and left.

Next stop, Tony Canzoneri's Paddock Bar and Grill at 1634 Broadway, near 50th Street in the Winter Garden building. During the short walk, the quartet shared their disappointment at not seeing Jack Dempsey, but the possibility of encountering Canzoneri was exciting. As soon as the group passed through the front door, they spotted a crowd of folks in one corner. And there he was, Tony Canzoneri. Immediately, one member of the group turned to the others and said, "He does look like Babe Ruth," prompting another member to comment, "How would you know? You never saw 'The Babe' in person." Canzoneri did indeed resemble a compact version of "The Bambino." No longer scaling at 135, the three-division champion was smaller than the group imagined (5'5"). He was moon-faced, pug-nosed, and dressed to the nines, and you could sense that he was somebody even if you didn't know boxing. His trademark smile spanned nearly the width of his countenance, while a cigar dangled and danced from the left corner of his mouth. Among the few women in the bar, not a single female eye left the handsome former champion.

As the group grabbed some drinks, they slowly drifted toward the champion to eavesdrop on the conversation. Noting the action, the experienced host appeared to turn on the charm while boosting the volume. The quartet, who caught a few names such as Barney Ross and Jimmy McLarnin, did their best to discreetly decipher the conversation—although it didn't matter, it reduced their anxiety.

Standing close to one of the most popular figures of the 1920s and 1930s, the gang was star-struck. As one member of the group remarked, "The only fighter more fashionable than Tony Canzoneri was Jack Dempsey." That was why the surname Canzoneri rolled off the tongues of sports fans like the best athletes of the era, including Ruth, Grange, Tilden, and Jones.

At one point, Canzoneri excused himself and headed toward the front door. As he walked by the foursome, he said, "Hi, fellas." Lost for words, only one member of the group managed to mumble, "Hi, Champ." And with that, the former pugilist disappeared among the other patrons. The quartet finished their drinks and left. For the remainder of the evening, and for years to come, the popular fighter was the topic of conversation. He was no longer Tony Canzoneri, simply "Canzy."

Unforgettably, the immensely talented Tony Canzoneri had it: that look, charm and swagger that exuded class. The dames loved him. Popular, the former champion could talk the talk and walk the walk. He was a champion's champion, a man everyone wanted to be around. A glorious figure and a hero who did what heroes were supposed to do.

Strangers in a Strange Land

> Two miles down the river, anchored in midstream, gently swaying and rocking with the tide, her great hulk looming dark in the bright sunlight, lies the steamship *Manilla*. On board this great ship are some 1,300 immigrants, men, women, and children, who have come to this strange country from the sunny shores of Italy to seek their fortune.[1]

From every corner of the ship, passengers pushed to the rails to catch a glimpse of the shore. Many, especially those who had never left Italy, were as curious as they were apprehensive. For those who had relatives in this country, there was a sense of belonging, even if they weren't familiar with the customs or language. It was strength in numbers, or a security blanket, and it was manifested by those with only the clothes on their backs. The unconquerable desire they possessed to get here, they believed, would be enough to reach their dreams.

Considered an economic and commercial hub for the broader Gulf Coast region, New Orleans, with a population of more than 300,000 in 1903, would increase by more than 18 percent during the decade. This ship, like many, would contribute to that growth. *The Times-Democrat*, a local journal, noted their arrival:

> To seek their fortunes—it is so romantic—to them: and there is such a spirit of strange adventure in it—in the great voyage, the mystery, and the uncertainty of coming to a

strange land. For years they have been saving up in their little purses, the pittances which they received for their labor in foreign lands, preparing for the one supreme event—the journey across the Atlantic to the new world, and the purpose has lived before their eyes in vague dreams and in confidential whispers with their fathers, mothers, and sweethearts.[2]

The sight of diminutive skiffs rowing out to the steamship turned to unbridled excitement when those aboard the ship recognized the faces of friends and relatives and frantically waved their arms and shouted greetings in Italian. It was a gratifying vision. Continuing their observations, the *Times-Democrat* confirmed:

> The *Manilla* left Italy on the 17th of last month [September]. Wednesday, at about half past one o'clock, she streamed out of the Gulf and came up the river. She arrived at her anchorage at about 7 o'clock yesterday morning. Her voyage was without mishap. All who came with her, including eleven stowaways, were in the best of health when she lowered her anchor in the waters of the Mississippi.

For the immigrants, the final step of the journey was an examination. One by one, they approached a long table at which sat inspectors, along with an interpreter. They were questioned regarding their mode of living, how much money they had, and if they were free from contract. The systematic process—as long and tedious as it may have been—was a small price to pay for a protracted journey that concluded on October 9, 1903.

A short and casually dressed young man, stout in build, with light brown hair and brown eyes, looked nervous as he approached the table. At 27 years of age, he

A view of Canal Street in New Orleans, Louisiana, ca. 1903 (Library of Congress).

claimed Palazzo Adriano, Città Metropolitana di Palermo, Sicilia, Italy, as his birthplace. Hoping to use his skills as a merchant to make a living, he felt he was in the right place at the right time. Upon conclusion of his interrogation, Giorgio Canzoneri, born on December 20, 1875, took his first steps on American soil.[3]

It wasn't long before Giorgio, or George, caught a glimpse of the beautiful Giuseppa, or Josephine, Schiro, the daughter of Antonio and Rosalia Schiro. Josephine, born in 1884, was living with her uncle in the Sixth Ward of New Orleans. After a short courtship, the pair were married. As a meat cutter, Giorgio kept busy while Josephine tended to the domestic duties. It was a challenging lifestyle but characteristic of the period. Since only New York City had a higher population of Sicilian Americans and Sicilian immigrants than New Orleans, it felt comfortable. It was the perfect environment, so George and Josephine Canzoneri believed, to settle down and start a family.

Anthony Canzoneri was born on November 6, 1908, in Slidell, Louisiana. As the third of six children, he had two older siblings, Lena (1905–1996) and Joseph (1907–1967), and a younger sister, Lillian (Lillie, Lily, 1911–1996), along with two younger brothers, Cyrus (Cy, 1913–1999) and Jasper (Jay, 1916–1985). All the children were born in the state of Louisiana.[4]

The population of Slidell, today considered part of the New Orleans-Metairie-Kenner metropolitan statistical area, was about 2,000 in 1908. The area was undergoing a period of economic and industrial growth thanks to the manufacture of bricks,

A New Orleans milk cart making an early morning delivery, ca. 1903 (Library of Congress).

lumber, and ships. Enhanced by transportation improvements—interstates 10, 12, 59—traversing the Gulf states, it didn't take a rocket scientist to envision the area being swallowed by New Orleans.[5]

Both Giorgio and Josephine stressed the value of hard work and family values by setting an example. All the Canzoneri children respected their parents and, as they got older, marveled at their productivity.

Tony's first memories were of the French Quarter and its exhilarating lifestyle. From 1884 until 1924, nearly 300,000 Italian immigrants, a great number of them from Sicily, arrived in New Orleans and settled in the French Quarter. "Little Palermo," as it was soon nicknamed, took on a flavor all its own. Irish immigrants also settled in the Esplanade area which was called the "Irish Channel."[6] With the common denominator Catholicism, the ethnic mix worked as best it could for the times.

Giorgio opened a grocery store in the Italian section and gradually brought the children into the business. It provided everyone in the family a sense of ownership. For example, when oldest son Joe, who loved boxing, wasn't pounding a heavy bag at a local gym, he was grinding and cutting meat at the market. It was Joe's influence that turned Tony toward the sweet science—the youngster looked up to his older brother. Thankfully, the patriarch of the family seconded the motion.

Pete Herman

The Canzoneri family lived three blocks from the home of former bantamweight champion Pete Herman (Peter Gulotta), aka Kid Herman. Peter Gulotta was born on February 12, 1896, in Convent, Louisiana.[7] Boxing out of the Orleans Athletic Club, he turned professional at the age of 16. Winning only one of his first five battles, he had a rocky start. But Herman quickly turned it around and won eight of his next 10 contests.

Two years after his first bout, he conducted a magnificent performance during a 10-round, no-decision bout against Kid Williams, world bantamweight champion. It happened on June 20, 1914, at the Pelican Stadium in New Orleans. It was a gallant effort even if the bout, in the opinion of the local *Times-Picayune*, was dominated by Williams. Winning eight of his next 10 bouts, Herman remained competitive. He closed out 1915 by defeating fellow New Orleans boxer Eddie Coulon via a fourth-round knockout. Both boxers weighed 116 pounds.

On January 9, 1917, Pete Herman defeated Kid Williams to capture the world bantamweight championship. Taking a 20-round points decision at the Louisiana Auditorium in New Orleans, Herman scored knockdowns in the fifth and 12th frames. Though Williams was the aggressor throughout the fight, Herman had little trouble dodging the former champion's blows. The irony of the event was that Williams selected his own referee, with hopes of getting the nod if the battle was close. Herman had reached the pinnacle of his career and looked unbeatable.

Like many champions of the era, Pete Herman wasn't an advocate of title defenses. But he also didn't avoid quality opposition in the form of Johnny Coulon, Joe Lynch, "Jersey" Frankie Burns, Frankie Mason, "Young" Zulu Kid, and Johnny Ertle.[8]

On December 22, 1920, Pete Herman lost his bantamweight title, via a 15-round unanimous decision, to Joe Lynch at Madison Square Garden. Using his height along with a four-inch reach advantage, Lynch dominated the bout. The following day, Herman, no worse for wear, sailed for London to face the incomparable Jimmy Wilde. Had Herman intentionally lost the Lynch fight so the title would remain in America?[9] Many fight critics believed that was precisely the case.

The Wilde-Herman fight, on January 13, 1921, at Royal Albert Hall in London, was boxing at its finest. Close after 14 rounds, Herman managed to hurt Wilde in the 15th. Fighting with an eight-pound weight advantage, Herman continued to leverage his strength and wear down the legendary Welsh flyweight world champion. Sending Wilde through the ropes three times in the 17th round, Herman put an end to the fight. Afterward, both men said it was the toughest bout of their careers.[10]

On July 25, 1921, Pete Herman decisively defeated Joe Lynch in a rematch for the world bantamweight championship. Both boxers tipped at 116¾ pounds for the Ebbets Field contest. Herman's decisive points victory—many scored 13 of 15 rounds for the Louisiana pug—again fueled speculation that he had thrown the first fight. Despite failing eyesight, Herman forced the fighting right from the opening bell.

Inside Madison Square Garden on September 23, 1921, Pete Herman lost his bantamweight title when he was outpointed by Johnny Buff over 15 rounds. Having compiled a Hall of Fame career with a record of 67–12–8, with 57 no-decisions, Pete Herman retired in 1922.

After his boxing career, Herman, who gradually lost his eyesight, became a successful businessman in New Orleans.

Peter Gulotta, aka Pete Herman, shown here in 1917, was one of the all-time great bantamweight world champions and a mentor to Tony Canzoneri.

The racially segregated neighborhoods where the Canzoneri family lived were prone to contentiousness. To little surprise, seven-year-old Tony was initiated into a gang as a form of protection.

By age 11, Tony was in a boxing ring and garnering accolades. Unlike with some amateur fighters, his father was supportive of the avocation. Giorgio was proud of Tony and frequently bragged of his son's ring prowess. Club owners couldn't pay the amateur boxers who appeared on their fight cards, so many would award the popular boxers prizes such as watches. Later, if a kid needed money, a promoter would buy it back or the fighter would hock it. With each passing bout, Tony's confidence grew.

While it was brother Joe's influence that turned Tony Canzoneri toward the ring, it was Pete

Herman who convinced the talented youth it was the proper direction. The encouragement from the ex-bantamweight champion had a profound impact on Tony Canzoneri. A friendship between the two gradually blossomed, with Pete Herman spending hours instructing his protégé at Joe Mandot's gymnasium.

Another local pug who took an interest in Tony Canzoneri was Basil Galiano.

Basil Galiano

Born in New Orleans in 1903, Basil Galiano (aka Bazilo, also Bazile, Anthony Gagliano) was, as Canzoneri always referred to him, a big shot in the neighborhood. Popular before he even turned to the ring, he saw boxing enhance his reputation.

View of Shibe Park (Stadium), located at 2701 North Twenty-first Street in Philadelphia (Library of Congress), ca. 1930s. Basil Galiano (bottom left) fought at the park on July 16, 1925. Eddie Shea (bottom right) sparred with Canzoneri in 1925. Both are shown here in the 1930s.

Galiano, who began his professional career on January 6, 1919, fought out of the Orleans Athletic Club. Posting a record of 23–2–1 entering 1922, he was improving with each bout. By the end of February 1925, Galiano had held elite fighter Johnny Dundee to a draw and took victories over Pal Moran, Mel Coogan, and Cuddy DeMarco. However, on March 9, 1925, he suffered a devastating points loss to Benny Valger; moreover, it happened during a lightweight title elimination bout held in Madison Square Garden. It was a great opportunity even if it didn't turn out as planned.

Promoter Herman Taylor signed Galiano to an undercard battle at Shibe Park in Philadelphia. Scheduled for July 16, 1925—the main event was Tommy Loughran tackling Jack Delaney—it was a wonderful opportunity. After Galiano defeated Joe Tiplitz in a 10-round unanimous decision, his career spiraled downward. He lost 12 consecutive bouts before assuming the role of the perfect set-up fighter—without hurting his opponent or being knocked out, he could make distance. Basil Galiano hung up the gloves in 1930 and died from complications of influenza on August 21, 1939.

Galiano, who always referred to Tony Canzoneri as "the Italian Terror," believed the juvenile should consider New York City as an outlet for his talent. Canzoneri was that good, and Galiano knew it.

When the business profile changed in New Orleans (about 1918), the Canzoneri family, all or part, briefly moved to Johnston City, Illinois.[11]

New York City

While "the Roaring Twenties" were still roaring (mid–1920s), Giorgio and Joseph Canzoneri decided to head to New York City and open a grocery store. It wasn't a spontaneous decision, but one they had discussed at length. Both felt that the ambitious undertaking would be good for the family. Once established, they would send for the rest of the clan.

New York City was the land of opportunity or, as Tony always claimed, a place where they had solid gold manhole covers. Perhaps he was correct as prosperity and transformation filled the air: Wall Street's Dow Jones Industrial Average closed 1923 at a new high of 120.51. R.H. Macy Company turned to a costly promotional parade that marched two miles from Central Park West down Broadway to Herald Square, and hoping to better control traffic, the city installed traffic lights at 50 intersections.

If there was a heaven for pugs, New York City was it. In 1923, city venues hosted Gene Tunney's impressive victory over Harry Greb, Pancho Villa's shocking kayo of the incomparable Jimmy Wilde, Jack Dempsey's dramatic finishing blow to Luis Firpo, Eugene Criqui's coup de grâce of Johnny Kilbane, and Johnny Dundee's long-awaited victory over Eugene Criqui. The road to a boxing title was always through the metropolis, and every pugilist knew it.

Landing in Brooklyn, Giorgio and Joe befriended welterweight Paul Doyle and his manager, Tony Palazolo—no doubt a common interest and language, not to mention a Sicilian heritage, played into the attachment. Becoming good friends, Giorgio never hesitated to brag about Joseph's pugilistic skills, and even those of his younger brother. Portrayed as a champion New Orleans fighter, Tony was on the cusp, or so

Giorgio believed, of conquering the world. To Doyle and Palazolo, the youngster soon sounded bigger than life.

When the remainder of the family was scheduled to arrive by train at Pennsylvania Station, awaiting their arrival on the platform were Giorgio and Joe, along with Paul and Tony—the last two curious to view the lauded Tony Canzoneri. After all the kisses and tears subsided, nobody could find little Tony. It was then that a youngster wearing a lace-collared shirt, short pants, and patent leather shoes popped out from behind his mother. It was all Doyle and Palazolo could do to stop laughing. "That's your idea of [a] champion?" both asked Giorgio. The teenager was humiliated and never forgot the incident.

Living in a spacious but not palatial house in Brooklyn, the family gradually acclimated to the city borough. Joe and Tony immediately got to work transforming the cellar into a gymnasium. With only a few amateur fights—he claimed 17, all taking place in New Orleans—under his belt, Tony felt like a stranger in Brooklyn. Not a surprise considering that Brooklyn had an estimated population of more than 2.2 million. Still oppressed by the comments of Doyle and Palazolo, Tony chose to hone his boxing skills from home. Nevertheless, one day a relative of his witnessed him sparring with Joe in the basement and asked him why he hadn't joined a boxing club. When Tony gave what seemed to be excuses, the relative of his took control of the situation and contacted the National Athletic Club, arranging for Tony's membership. The door was opened.

The next question was one of balance: Could the youngster find a footing for boxing while both attending school and working? Being set back a grade—common when relocating from one school system to another—didn't affect Canzoneri much. However, landing a job with the American Tobacco Company, making Lucky Strike cigarettes, complicated matters. His daily regimen, unusual for someone not yet 16, involved school by day and work by night. This left a couple of evenings a week to dedicate to boxing. Adapting to the schedule, Canzoneri appeared tireless.

Improving his skills at the National Athletic Club was the springboard Tony Canzoneri needed for a successful amateur career. His fight frequency increased almost five-fold in the first year. Absorbing instruction like a sponge, he dramatically improved his ring mobility while developing a style all his own. It didn't take long for his name to become synonymous with winning.

1925

1925 New York State Amateur Boxing Tournament

The annual New York State championship tournament held in Madison Square Garden was one of the premier events in boxing. Amateur mitt wielders, in every class from flyweights to heavyweights, prepared for months for the event. And why not? It attracted many prominent figures in the sport and yielded enormous publicity. As a catapult to a professional career, every Empire State pug hoped to be selected to represent their athletic club. Yet the odds, as most understood, were against them. The National Athletic Club entered five men: Tony Canzoneri (bantamweight), Ted Currier (lightweight), John Killoran (middleweight), Jack Gallagher (light heavyweight), and John Halbey (heavyweight). It was a confidence builder for all five participants.

The bantamweights conducted business on January 8, 1925, all three bouts taking place the same day. Tony Canzoneri defeated Henry Usse, followed by Peter Burns, both by three-round decisions, to make it into the finals. There he met Joe Scalfaro, aka "the Fighting Chemist," who hailed from Harlem. The hard-hitting Scalfaro, known for his durability, could put away an opponent with one punch. Understanding this, Canzoneri planned to outbox him. After three rounds, Tony Canzoneri, having conducted an impressive performance, was crowned the 118-pound champion.[12]

Besides Canzoneri, those taking home New York State boxing titles included Harry Traub (112 pounds), Ted Rotzmore (126 pounds), Thomas Lown (135 pounds), Mike Reilly (147 pounds), Arvid Mevik (160 pounds), William Freeman (175 pounds), and Jack Coleman (heavyweight).

Carrying the title of New York State 118-pound champion garnered Tony Canzoneri a level of notoriety, and he relished it. So did his father, who routinely picked up multiple copies of the *Brooklyn Daily Eagle* whenever Tony's name appeared. Club dates filled the gap until mid–March, when the Amateur Athletic Union championships began.

Picking up solid victories—over Jimmy Mendoza, Nick Del Genio, Jimmy McNamara, and a few others—was the perfect prelude to the junior national Amateur Athletic Union (AAU) tournament.

Junior National Amateur Athletic Union Tournament

Ten Metropolitan Association boxers, including Tony Canzoneri and three other New York State ring champions (Harry Traub, Tommy Lown, and Murray Israel), headed south to Baltimore to participate in the junior national AAU championships. The bouts took place at the 104th Medical Regiment Armory. On March 11, Canzoneri delivered William Jones via knockout to advance to the finals. The following day, he faced Sidney Lampe, a far tougher opponent who hailed from Baltimore. At the opening bell, the pair set a quick pace and sustained it during all three rounds of the contest. Whereas the judges split on the result, Referee Spike Webb saw it for Canzoneri. On to the metropolitan AAU championships.

Metropolitan AAU Championship

The preliminary rounds of the metropolitan AAU championships were held on March 18 at Madison Square Garden. Tony Canzoneri faced Sammy Tisch, who represented the Bronxdale Athletic Club. Preferring to take the early rounds, Canzoneri did that. With both the first and second rounds in his favor, he finished strong. Tisch, who was no match, was rocked several times during the battle and even dropped once.

Next up was Ed Healey, representing the Hudson Guild. Having devoured his opponent, Morris Musky, in 14 seconds in the opening round, Healey was confident he could do the same to Canzoneri. He could not. However, in a losing effort he did manage to inflict considerable damage to the countenance of his adversary.

Canzoneri's right eye was so badly cut that he could not compete in the final round. The title went to Tommy Lorenzo by default.

Unfortunately, Canzoneri could not heal quickly enough to participate in the March 23 tournament held at Rink Arena on Clermont and Myrtle avenues. Jimmy Mendoza, who was scheduled to meet Canzoneri, fought brilliantly and won the 118-pound class.

State Finals, National AAU Representative

Healed, Tony Canzoneri won the right to represent the metropolitan AAU as a competitor in his class. Knocking out Tom Donnelly in the opening round of their contest, he not only felt good but looked stronger than ever. The bout was held on April 6 at the New York Athletic Club. With the victory, Canzoneri was off to Boston, where he competed in the annual tournament of the national AAU.

National AAU Championship Tournament

Approximately 6,000 enthusiastic fans turned out for the first evening of the national amateur championships, held in The Hub. Six hours of continuous boxing saw the wheat separated from the chaff, as they say. Participating in the 118-pound class, Canzoneri got by Carl Kenney in the first round of the tournament but lost to August "Augie" Gotto in his next contest.[13]

Semi-Monthly Amateur Boxing Tournament

Disappointed, Tony Canzoneri headed back to New York and settled into his routine. Most of his better performances occurred at the Crescent Athletic Club's semi-monthly amateur boxing tournaments (SMABT). In May, he knocked out three of four opponents in the opening round. He also picked up a three-round decision victory over fellow Brooklyn pug Frankie Neve.

Canzoneri grabbed two decision victories at the SMABT in June, over Vinny LaGuardia and Tommy Lorenzo. As it was LaGuardia's amateur debut, many spectators figured he was nothing more than a set up for Canzoneri. It proved far from the truth. Canzoneri, exhausted following his previous three-round victory, was dropped in the second round and severely cut over his left eye. It turned out to be a challenging prelude to Tommy Lorenzo, the metropolitan AAU titleholder. Yes, that Tommy Lorenzo, whom Canzoneri was scheduled to meet before his swollen eye forced him to default. At the opening bell, both fighters went at each other hammer and tongs, as they used to say. The action quickly brought the crowd to their feet. Cut and bleeding from the opening salvo, neither pugilist was willing to give ground. After three taxing rounds, Canzoneri managed to take the decision.

Picking up a copy of the *Brooklyn Daily Eagle* on June 26, 1925, Tony Canzoneri learned that his old pal, Basil Galiano, was fighting on the undercard of the Babe Herman versus Jose Lombardo feature at Coney Island Stadium. As the fight wasn't until June 30, he decided to track down his old friend. Eager to share stories of his amateur success, Canzoneri headed to Stillman's gym, where Galiano was training.

Taking the subway to New York, Canzoneri reached Stillman's and learned that it cost a quarter to gain entry. Without the money to pay admission, he decided to sneak inside and did, courtesy of a heavyweight who distracted the doorman. Once upstairs, he began scanning the smoke-filled room for Galiano. It was like the land of the giants, as everyone appeared larger than the 118-pound amateur. Finally, Canzoneri caught Galiano shadow boxing behind the ring—he was in a section off limits to spectators. Concluding his workout, Galiano began walking across the gym. That was when Canzoneri managed to intercept him.

"Hey, Basil," screamed the youngster, "I'm Tony Canzoneri from New Orleans."

Galiano paused briefly, as though to let the engines restart, a big smile painting his face. He recalled the youth he used to pat on the head.

"The Italian Terror," he remembered.

Before Galiano could utter another word, Canzoneri began reciting his amateur fighting accomplishments, in a minute or less. Facetiously, he asked his friend if he could spar with him. Never in his wildest dreams did he believe it would happen. Yet Galiano agreed and suggested the following day.

Canzoneri arrived early with his fight togs in tow. Since it was Sunday, Stillman's wasn't busy. Finding the same individual manning the front door, Canzoneri wasn't certain what to expect. When he stated he was at the gym to see Basil Galiano, he was instructed to go on in. Welcomed by his friend, Canzoneri was enthusiastic. His first introduction was to Isadore "Izzy the Painter" Faber, Galiano's trainer.[14] Then it was off to the dressing room to change.

Three quick rounds concluded before Faber called time. Having gone easy on the young amateur, Galiano was impressed; incidentally, so were numerous inquisitive boxing managers who happened to witness the performance. Stopping the youngster in his tracks, onlookers directed a barrage of questions at the pugilist. What was his name? Who was his manager? That was when Faber called off the dogs by stating emphatically that Canzoneri was spoken for by the perspicacious Sammy Goldman, who managed Pete Herman and Basil Galiano. Having never spoken to or even met Goldman, Canzoneri was shocked and bemused. Everyone around the fight game, or so it was believed, knew Sammy Goldman or his younger brother Charley.

Sammy Goldman (1890–1964)

Sammy Goldman was born on January 7, 1890, in St. Louis. He grew up in the tough Red Hook section of Brooklyn. He and his brother, Charley, learned the art of self-defense not as an avocation but a form of survival. Sammy Goldman broke into boxing in New Orleans, where he was a sportswriter for *The Item* and a referee. He met Pete Herman in New Orleans and guided him to the world bantamweight title.

A handsome man who stood 5'6", Sammy Goldman had an oval face complemented by brown eyes and brownish black hair. He married Hannah Newfield (1895–1976) in the Bronx on June 7, 1917. The couple had two children, son Alfred Goldman and daughter Anita Shirley Goldman (Coppel). It was unusual for his wife, and even children, to accompany him on overseas business trips, as they did in December of 1920, when he traveled to London and Paris.

After the sparring session, Canzoneri told Galiano that he would love to see him fight Archie Walker, Brooklyn's leading lightweight, on June 30. Galiano smiled and promised to leave a ticket in the youngster's name at the box office. Arriving at the Coney Island fight club around 7:30 p.m., Canzoneri went straight to the box office. But there was no ticket left in his name. Frantic, he saw a gentleman he recognized from Stillman's and asked him the whereabouts of Sammy Goldman. Scanning the crowd, the acquaintance pinpointed Goldman.

Canzoneri cautiously approached the well-dressed man and introduced himself. After a visual inspection by the fight manager, almost as though the youth was a race-horse, Goldman claimed he couldn't spell Canzoneri, so he left a ticket in his name. With his hands clutching the stub, Canzoneri found his seat and reveled in the atmosphere. It was the first time he viewed a professional fight.

Sitting through the first two preliminaries—George Nickfor versus Nick Mercer and Giovanni Salerno versus Joe Kestner—Tony Canzoneri couldn't believe he was watching professional boxers. Since he had fought far more talented pugs in the amateur ranks, the designation didn't seem appropriate. During the third preliminary—Sammy Aaronson versus Jack McFarland—Sammy Goldman came over and sat beside Canzoneri. Trying not to be boastful yet honest, the youngster told the boxing manager he was not impressed by any of the fighters he had seen thus far and could lick the lot. Always discreet and composed, Goldman exhibited no emotion. He paused for about a minute, then asked the kid how he liked New York.

Basil Galiano, with a record of 42–8–6, knocked out Archie Walker, with a record of 33–11–2, in the opening round. Ecstatic, Canzoneri headed to the dressing room to congratulate his friend. After the excitement of the evening faded, Galiano and Canzoneri headed for their desired form of transportation. That's when Goldman spotted them and asked if they would like to share a cab ride home. Thrilled, they both accepted.

Galiano, Goldman, Izzy the Painter, Canzoneri, and a guy unfamiliar to Canzoneri piled into a cab. For Canzoneri, the cab ride provided the most excitement of the evening. All ears, the youngster listened to the fight assessment, promoter criticisms, and future predictions. Distracted by the conversation, Canzoneri ended up taking the cab far beyond his destination. As he finished his ride home via subway—worth the inconvenience created by his failure to recognize where he was—his mind replayed the evening for hours.

From this point forward, Tony Canzoneri was never a stranger at Stillman's. Watching Galiano train was an education in the art of being a professional fighter. Meanwhile, discerning Canzoneri's every action and reaction was the vigilant lens of Sammy Goldman. He was assessing the youngster's strengths and weaknesses as part of his development. The boxing manager introduced Canzoneri to a plethora of individuals associated with the fight game and explained their various roles. The fight manager understood that the more familiar Canzoneri became with the vibe, the less likely that nerves could impact his ring performance or that he would make an avoidable mistake. When the savvy fight impresario believed the youngster was ready for his professional boxing debut, he would make the call.

Galiano was inked to an outstanding fight card being promoted by Herman Taylor and Bobby Gunnis in Philadelphia. Set for Thursday, July 16, 1925, at Shibe Park, it had all the makings of a fabulous evening of boxing: Pete Zivic versus Sammy Novia would open the show, followed by Basil Galiano versus Joe Tiplitz, then Lew Tendler versus Joe Dundee, and finally Tommy Loughran versus Jack Delaney.

Out of the blue, Sammy Goldman offered Tony Canzoneri an all-expenses-paid trip to the fight. From meals to hotel room, Goldman picked up the tab. Speechless, the youngster was thrilled. Once Galiano picked up his 10-round unanimous decision over Tiplitz, Canzoneri settled into his seat to watch Tendler battle to a draw with Dundee and Delaney beat Loughran. The latter bout ended in controversy when Charlie White of the athletic commission changed the decision to a draw after an hour delay. Hey, it's boxing.

The following day, Canzoneri and Goldman rode back to New York with Bob Levy. Although Levy worked Loughran's corner the previous evening, he was best known as a matchmaker for the Rockaway arena. When the ride reached the New Jersey border, Goldman asked Levy about his next promotion. Before Canzoneri could even figure out what was happening, he was signed to a four-rounder with Levy's opponent of choice.

Tony Canzoneri couldn't wait to sit down with his father and tell him the news. Euphoric, Giorgio wanted to inform everyone, especially Tony Palazolo. In his broken English, he kept reminding his son that he was going to be a champion and make lots of money. And that, as far as Tony was concerned, was fine.

Going right to work in Stillman's, Canzoneri began training with Izzy the Painter. Instructing his pupil to smooth it out, Izzy believed his fighter was training too fast. He was trying to work on everything all at once, instead of pacing himself and taking it one step at a time. When bantamweight contender Eddie Shea, who was fighting Charley Phil Rosenberg for the world bantamweight championship, contacted Izzy about working with his pupil, the trainer approved. Still an amateur, Canzoneri collected $10 a day for his sparring sessions. They weren't easy, as Shea was an old-fashioned banger like Battling Nelson or Ad Wolgast. In retrospect, Canzoneri didn't learn much from Shea—as for the latter, he was knocked out by Rosenberg in the fourth round on July 23, 1925, at the Velodrome in New York.[15]

The door was open, and it was now up to Tony Canzoneri to pass through.

Two

Early Rounds, 1925–1926

"Age is never so old as youth would measure it."—Jack London

First Professional Fight

Summer 1925 felt like a rebirth for sports, as it was out with the old and in with the new: Madison Square Garden was demolished after 35 years and replaced with a new, $5.6 million facility operated by impresario Tex Rickard. Opening November 28, and located between 49th and 50th streets, the facility was designed primarily for boxing. Over in the Bronx, a Columbia graduate named Lou Gehrig took over for a slumping Wally Pipp at first base for the New York Yankees. A New York–born swimmer, Gertrude Ederle, 17, was breaking swimming records with regularity. If news was being made in sports, it was likely taking place in New York City.

Matchmaker Bob Levy, fulfilling his promise to Sammy Goldman, put together an entertaining evening of boxing on Friday, July 24, at the Rockaway Beach arena. Included on the fight card: a svelte and confident Tony Canzoneri making his professional debut at 119 pounds. It was time to step up a level, and the 16-year-old pugilist was ready. In his corner was an arsenal of four qualified seconds, including Goldman and Izzy the Painter—the expertise was there if required. Fortunately, Canzoneri didn't need it. In the opening round, he sent a blistering right cross that caught Jack Gardner—aka Jack Grodner or Levy's hand-picked, two-pound-heavier Brooklyn adversary—perfectly and dropped him like an anvil to the canvas. The sensational first-round knockout, in the initial preliminary bout, thrilled the audience and ignited Canzoneri's professional career. Goldman's nurturing of the youngster had paid off.[1]

Delighted with his performance, Tony Canzoneri believed he had found his calling. Sammy Goldman, fearing overconfidence, quickly signed his fighter to a four-round preliminary, on August 5, at Bayonne Stadium in New Jersey. After outpointing Ray Cummings of Staten Island, Canzoneri got another satisfying taste—his first decision victory—of the professional fight game. The result was precisely as Canzoneri's team had hoped. After his bout, Canzoneri took a seat ringside to witness Hong Fong Lee, of China, knockout Gene Travers, of Long Island, in the opening round of the semi-final. But his interest was not only in the bout, but in the presence of referee Joe Jeannette, the former world colored heavyweight champion. Jeannette owned a boxing gym on 27th Street and Summit Avenue in Union City, New Jersey. Having heard stories of Jeannette's ring prowess, Canzoneri was delighted to meet the great heavyweight. At the conclusion of the Lee victory, the crowd, estimated at

The Brooklyn Bridge (shown here around 1905), opened in 1883, spans the East River connecting the boroughs of Manhattan and Brooklyn. In the foreground is the New Haven/Bridgeport line traveling to Connecticut (Library of Congress).

2,000 fight fans, got restless. Seems the main event participants disagreed with the financial arrangements. After nearly an hour delay, Louis "Kid" Kaplan, of Meriden, Connecticut, defeated Billy Kennedy, of New Orleans, over 12 rounds.

Taking another four-round curtain raiser, Tony Canzoneri defeated Henry Usse on August 8, 1925, at Ridgewood Grove in Brooklyn. The decision wasn't exciting but efficient, as Canzoneri's handlers were teaching the fighter to pace himself. Sammy Goldman understood that young fighters learn more from a well-executed display of skills than a quick knockout. Better said: There was a time and place for the latter. The main event saw Roscoe Hall victorious over Jamaica Kid via a final-round foul. Henry Usse was positioned as a rival to Canzoneri by the press, which was a stretch but understandable—both fighters had participated in the year's New York State Amateur Boxing Tournament, 118-pound championship. Nevertheless, the matchmakers liked it and booked the pair for a rematch on August 22. This time the journey would be over six rounds. Regardless of the length, the results were the same: a decision victory in favor of Tony Canzoneri.

Ridgewood Grove

Ridgewood Grove in 1925 was not the "New" Ridgewood Grove that most would become familiar with. Clarence S. Gillespie, vice president and general manager of the Ridgewood Grove Sporting Club, witnessed the drawing power of the sweet science and purchased a large piece of land adjacent to the venue. Wanting to capitalize on the attraction, he hoped that an expansion, once completed, would take the seating capacity of the arena to 6,000.[2]

The famed "New" Ridgewood Grove opened in 1926. Located at (341–343) St. Nicholas Avenue and Palmetto Street, on the Brooklyn/Queens border, it attracted thousands of residents for events, especially prizefighting. Thanks to competitive fight cards, fans flocked to the venue. It wasn't long before Saturday night meant one thing: boxing at "the Grove."

As a thoroughfare for local talent, every pug, including Tony Canzoneri, dreamed of taking their licks inside the venue.

Staying at Ridgewood Grove, Tony Canzoneri was inked to a six-rounder against Paulie Porter on September 12—this would be his first opponent with more than 25 bouts' worth of experience. Although Porter had lost to Danny Terris, the younger brother of popular pugilist Sid Terris, he was fighting for a paycheck and not notoriety. Despite a competitive showing by his spirited adversary, Canzoneri took control and scored a technical knockout in the fifth frame. The main event of the six-bout fight card saw "Irish" Tommy Jordan battle to a draw with veteran Paul Doyle—by the way, Doyle was no longer making fun of Giorgio's little champion. There are times in life when what goes around does come around.

On October 10, Tony Canzoneri was signed to meet seasoned boxer Johnny Huber at the Commonwealth Sporting Club at 14 East 135th Street. Formerly known as the Harlem or the Olympic, it was a loud and popular haunt during the 1910s and 1920s. The club's regular Saturday night shows, of which this was one, drew from over all the city. Huber, who had an inflated record of 24–5–7, would quickly learn that his opposer was no tomato can (a boxer of diminished skill). Looking sharp, Canzoneri took the six-round points victory. The evening's excitement took place during the main event: Lew Hurley's technical knockout victory over the popular Harry London. While the latter was taking a beating, Mrs. London, his spouse, passed out on the ringside floor. Thankfully, Mrs. London was fine; as for her husband, he claimed a broken left hand. This was one of the final shows conducted by Jess McMahon, who had recently been appointed matchmaker at the new Madison Square Garden.

Pete Passafiume, another star in the amateur ranks, was scheduled to meet Tony Canzoneri on November 7 at Ridgewood Grove but was replaced by novice Henry Molinari. It was unfortunate, as both Canzoneri and Passafiume remained unbeaten. Wasting little time, Canzoneri put Molinari's lights out in the opening session courtesy of a solid right hand. It was a belated birthday gift but the type of present Canzoneri enjoyed.

The Broadway Arena, on 944 Halsey Street in the Bushwick section of Brooklyn, conducted a show featuring all new talent on November 12. One of the 10 bouts on the fight card: Tony Canzoneri versus Harry Brandon—the latter had nearly five times the number of bouts as his opposer. Thankfully, it didn't matter. Elusive and accurate, Canzoneri, who scaled at 117¾, fired combinations at will. Brandon, who tipped a pound heavier, failed to mount a defense and lost the four-round battle, his seventh consecutive loss. The *Brooklyn Standard Union* saluted the event with the headline "Canzoneri Takes Fast Four Rounder from Brandon at Broadway Arena."[3] Putting on a good show in front of his peers gave the youngster a sense of pride.[4]

In 1925, Thanksgiving afternoon meant a hearty meal followed by boxing.

A popular summer spot for the Canzoneri boys was Brighton Beach, a neighborhood in the southern portion of the New York City borough of Brooklyn, shown here ca. 1915–1920 (Library of Congress).

Matchmaker Clarence Gillespie of Ridgewood Grove assembled a 10-bout Turkey Day matinee complete with all the trimmings. Consisting of eight four-round bouts and a feature six-round battle, it promised to be a memorable evening in Brooklyn on November 26. Tony Canzoneri, who scaled at 118 pounds, or four pounds lighter than his opposition, outpointed Ralph Nischo in the four-round semi-final. Ringside had the fight even after the opening round, but that quickly changed. Stepping up his game in the second term, Canzoneri was unrelenting. The feature bout ended in controversy as bantamweight Jackie Nichols held Benny Hall to a draw. Unfortunately, the verdict was overturned in favor of Hall.

Brooklyn Teenagers in the 1920s

Young adults, or teenagers, lived in stark contrast to their parents during the 1920s. Canzoneri, like other boys, dressed in inexpensive, light-colored suits, colorful shirts, and dress boots—typically hand-me-down clothing. As jobs were plentiful, many teens didn't finish school, opting instead to work in family businesses where they could learn a trade. Model-T Fords (roughly $260 each) were the rage and, like all automobiles, revolutionized dating—men no longer had to call on women only at home but could receive permission to travel elsewhere. Thus, vaudeville shows, social events, ice cream parlors, and movie houses grew in popularity. Life was good: World War I had ended, technology was around every corner, and the economy was booming.

Tony Canzoneri was back at the Broadway Arena on Monday, December 7, to battle a talented Danny "Spider" Terris over the six-round distance. The competitive fight card promised lots of action and delivered. Appearing in one of the six-round openers, Canzoneri, tipping at 118¼, captured a points victory over Terris, who scaled at 122. In 13 professional bouts, it was the second loss for Terris. As Terris was fast afoot, it was a great opportunity for Canzoneri, and his team, to gauge his ring speed. He proved quicker than anticipated. Aggressive, Canzoneri had his opponent in trouble numerous times. However, Terris always managed to counter the assaults. All six rounds were action-packed and impressive enough to garner the pair a Madison Square Garden rematch on December 23. Despite Canzoneri's solid performance in this billed "new talent show," the *Brooklyn Standard Union* misidentified him. Nevertheless, Tony Canzoneri was certain that would change.

Premier Professional Performance at Madison Square Garden III

The incomparable George Lewis "Tex" Rickard, boxing impresario and builder of the third incarnation of Madison Square Garden in New York City, in 1921 (Library of Congress).

From 1925 through 1967, there wasn't a boxer born who didn't dream about one day fighting in Madison Square Garden—the Mecca of boxing. Located on the west side (825) of Eighth Avenue between 49th and 50th streets, the large main floor was surrounded by banked seating. To reach a capacity of 18,500 for boxing, a mezzanine and a 10-row balcony were added to the initial design. For boxing impresario Tex Rickard, who understood boxing promotion, this was his kingdom or "the House That Tex Built."

For Tony Canzoneri, it was one thing to box in Madison Square Garden II as an amateur. It was another thing to boxing professionally in the "New Garden," as everyone referred to it. Thrilled when Sammy Goldman gave him the news, the youngster couldn't wait to tell his family. It even prompted a smile from his mother, overjoyed at the announcement.

Trying hard to keep his nerves in check, Tony Canzoneri

concentrated on his opposition—it helped that he had recently faced and defeated Danny Terris. As the four-round curtain-raiser for the charity event (the Christmas Fund), he had a job to do, and he knew it. Weighing 121 pounds, Tony Canzoneri knocked out Danny Terris, who tipped at 119½, in the fourth round. Having dropped Terris for a three count early in the session, Canzoneri immediately floored him again with a convincing right. Referee Kid McPartland, no stranger to a boxing ring, counted out Terris before dragging him to his corner—the end came at 53 seconds of the fourth round.[5]

Attracting a large crowd for the show that began at 8:15 p.m., promoter Rickard was pleased. Tickets were scaled from $1.10 to $11.00. The preliminary bouts, as was often the case, catered to those who arrived early and consisted primarily of general admission ticket holders. Those sitting ringside gradually found their seats by the "wind up" bout. Not a surprise, as the action inside the Garden was not only in the ring, but outside it.

The outing became famous not for Canzoneri's bout but because of a bonehead decision rendered in the main event. Mike McTigue, a White boxer, was handed a decision victory over Tiger Flowers, a Black pugilist, even though the latter took most of the rounds. The crowd was furious, and you could hear the boos all the way to Staten Island. It was as pathetic as it was unjust. In addition to the two bouts mentioned, Fidel LaBarba took a six-round points victory over Lew Perfetti, Corporal Izzy Schwartz drew Ernie Jarvis, and George Godfrey took a points victory over Martin Burke.

To end the year with a victory inside Madison Square Garden was a dream come true for young Tony Canzoneri. Pocketing an impressive payday, the undefeated pugilist, with a professional record of 11–0, could now sit back and enjoy the holidays.

1926

Living in, or even visiting, New York City in 1926 was exciting thanks to the incomparable Mayor James J. "Jimmy" Walker. Part of the powerful Tammany Hall political machine, Walker was a liberal Democrat who was hellbent on shaping the city his way. As Walker was the sponsor of a boxing reform bill back on March 24, 1920, suffice it to say that fans of the sweet science were delighted by his election. Boxing thrived after Governor Al Smith signed Walker's edict into law. No better evidence existed than the more than 6,000 licensed boxers a mere four years later.

Hosting its fair share of great boxing matches, New York City witnessed Tiger Flowers picking up a points verdict over Harry Greb, Ace Hudkins making a miraculous recovery to knock out Ruby Goldstein, and Jack Sharkey's disqualification victory over Harry Wills. While Jack Dempsey was still the most popular heavyweight in the metropolitan area, Gene Tunney, who defeated "the Manassa Mauler" in Philadelphia, remained a close second.

Unknown, Tony Canzoneri basked in the obscurity, but the situation proved to stimulate him. Having faith in the management of Sammy Goldman, Canzoneri understood that the fight manager knew how to construct a champion. Both agreed that fighting twice a month, on average, was realistic barring an injury. Thankfully, there was plenty of opportunity in the metropolitan area—Broadway Arena,

Ridgewood Grove, and Dexter Park Arena—and the exposure lent itself to options and even notoriety.

Tony Canzoneri began his year at the New Manhattan Sporting Club on January 13. Although it was the reopening of the club, it drew a small crowd of fight fans—part of the reason was a weak fight card topped by light heavyweight Billy Vidabeck of New Jersey. Scheduled for six rounds, Canzoneri, who tipped at 120¼, needed only four. Slicing a large cut over the eye of his opposer, George Nickfor, who scaled a pound lighter, was a prelude to a short evening. Ineffectual at halting the bleeding, the West Side boxer was unable to continue.

In contrast to his previous bout, Tony Canzoneri next tackled Kid Rash in the feature contest of a 10-bout fight card at the New Broadway Arena. In addition to Canzoneri, Willie Garafola and Harry Ebbets were the better boxers on the bill. Scheduled for January 21, five of the bouts included boxers making their professional debut.

Kid Rash, aka Randolph Rasch, began his career back in 1916 and brought a losing record into the ring against his undefeated opposer—trying to transform himself into a contender, he had failed thus far. He continued that path by losing a four-round decision to Canzoneri. Taking command early, Canzoneri, who tipped at 118¼, used his left jab with precision to set up his forceful right. As the jabs began taking a toll on Rash, who scaled at 116, it was a matter of time before Canzoneri moved to the cannonry. Rash countered by taking close quarters to avoid the heavy blows. Reacting to the action, Canzoneri took a step back and unloaded a barrage of straight lefts and right crosses to quell the aggression.[6] As the cumulative damage continued to mount, Rash had little choice but to grab and hold to stay the distance.

For the first time ever, media members at the *Brooklyn Daily Eagle* believed Canzoneri had all the makings of a three-division (bantam, feather and lightweight) champion.[7] Profound, wouldn't you say? Even at this early stage of his career, his ability, charm, good looks, and lucky purple trunks were having an impact—they even landed him a handsome portrait in the *Daily News*.[8]

Lew Raymond, matchmaker at the Pioneer Athletic Club, signed Canzoneri for his last bout of the month. He would meet Mickey Lewis on January 26. Nine four-rounders made up the fight card, with Canzoneri, Lewis, Andy DiVodi, Paul Gulotta, and Nick Fadil the best of the lot. Ever consistent, Canzoneri, who scaled at 117, took a points victory over Mickey Lewis, who tipped at 119½. However, it was no walk in the park as his opposer would not relent. In the third round, Canzoneri found his range and delivered Lewis to the canvas twice. Targeted right hooks accounted for the damage. Taking nine counts each fall, Lewis had little choice but to hold to make distance.

Even though February was a short month, Tony Canzoneri took two battles. He met Romeo Vaughn (also spelled Vaughan) at Ridgewood Grove on February 13 and Al Scorda at the Broadway Arena five days later. As both opponents had winning records and more experience, the matches looked solid on paper. Undefeated, Canzoneri was keeping his emotions in check.

Vaughn, like Canzoneri, was being groomed for bigger and better things. It was no surprise that matchmaker Jack Clifford, now handling matters at Ridgewood Grove, promised the winner a match against Vic Burrone, the latest bantam sensation. In a tight battle, when it went to the cards, the six-round bout fell in favor of

Canzoneri. Since Vaughn was a slow starter, Canzoneri took the early frames. In the end, he was glad he did. As for the Burrone offer, Goldman wisely turned it down. As tempting as it was to take the proposition, a good boxing manager doesn't rush the development of his boxer. Canzoneri wasn't ready.

Five days later, Tony Canzoneri, tipping at 118½, returned to the Broadway Arena to battle four rounds against Al Scorda, who weighed in at 120¼. Canzoneri's straight left prevented Scorda from scoring; consequently, Goldman's fighter seemed content to hold back the heavy ordnance until the final two rounds. In the third frame, he tried hard to deliver his opposer with accurate right hooks but was unsuccessful. In the end, Canzoneri took the points victory. However, a wild right hand by Scorda managed to catch his adversary and cut his mouth. The 10-bout fight card made for a long evening.

Canzoneri's first five victories of the year had all been against local fighters in New York City venues. Kid Rash, the most experienced opponent he faced, was the only one with a losing record.

The First Speed Bump

Canzoneri didn't plan on taking four bouts in March, but that was how it played out. Signed to a six-round bout against Bobby Wolgast, aka "the Philadelphia Wildcat," at Ridgewood Grove on March 6, he prayed his mouth healed in time. A seasoned fighter, Wolgast had met a sprinkling of the best in the division, including Vic Burrone, Bud Taylor, and Benny Schwartz. Canzoneri, scaling at 118, was far quicker than the surprisingly lethargic Wolgast, who tipped to a five-pound advantage. The highlight of the evening, a double knockdown, came in the fourth round. It was an exciting occurrence even though both fighters were quickly back on their feet. As Wolgast began to tire, his holding prompted numerous warnings. In the end, the decision went to Canzoneri.

In another 10-bout fight card at the Commonwealth Sporting Club, Tony Canzoneri straightforwardly defeated Cuban novice Jacinto Valdez over four rounds. Both fighters tipped at or about 119 pounds. Outclassing his adversary from the opening bell, Canzoneri used the bout as target practice. A mismatch, the fight was taken as a favor to the promoter.

Back at the Grove, matchmaker Clifford signed Canzoneri to a six-frame feature, on March 20, against Tommy Milton, a flyweight and bantamweight contender with twice the experience. Although Canzoneri took the decision, the overhyped fight didn't live up to expectations. The overzealous media had not put the bout into proper perspective. Nevertheless, it was off to Madison Square Garden on March 25.

Signed to the undercard of the Young Stribling versus Jimmy Slattery feature bout, Tony Canzoneri was thrilled to appear at the Garden once again. His opponent, over four rounds, was Michael "Mickey" Esposito, the brother of Connecticut fighter K.O. Morgan. Esposito's previous performance was a four-round victory over George Cuneo at Madison Square Garden. Neither fighter appeared nervous, as both fought evenly over the distance to a draw. Adding a draw to an undefeated record was never easy, the only conciliation being that it wasn't a loss.

Needing well-deserved recovery time from a busy month, Tony Canzoneri stayed out of the ring in April. Folks forgot that he was still a teenager, though his mother never hesitated to remind him.

Sammy Goldman booked his fighter for two dates in May, the first against Benny Hall at Ridgewood Grove on May 8, and the second opposed to Brooklyn boxer Sammy Nable at Coney Island Stadium in Brooklyn on May 28.

Benny Hall, who had twice as many wins as losses, was a St. Louis pug now living in Long Island City. Having recently campaigned as a featherweight, he felt he was a natural bantam. Matchmaker Clifford, who spun a tale as a spider spun a web, made him out to be the next Terry McGovern. He wasn't, but he wasn't bad either, as he held Canzoneri, who scaled a pound heavier at 120, to a draw over six rounds.

Consecutive draws left Canzoneri with mixed emotions. Replaying both fights over and over in his head helped him real-

This ticket stub, from Madison Square Garden, was for the Young Stribling v. Jimmy Slattery bout. Tony Canzoneri drew Mike Esposito in one of the four round preliminary bouts.

ize the importance of timing and execution. Both became critical factors as his bouts increased in rounds. The days of riding to a victory solely on his talent were ending. It was time to fight to a strategy.

Coney Island Stadium, located on Surf Avenue near West 6th Street, in the Coney Island section of Brooklyn, was a popular open-air venue. (Later, during the 1930s, it was called Fugazy Bowl, when boxing promoter Humbert J. Fugazy sought more notoriety.) In one of those "I can't say no" bouts, Tony Canzoneri signed to meet veteran Sammy Nable. But it wasn't Nable who caught Canzoneri's interest. Also on the fight card were two familiar names: Basil Galiano, who would tangle with Lew Tendler, and Paul Doyle, who would scrap with Tommy Freeman. As Canzoneri saw it, fate had given him the perfect showcase.

Performing brilliantly, Canzoneri, or Williamsburg's (also spelled Williamsburgh) wonder boy, who tipped at 122 or to a two-pound advantage, dropped Nable, the Harlem veteran, to two nine-counts: first in the opening round and again in the fourth frame. It was Canzoneri's marvelous right hands to the chin that did the damage. Referee Patsy Haley, witnessing enough destruction, stopped the battle after one minute and 40 seconds of the sixth round. Ecstatic over the victory, his 20th, Canzoneri had a smile cemented on his face. When both Basil Galiano and Paul Doyle lost 10-round decisions, it dampened the evening, but it didn't ruin it.

In June, the outdoor season in New York was all about opportunity. It provided a chance for fighters, even with limited experience, to be signed to large promotions at impressive venues for big paydays. As fighters are often booked with short notice, pugs comparable to Canzoneri needed to be on call. Manager Sammy Goldman, seeing it also as a chance to step up the competition, inked his fighter to three six-round fights: Sonny Smith on June 16, Willie Suess on June 21, and Archie Bell on June 25. All three boxers had more than 30 professional bouts and twice as many victories as defeats.

First on the docket was Sonny Smith, a neighborhood rival, who held a 12-round victory over champion Charley Phil Rosenberg and performed skillfully against many others, including Cannonball Eddie Martin. Canzoneri, who tipped at 120 or to a pound disadvantage, pounded his way to a points victory. Apprehensive at first, he took command in the second frame and held it until the fifth. To his credit, Smith delivered enough counters to force his adversary to rally in the final round. In front of a capacity crowd at Golden City Arena in Brooklyn, it was an impressive victory for Canzoneri.

Dexter Park Arena, located at Jamaica Avenue between Elderts Lane (Dexter Court) and 76th Street, staged boxing matches from 1925 until about 1950. Having heard much about the venue, Canzoneri was excited about battling in the multi-purpose facility. In the second four-round opener, Canzoneri, tipping at 121, took a decision over Willie Suess, who scaled at 119¼. Suess was overwhelmed by the mobility of Canzoneri and could not mount an offensive. The only excitement came before either boxer entered the ring, as the handlers for Suess refused to allow their fighter to work more than four rounds—the fight was scheduled for six. It wouldn't have made any difference as Suess was overmatched.[9]

Returning to Coney Island Stadium, Tony Canzoneri scored a technical knockout over Archie Bell when referee Jim Crowley halted the contest in the fifth round. Bell's right eye was severely gashed because of a furious third-round exchange. Crowley had no alternative but to end the contest. Butting heads in the frame, both fighters sustained cuts; however, Bell got the worst of it. It didn't help that Canzoneri pounded Bell's countenance much the same as a butcher would a cube steak. Up to the point of the incident, it was a competitive and action-packed fight that could have fallen either way. An estimated 15,000 fight fans enjoyed the fight card that was topped by Ace Hudkins' fourth-round knockout of Ruby Goldstein.

Giving his fighter a chance to catch his breath, Sammy Goldman booked Canzoneri for one contest the following month. He would return to Dexter Park Arena on July 25 for a bout against Manny Wexler. Far from a tomato can, Wexler had been in the ring with Charlie Phil Rosenberg, Frankie Genaro, and Ernie Jarvis. He was competitively matched against Canzoneri, and he knew it.

At this point in his career, the press believed that Canzoneri was being fully challenged, or put to the acid test, with each fight. Granted, Goldman was working him up in competition, but the press found it hard to believe Canzoneri was as good as he was.

Scaling at 121½, Tony Canzoneri scored an impressive knockout over Manny Wexler, who tipped at 117, in front of 5,000 enthusiastic spectators. Canzoneri dropped Wexler to a nine-count in the fifth frame, then reloaded. A hard right to the jaw silenced his opponent. The end came after two minutes and 45 seconds of the fifth round. Wexler, who was also dropped in the second round by an accurate right hand, was stunned by the result—as were the gamblers. It was the first time Wexler had been knocked out.

Was Canzoneri ready to journey further than six rounds? Many, including Sammy Goldman, believed he was. However, the New York State Athletic Commission (NYSAC) adopted a rule on June 1, 1922, prohibiting boxers under the age of 20 from participating in bouts of more than six rounds. NYSAC *still* had no idea that Canzoneri wouldn't turn 18 until November 6, and nobody was about to tell them.

Goldman signed Canzoneri for three bouts in August: Young Montreal on August 9 at Dexter Arena; Buck Josephs on August 14 at Ridgewood Grove; and Georgie Mack on August 28 at Queensboro Stadium on Long Island. All three bouts were against out-of-state opponents.

A seasoned boxer with more than 100 professional bouts, Young Montreal, New England bantamweight champion, won twice as many bouts as he lost. It was a fact that his undefeated opposer tried to forget. Taking immediate control with a stiff right to the jaw of Montreal, Canzoneri delivered the first message. Unfazed, Montreal shook it off. Ageless, the veteran pugilist was always dangerous inside the ring and quickly proved it. Firing a hard left to the face of his adversary in the third round, Montreal shook Canzoneri. Blood, from a variety of old cuts, began streaming into his eyes. Sensing a momentum change, Montreal took control in the fourth and fifth rounds. Canzoneri briefly lost his range and began misfiring. As the veteran began to tire, combinations and speed were what won Canzoneri the six-round decision. There were no knockdowns, though Canzoneri slipped to his gloves at one point. Both fighters weighed 121 pounds.

Buck Josephs, aka Joseph Barone, was a New Jersey bantamweight who had grown popular with Ridgewood Grove fight fans since his debut in 1921. Winless in his previous nine contests, Josephs was there to put fans in the seats. He accomplished that, despite his six-round loss to Tony Canzoneri.

Queensboro Stadium (or Arena), located at 29–49 Northern Boulevard in Long Island City, was a popular outdoor site with seating for about 4,000. Matchmaker Tom McArdle put together a solid fight card—three ten-rounders, one six-rounder, and a four-rounder—topped by Babe Herman facing Petey Mack. Sammy Goldman also liked the card and accepted the six-round slot for his fighter: Canzoneri would meet Georgie Mack, a brother of Petey Mack and Baby Mack. In the wake of two postponements, the show finally took place on August 28.

Having recently taken a newspaper decision (a general agreement of sportswriters attending a bout after it had ended inconclusively with a "no decision") from Willie Spencer, Mack was slotted against Canzoneri. Honestly, Canzoneri wasn't worried about his opponent—that is, until he got into the ring with an opposer who would not concede defeat. Each time Canzoneri thought he had trapped his adversary, Mack escaped. Both fighters battled hard to an even verdict, though ringside felt Mack had the edge. It was Canzoneri's third draw of the year. Having injured his eye during the conflict, Canzoneri was forced to cancel his bout on September 3 against Murray Layton.

As the summer season was winding down, Sammy Goldman signed Tony Canzoneri to an all-star show of six-round battles on September 20. Canzoneri was slated to meet Georgie Marks, another popular Brooklyn fighter. As the closing event of the season, a large crowd was anticipated at Dexter Park Arena.

On September 16, Tony Canzoneri, who was in training for the contest, received a telegram from an old friend, Pete Herman. The former bantamweight champion was headed to Philadelphia for the Dempsey-Tunney battle on September 23 and thought he might pay a visit to Dexter Park and root for his protégé. To say the news invigorated the boxer would be an understatement.

In front of 10,000 fans, Tony Canzoneri, who scaled at 123, defeated Georgie Marks, who scaled at 120. Canzoneri performed with style and precision. As the closing bell of the sixth and final round sounded, he dropped Marks to the canvas comparable to a wrecking ball hitting a brick wall—an accurate right cross did the damage. Although it robbed Canzoneri of a knockout victory, it impressed everyone in attendance. As the mentor hailed the victory as part of a standing ovation, the student saluted him with a wink.

The Pioneer Athletic Club hosted an evening of six-rounders on October 5. The final three bouts all featured undefeated fighters, and as fate had it, all stayed that way at the end of the evening. Andy DiVodi defeated Henry Goldberg, Tony Canzoneri was victorious over Benny Hall, and Sammy Dorfman defeated Lew Hurley. All three bouts were points victories. In the fourth frame, Tony Canzoneri, who scaled at 122 or a five-pound advantage, was sent to the canvas by Hall. Embarrassed by the action and acting as though he knew better, he immediately returned to his feet without a count. Canzoneri could not avoid the commanding left hand of his adversary, leading some ringside to believe Hall should have been given the verdict. It was that close a contest.

Angelo Geraci, aka Bushy Graham, shown here in the 1920s, won the world bantamweight championship in 1928, then vacated it the following year.

On November 6, Tony Canzoneri's birthday, the Brooklyn fighter was matched against Davey Abad, a tough boxer born in Panama, at the grand opening of the *New Ridgewood Grove*. According to the *Daily News*, it was Canzoneri's 21st birthday, thus the match would be over the 10-round distance. Truth be known: It was the fighter's 18th birthday. And it was also the boxer's first journey over the distance. Abad, who also called the Williamsburg section of Brooklyn his home, was not a wise choice to test drive a fighter over 10 rounds; moreover, he had recently lost a 10-round war against Bushy Graham, the tough Utica bantam. Thus, Abad was primed to wage battle against Canzoneri.

Davey Abad, scaling at 119½, won a close decision over Tony Canzoneri, who tipped at 120½. Making the jump from six rounds to 10 was far more difficult than Canzoneri imagined.[10] This, the fighter believed, was because of losing the weight he had accumulated since his last bout. As he slowed, he became an easier target to hit and was outscored. Some of the writers ringside gave the fight to Canzoneri, the margin of victory was that thin. To top it all off, an 18-year-old Canzoneri never should have been in the 10-round contest to begin with. In retrospect, Canzoneri felt it was good to taste defeat at this stage of his career.

Tony Canzoneri was signed to rematch with Georgie Mack at the New Walker Athletic Club, located at 125th and Lenox Avenue (now Malcolm X Boulevard), on November 13—an opportunity for redemption after the six-round draw. But Mack backed out to prepare for a bout against Charley Phil Rosenberg. Canzoneri was next matched with Monk Kelly. However, that fell through. On the day of the fight, nobody was certain whom the teenager was going to meet. Tipping at 122, or four pounds lighter than his opposer, Tony Canzoneri stopped Enrique Savaardo in the fifth round by way of technical knockout. The one-sided, not to mention mismatched, bout was slated for 10 rounds—Savaardo had only won three of his 48 professional bouts.[11]

Enter André Routis, a demanding fighter who had become familiar to many. Winning the French amateur bantamweight championship in 1918, Routis turned professional that same year. Quickly establishing himself as a contender, he was running out of French competition. With an endless arsenal of combinations, Routis traveled to America for the first time as a professional in August of this year. Having won three bouts in a row—two over Cowboy Eddie Anderson and one over Allentown Johnny Leonard—he hoped to add Canzoneri's name to the list when the pair squared off at the New Broadway Arena on November 22. Routis, who was a 3–1 favorite, was handled by Joe Jacobs, who also handled Ted Moore, Frankie Genaro, and Mike McTigue.

In his first bout at 12 rounds, Tony Canzoneri, tipping at 122½, took a points decision victory over André Routis, who scaled at 124½. Each fighter bounded from his respective corner to the middle of the ring and threw punches until the bell sounded to end the round, then repeated. It was a sensational performance by two talented warriors. Routis stuck with his machine-gun combinations mixed with solid body punches, while Canzoneri opted for control with the left jab, saving the heavy weapons for choice opportunities. Routis, who looked tired after 10 rounds, caught a Canzoneri right hand that opened cuts over one eye. At one point in the 10th frame, the local youngster appeared to shake Routis. Yet he could not capitalize on the situation. During the final rounds, Canzoneri turned to his right uppercut to inflict damage—Routis had done an excellent job blocking many of his rival's other punches. With this bout, Tony Canzoneri debuted in the featherweight division, which had a limit of 126 pounds. Even though there were no knockdowns, the estimated crowd of 4,500 spectators enjoyed every moment of the contest.[12]

After the battle, it was rumored that Canzoneri would head to Waterbury, Connecticut, to battle Mike Esposito. But that was before Sammy Goldman heard from Jess McMahon. Constructing an all-bantamweight fight card at Madison Square Garden on December 17, the matchmaker wanted to sign Canzoneri to a 10-rounder against Bud Taylor. Goldman accepted the offer and pulled his fighter from the Connecticut event. On December 10, McMahon was notified by Taylor's camp that an eye injury required an operation. Since he would be out of the ring for at least six weeks, he could not meet Canzoneri. McMahon signed Utica boxer Bushy (Bushey) Graham, aka Angelo Geraci, to replace Taylor.[13]

Was Canzoneri ready to face an elite fighter like Charles "Bud" Taylor? Many fight critics believed he was not, and thankfully the fight didn't take place. As the *Evening Star* noted: "Why this match should be made is causing no end of talk. Canzoneri has no business in the lighter class, especially against a chap like Taylor. Managers make foolish moves sometimes. Time will tell whether this is one of them."[14] Folks cringed at the thought of Canzoneri's smile being relocated during an encounter with Bushy Graham. However, Goldman insisted that his fighter was ready. Roll the bones.

In a masterful upset, Tony Canzoneri, tipping at 120, took an impressive 10-round points victory over Bushy Graham, who scaled at 118½. Taking seven of ten rounds, the Brooklyn boxer brilliantly countered every offensive by Graham, who was a 4–1 favorite.[15] Canzoneri was spry and on his toes the entire bout, his movement graceful. The veteran, figuring he would take the later rounds to win the fight, figured wrong. While pressuring his opponent in the seventh frame, Graham took a left hook that badly sliced his right eye. Constantly moving forward, Canzoneri was unintimidated by any aspect of the old hand's tactics. Capturing the seventh, eighth and ninth rounds, he gave Graham the final frame. Of the 8,000 spectators on hand at the New Garden, nobody left disappointed.[16]

Graham was scheduled to meet Charley Phil Rosenberg on January 7 for the NYSAC world bantamweight championship. How, or even if, the result of this fight would play into the picture was anybody's guess. Sammy Goldman decided to go to NYSAC and press the claim that his fighter should be meeting Rosenberg instead of Graham. Graham's camp reminded NYSAC that their fighter was a substitute and fought at catchweight (meaning a weight limit that does not adhere to the normal weight for weight classes). Regardless, Jess McMahon, no stranger to opportunity, signed Canzoneri to three Garden fights.

Seventeen months and seven days into his professional boxing career, Tony Canzoneri, age 18, took a ring record of 31–1–3 into 1927. Having made a name for himself in New York City—even having his handsome countenance adorn the sports pages of the *Daily News*—he was known in Northeast fight circles, popular in Brooklyn, and fighting at the level of a contender. Receiving four times more publicity in 1926 than he did the previous year, he was turning heads. And it wasn't a surprise as his ring prowess was matched by his movie star looks.

THREE

Breakout, 1927

"Nobody owes anybody a living, but everybody is entitled to a chance."—Jack Dempsey

From commerce, culture, and gangs to jazz, illegal booze, and the Yankees, New York City had it all and more in 1927. Charles Lindbergh flew *The Spirit of St. Louis* across the Atlantic nonstop and solo, from Roosevelt Airfield, Long Island, to Le Bourget Aerodome, Paris, in a single-seat, single-engine, high wing monoplane. If that wasn't enough to convince you that the times were changing, a two-and-a-half-mile-long tunnel under the Hudson River was opened, connecting New York State to New Jersey.

With Yankee Stadium hosting its fair share of ring battles, New York fight fans—an estimated 80,000—turned up there on July 21 to watch Jack Dempsey tackle Jack Sharkey. Dominating the early rounds, Sharkey, as cocky as ever, looked unstoppable. Frustrated, Dempsey landed a series of low blows in round seven. At close quarters, Sharkey turned to the referee to protest, and Dempsey knocked him out with a left hook to the chin. It was classic Dempsey, or Jack being Jack. The end came at the 0:45 mark of the seventh frame. On December 12 at Madison Square Garden, Tommy Loughran successfully defended his light heavyweight title against Jimmy Slattery. The 15-round majority decision wasn't easy as Loughran claimed his Buffalo opponent moved quicker than any opponent he ever faced. For the victorious "Phantom of Philly," who finished the year 10–0, it was an impressive display.

Fight followers saw Bud Taylor as the best of the bantamweights in 1927, followed by Angelo Geraci, aka Bushy Graham, Andy Martin, Dominick Petrone, and Pete Sarmiento. Stepping up a division, Charley Phil Rosenberg was the boxer to beat among the featherweights, followed by Benny Bass, Red Chapman, Sam Dorfman, Honey Boy Finnegan, Babe Herman, Chick Suggs, and Al Winkler. Canzoneri, as many believed, was young and competitive, but his victory over Graham was considered more luck than talent. It was an assessment the Brooklyn boxer didn't appreciate.

Tipping at 121, Tony Canzoneri drew Joe Ryder, who scaled at 123½, over 10 lackluster rounds at the New Manhattan Sporting Club/Casino. The January 12 bout looked like two fighters going through the motions rather than battling one another. This was not the same Canzoneri who ducked in and out of range against Bushy Graham, and it needed to be, considering he was meeting Vic Burrone on January 22. Burrone, who hailed from Greenwich Village, was an aggressive two-fisted warrior who was willing to take two punches to deliver one. Facing Bud Taylor the previous

October, Burrone gave him a heck of scrap; consequently, many spectators were stunned when Taylor got the nod.

Managing to keep the contest close during the first half of the fight, Vic Burrone succumbed to Canzoneri's aggressiveness during the second half. Mindful of Burrone's forceful infighting, Canzoneri wisely stayed on the outskirts of town, as they say, and it gained him a victory. Tony Canzoneri, scaling at 122½, captured a 10-round decision over Vic Burrone, who tipped at 121, at the Ridgewood Grove Sporting Club.

Before the Burrone fight took place, Canzoneri was inked to a battle against Johnny Green. The bout was to take place on the undercard of the Charlie Phil Rosenberg versus Bushy Graham world's bantam title tilt at the Garden on February 4. As this was Canzoneri's fourth Garden battle, he was aware that a strong performance could yield future benefits. That was what he gave as he whipped Green in the eight-round semi-final; moreover, dropping his opposer four times—in rounds one, three, five, and seven—to the canvas made a powerful statement to the near 14,000 in attendance.

Pushing hard to match his fighter against Bud Taylor, Sammy Goldman was hitting numerous, but not surprising, obstacles along the way. First, Canzoneri had to go through, or fight, Midget Smith. Then there was the battle over weight limits. Understandably, Team Canzoneri wanted the fight at the limit of 118 pounds. Although the fight manager could make a match at 121 pounds, Goldman wanted the fight at the lower tier. Finally, Taylor's manager, Eddie Long, agreed to a February 24 bout.

Unfortunately, Tony Canzoneri suffered a foot injury on February 13, and it forced the cancellation of his bout against Bud Taylor. Since the Terre Haute fighter's bantamweight title—it was recognized in Illinois and 17 other states—was on the line, Goldman didn't want his fighter in the ring unless he was healthy. Promoter James C. "Jim" Mullen of Chicago contacted the Illinois boxing commission about a possible March date for the battle.[1]

Finally, March 26 was agreed upon for Canzoneri's title contest against Taylor. Believing his fighter needed a warm-up contest, Goldman inked him to a 10-round bout at the Broadway Arena on March 7 against "California" Joe Lynch. The action upset Jim Mullen, who attempted to postpone Canzoneri's bout against Lynch—surprisingly, Mullen wasn't concerned that Canzoneri would get hurt but worried about a possible upset by Lynch. While Lynch had 11 more career victories than Canzoneri, he also had 31 more losses. Nevertheless, the fight took place.

Tony Canzoneri outpunched California Joe Lynch over 10 rounds at the Broadway Arena to pick up a points victory. Both fighters scaled at 121 pounds. After the contest, it was clear why Jim Mullen had been upset. The battle wasn't without its share of damage, as Canzoneri suffered a cut right eye and Lynch had a large gash opened over his left eye. It wasn't the cleanest battle; frustrated at his inability to slow his opposition, Lynch resorted to low blows and backhanded punches. An impressive crowd of 4,500 fights fans turned out for the event.

Charles "Bud" Taylor

Dubbed "the Blonde Terror of Terre Haute," Charles "Bud" Taylor was born on July 22, 1903. Turning professional in 1920, he clearly fought as an outlet for his aggression. His impressive skills, accompanied by his ruthless style, were tough to overlook—nobody wanted to get into a ring against the teenager. Prolific, heartless, and belligerent, Taylor met Memphis Pal Moore four times from June 1922 to February 1923. Fighting during the no-decision era, Taylor impressively competed against Moore, who was a veteran of more than 180 bouts. (The no-decision era was from approximately 1911 to 1920; a no-decision happened when, either under rules of state boxing law or by an agreement between the boxers, both fighters were still standing at the end of a bout and there had been no knockout or no official decision, and neither fighter was declared the winner.) In 1923, he took newspaper losses to Frankie Genaro and Pancho Villa. Defeating Charley Phil Rosenberg (1923), Pancho Villa (1924), and Eddie Coulon (1924), Taylor began turning heads. Winning his first eight fights in 1926, he took victories over Abe Goldstein (NWD 10, newspaper decision), Jimmy McLarnin (W10), and California Joe Lynch (W10). He was also the first fighter to defeat McLarnin—the division's bellwether opponent—and the first boxer to defeat him twice. (Later, Barney Ross would become the second.)

Both Canzoneri and Taylor worked hard in preparation for their March 26 contest at the Coliseum in Chicago. Early reports saw Canzoneri a slight favorite owing to his speed. But that was a subjective observation. Adding more incentive to the picture, Jim Mullen added a $2,500–$4,000 diamond belt to the winner's share. But was the title on the line?

Barred in New York and Illinois for failure to make the championship weight, Charley Phil Rosenberg was suspended for a year. But was he out of the title picture? Bud Taylor was awarded the crown by the Illinois Athletic Commission; thus, he would be making his first defense. Since it was a nontraditional title transfer, critics viewed the title as remaining vacant.

In a "Tale of the Tape": Taylor was taller (+2½"), older (+2 years), and had a reach advantage (+3¼"). Taylor had a larger chest, waist, thighs, claves, and forearms. Taylor also had a slight weight advantage at 118 pounds (+1).[2]

Tony Canzoneri v. Bud Taylor, NBA Bantamweight Title

The Associated Press called the fight a "fierce draw."[3] The partisan Midwest crowd, estimated at 7,000, gave a slight edge to Bud Taylor. Since Tony Canzoneri answered every assault punch for punch, any conclusion other than a draw would have been questionable. Let's take a closer look.

Canzoneri, who tipped at 117, looked nervous in the opening round. Missing a wild shot to the head, he took a deep breath to calm down. He then moved to combinations over heavy ordnance. Meanwhile, Taylor, who scaled to a pound advantage, went to the body. Both fighters were bleeding from their right eyes at the end of Round One.

Landing with the left, Canzoneri stayed above the shoulders with combinations. Taylor, successful delivering lefts to the body, maintained that strategy in Round Two.

Canzoneri broke ground and backed into the ropes for the first time in the bout—the body blows, no doubt, the reason. Yet he continued to trade punches. Taylor continued to have success with the left in Round Three.

Both antagonists continued their fight strategies in Round Four. Canzoneri appeared stronger at the beginning of the round, while Taylor finished in spirited form.

As Round Five opened, Canzoneri landed with sweeping lefts to the face. Yet

Taylor remained unfazed and continued his body attack. It was Canzoneri's best round of the battle. Reaching the halfway point of the confrontation, observers were wondering: How much more damage could Taylor's face endure? And could Canzoneri maintain his pace under such a fierce body onslaught?

Canzoneri began backing away from Taylor's body assaults in Round Six. An amalgam of punches by Taylor drove Canzoneri to the ropes. As both fighters exchanged blows, the session ended.

Taylor maintained his body barrage, and soon it was clear Canzoneri had slowed enough for Taylor to begin landing to the head. A furious exchange ended Round Seven.

Canzoneri sent Taylor to the ropes, courtesy of a powerful combination to the skull. Round Eight ended with each fighter delivering solid lefts to the opponent's countenance.

A brisk facial assault by Canzoneri forced Taylor to retreat. Though Taylor was missing high, he continued to land to the frame of his opposer. Round Nine ended with both warriors exchanging body punches.

After shaking hands, both gladiators traded assaults and held their ground. When the gong ended the battle, it looked even.

Some saw it for Canzoneri, giving him the first, fifth, sixth, seventh and eighth sessions, while calling it even in the second, third, fourth and tenth. If you do the math, don't forget to add the Chicago factor and include Taylor's position as title holder to the equation: It was a draw.

Referee Joe Choynski, the old-time heavyweight, and two judges were unanimous in their verdict. It was indeed a draw. Staying out of range, Canzoneri used his left with precision, and it kept him in the fight. It was a wonderful performance by both fighters.

Almost immediately after the bout, the telegrams poured in with offers for a rematch. New York wanted the fight, although it was a question whether Tex Rickard or Humbert J. Fugazy could entice the promotion. Naturally, Rickard wanted it for his new Garden, while Fugazy saw the Polo Grounds as the logical venue. While Goldman was leaning toward Fugazy, the offers weren't on the table yet. Then there was Jim Mullen, who was resolved at keeping it in Chicago. Besides, he still had *his* belt.

Tony Canzoneri wasn't eager to get back in the ring after facing Bud Taylor. It was understandable. Nevertheless, when he learned Jim Mullen was likely to take the rematch, he understood that he had to stay in shape. Goldman signed him to two battles in April. The first was against the mauler Vic Burrone on April 18 at St. Nicholas Arena, followed by Harold Smith on April 25 at the Broadway Arena. He would also meet Chick Suggs on May 3 in Chicago.

St. Nicholas Arena

During the 1920s, the most popular neighborhood fight club was St. Nicholas Arena, located on the northeast corner of 66th Street and Columbus Avenue (69 West 66th Street). It was a hop, skip and a jump east of Broadway. Built as an ice-skating rink in 1896, it became a prototype for such facilities in the United States. Boxing became an alternative in 1906. With its capacity of about 4,000, which included a balcony, it was a hit with fight fans. The smoke-filled venue, which drew obstreperous and occasionally intoxicated patrons, attracted everyone from businessman Diamond Jim Brady to wrestler Gorgeous George.

If Canzoneri wanted to stay sharp, fighting West Sider Vic Burrone could guarantee it. But why did it have to be right after the Taylor fight? Granted, Sammy Goldman was rumored to be unsatisfied with his fighter's performance—Canzoneri struggled to make weight—against Taylor, but putting him in the ring against Burrone was dangerous. Known for making distance along with punishing his opposers, the Boston-born Burrone was a dangerous gladiator.

A clamorous crowd of 3,500 fight fans watched as Tony Canzoneri, who tipped at 122, fought Vic Burrone, who scaled a pound lighter, to a 10-round draw. It was Canzoneri's debut at the Arena, and a memorable one at that, as many felt he was lucky to leave without a loss. Counting rounds, Canzoneri took the first six at lightning speed; however, he attempted to coast the final frames. Yet there was no coasting against a vicious fighter like Burrone. The West Side resident took all the ground he lost in the earlier rounds and made it a contest. Luring Canzoneri inside, Burrone lathered him with left hands. In the ninth round, Burrone struck with a damaging left hook, opening a nasty cut over Canzoneri's left eye. Although Burrone was relentless in the final round, it wasn't enough to take the fight.

Members of the press tried to paint Canzoneri "as fresh as a daisy" after his bout with Burrone, but those who saw the battle knew better.[4] After his second consecutive draw, not to mention being belted around like a pinball for four rounds, Canzoneri was looking forward to taking time off. Harold Smith, at least to Canzoneri, was a good fighter but not nearly as aggressive as Burrone.

As much a showman as a battler, Harold Smith was a fan favorite in Chicago. A victory over Canzoneri could push him into a title shot against Bud Taylor, and he liked the idea. But it would remain a fantasy as Tony Canzoneri, who scaled at 121¾, knocked out Harold Smith, who tipped at 120. The end came after one minute and 15 seconds of the third round at the Broadway Arena. Smith was staggered in the first round, dropped in the second, and out on his feet in the third. Referee Patsy Haley had little choice but to step in and stop the contest.

On May 3, Bud Taylor, the recognized bantam champ, captured a decision over veteran Abe Attell Goldstein inside the Coliseum in Chicago. The semi–wind-up of the evening saw Tony Canzoneri, who scaled at 121½, score a technical knockout against overrated local pugilist Ray Rychell (substitute for Chick Suggs) in the seventh round. More than 8,000 dedicated fight fans witnessed the closing indoor show at the Coliseum.

When the July 1927 of issue of *The Ring* hit newsstands, it featured the handsome countenance of Tony Canzoneri on the cover. His movie star looks and million-dollar smile almost guaranteed a sale to any female passerby, and editor Nat Fleischer knew it. Writer Francis Albertanti pushed Canzoneri into the spotlight, while reporting that he turned 21 on November 26, 1926. He did not.

The Marlboro Farm

In 1927, Tony Canzoneri purchased a farm in Marlboro, New York, for $25,000. It was a beautiful setting of about 144 acres where he hosted his family and hoped to retire one day. The farm produced apples, grapes and vegetables marketed to wholesalers. Later, other businesses were born from the property. Although his immediate concern was setting up an indoor and outdoor training camp, he hoped to add a swimming pool and a handball court. Pitching a regulation outdoor boxing ring on the property, he surrounded the area with all the necessary equipment. Since sparring partners were scarce in Marlboro, Sammy Goldman sent trainer Izzy "The Painter" into the city to recruit a hoard of punching bags.

Bud Taylor v. Tony Canzoneri, NBA Bantamweight Title

In an old-fashioned shootout, Bud Taylor withstood 10 rounds of toe-to-toe confrontation against Tony Canzoneri to successfully defend his title for the first time or to rightfully claim the vacant NBA world bantamweight title. Both fighters scaled at 117½ pounds. It was the main event of Jim Mullen's boxing show held on June 24 at Wrigley Field in Chicago, and it was one of the best displays of pugilism folks had seen in years.[5] Taylor, having profited from the lessons of their first battle, was a near constant aggressor. As a result, he took the unanimous decision. Referee Joe Choynski, along with judges Earl L. Cook and William R. Fetzer, made their united verdict in front of more than 15,000 dedicated fight fans.

Taylor started aggressively and drove Canzoneri to the ropes. As the pair traded lefts, the blood started to flow from Taylor's nose and Canzoneri's lips. Taylor also delivered a solid right to the jaw of Canzoneri. Nearly everyone ringside saw the opening session as even.

Catching Canzoneri flush on the jaw with a left hook was proof of Taylor's modified strategy. Unlike their first battle, Taylor didn't concentrate on merely the body. Round Two belonged to Taylor.

Canzoneri delivered solid combinations to the head and looked better than he did during the first two rounds. The left hook he caught last round was a wake-up call. Canzoneri's round.

Canzoneri delivered a left hook to the jaw, a solid right to the body, and three solid rights to the jaw. Taylor sent an accurate right cross to the face, firm combinations to the body, and two accurate left jabs to the face. Round Four was viewed as even.

Instructed to pick up the pace, Canzoneri complied. He sent two accurate left crosses to the jaw, a hard right to the chest, and two firm left hooks to the jaw. Frustrated Taylor sent a left to the body followed by a punch south of the border. A solid left to the jaw of Canzoneri was his last best punch of the term. Looking tired, Taylor began covering during assaults. Canzoneri's round.

Canzoneri came out headhunting in Round Six. Taylor moved to the uppercut and scored with it to the body and the jaw. The round was even.

Canzoneri continued headhunting. A firm Canzoneri right uppercut to the body, before burying a left hook to the solar plexus, surprised Taylor. Returning two firm left hooks to the jaw and a solid left hook to the body was Taylor's response. Most saw Round Seven as even.

The momentum was solidly with Bud Taylor in Round Eight and Round Nine. After delivering two lefts to the face and a right to the jaw, Taylor drew Canzoneri inside and gave him a robust lacing to the body. This forced Canzoneri to hang on. Taylor continued to pound Canzoneri's body unmercifully during Round Nine, and when he saw a shot at the head, he took it and scored. Both rounds favored Taylor.

After the two shook hands to begin Round Ten, Canzoneri released a salvo at Taylor's head and body. Taylor went to the head with firm left hands and solid right crosses. Canzoneri did manage to take Taylor to the ropes and deliver a few painful body shots. Although the round was even, the fight ended in Taylor's favor.

The fair-weather press, such as Jimmy Woods, took fewer than three days to declare neither Taylor nor Canzoneri the future bantamweight champion but instead opted for Filipino Ignacio Fernandez. It was a ridiculous assessment, yet typical of certain beat writers of the era. Granted, Fernandez was a skilled boxer and his victory over Abe Goldstein, on the Taylor-Canzoneri undercard, was impressive, but he would win only five of his next 17 bouts.[6]

Speaking of the press, Canzoneri was gradually becoming more comfortable with reporters. The teenager admitted to his nervousness against Taylor during their first meeting but overcame the anxiety during their rematch. Naturally, the loss, via unanimous decision, wasn't easy to take, but Canzoneri made no excuses. He got his licks in against Taylor, who happened to suffer a split bone over his left optic nerve that required surgery.

Goldman wanted his fighter back in the ring as soon as possible, therefore he inked him to another 10-round contest against California Joe Lynch. This time the show was held at the Olympic Arena in Cleveland on July 27. Lynch, a veteran of more than 100 bouts, was on the downside of a solid career. Canzoneri glided over the distance to capture a decision victory. Taking a solid beating, Lynch attempted to answer every assault and to his credit lasted all 10 rounds. Canzoneri, who went to

Fans lined up along Bedford Avenue outside Ebbets Field in Brooklyn in 1920 (Library of Congress).

the left hook for body blows, reserved the right for heavy damage. As usual, he controlled the bout with his jab.

Word came the first week of August that Tony Canzoneri would likely meet Red Chapman over the 15-round route at Ebbets Field. The winner would fill the vacancy caused by Connecticut featherweight Louis "Kid" Kaplan's title resignation.[7] Goldman confirmed his fighter could make 118 pounds to take the bout with Chapman. However, organizers insisted Canzoneri make a definitive statement over his next four fights before they completed the agreement.

It was over to Queensboro Stadium in Long Island City, as Canzoneri finally— Mother Nature having failed to cooperate in the past—met veteran Cowboy Eddie Anderson on August 9. Hailing from Wyoming, Anderson held victories over Johnny Jadick, Edouard Mascart, and Sammy Mandell (1922 newspaper victory). His brother, Buffalo Billy Anderson, was also a pugilist. Canzoneri, taking nothing for granted, was in outstanding shape and came in at 125 pounds, or one pound less than the featherweight limit. Anderson, always willing to rough it up, decided to fire at will in the first round with hopes of a short night. It was a bad idea, as Canzoneri withstood the assault. From the second frame until the seventh, the Brooklyn boxer pounded Anderson's countenance much the same as a hammer over a railroad spike. The bout was almost stopped in the fourth round by referee Tommy Sheridan, when there was a concern about how much blood Anderson was losing. Witnessing the disfigurement, Canzoneri appeared to pull back from his assaults in rounds eight and nine. Both fighters started the final round strong, but Anderson, who tipped at 127½, quickly faded. The 10-round verdict went to Canzoneri.

Returning to his farm in Marlboro, New York, Canzoneri prepared for his August 17 battle against Pete Sarmiento. Promoters Andy Niederreiter and Bill McGuire were staging a gigantic—their choice of an adjective which pushed the limit of the definition—boxing show at Ebbets Field. The extravaganza featured Joe Glick versus Andre Routis, Cowboy Eddie Anderson versus Sammy Dorfman, and two opening bouts. The *New York Daily News* couldn't resist the opportunity to adorn their Sunday, August 14, 1927, issue with a cover photograph of Tony Canzoneri driving cows on his farm—a change from the traditional image of a pugilist chopping wood.

More than 25,000 crazed fight fans poured into Ebbets Field in Brooklyn to view the phenomenon known as Tony Canzoneri, aka the future of the featherweight division. Having had two featherweight kings (Terry McGovern and Tommy Sullivan), Brooklyn was prepared to add a third. It looked very feasible judging by Canzoneri's prowess and performance. Sarmiento, who hailed from the Philippines, bounded from his corner with visions of victory dancing in his head. But the dance ended two minutes and 51 seconds into the opening round. That was when a crashing right hand to the head of Sarmiento had the lights blinking; moreover, the Filipino was stuck against the ropes of a neutral corner. Another crushing right to the jaw followed by a ramrod to the breadbasket dropped Sarmiento to his knees. On the canvas referee Lou Magnolia tolled the required 10 digits before assisting Sarmiento to his corner for resuscitation. No sooner had the fight ended when whispers of "set up" could be heard ringside. A mismatch? Yes. A conspiracy? No. Sarmiento hadn't fought in a few months, and it showed. Nevertheless, the fans loved it. Tipping at 124, Canzoneri needed the morale boost. Sarmiento, who scaled at 119½, hadn't won a bout since September 1926.[8] In addition to the feature, the semi-final of the evening provided a spirited encounter as Joe Glick, a (Williamsburg) Brooklyn junior light-weight, slugged it out over the 10-round distance to capture an action-packed victory over Frenchman André Routis.

Carrying his momentum out to Kansas City, Canzoneri "decisively outpointed" Mexican Joe Rivers over the 10-round distance at Convention Hall.[9] The uninspiring newspaper decision was a slow and systematic conquest. Rivers, who had more than a six-pound advantage, could do little more than watch Canzoneri dance to victory—Rivers lost a $500 weight forfeit to Team Canzoneri. Even if the 6,000-plus in attendance were unimpressed by Canzoneri's performance, they understood it was a rare appearance by a future ring star. East Coast pugilists seldom made it to Kansas City at this stage of their career.

Turning to the press: Damon Runyon found time to mention that it was he who first acknowledged the skills of Tony Canzoneri, thanks to a letter he received from matchmaker Silvey Burns, aka the Nostrodamus of the Brooklyn prize ring. Runyon confirmed that he agreed with Mr. Josephus Humphreys, who—unprofessionally and out of character—introduced Canzoneri at Ebbets Field as "the next champion of his class," even though Runyon wasn't certain as to which division he meant. Granted, Humphreys was the vocal barometer of the business, but Runyon facetiously claimed he couldn't excuse the announcer until he learned to be more specific.

Speaking of details, Eddie Anderson, scheduled to meet Tony Canzoneri on September 2 at Mills Stadium in Chicago, was facing a ring conflict of a different sort. Mrs. Anderson, not happy with the Wyoming cowboy, filed suit for separate maintenance from the fighter. "Madder'n a wet hen," Anderson turned his anger toward the boxing ring. He rode into the venue and picked up a victory over Canzoneri courtesy of a foul. All 8,500 fans appeared to agree with the call as there was little protest. The low blow came at the end of the second round, and Anderson remarkably managed to make it until the bell. If it was an alternative to an economic problem, it was a painful one. During the intermission between rounds, Dr. Edwin Wachlin, the boxing commission physician, examined Anderson and confirmed that he had been fouled. Referee Joe Choynski declared Anderson the victor via the action.

Canzoneri sent a blow south of the border in the opening salvo and was warned at the intermission. Early in the second frame, Canzoneri delivered Anderson to the canvas for a nine count with a similar low punch. The fight ending strike came about 15 seconds from the end of the second session. Even the press admitted the foul honors were about even when the end came. Unfortunately, the one-way vision of Choynski did not work in Canzoneri's favor. At the conclusion of the battle, Canzoneri was suspended for 90 days by the Illinois State Athletic Commission, and his state license was revoked.

After the fight, rumors flew that Canzoneri was close to being inked for a battle against Johnny Dundee, the world's (unofficial) featherweight champion. Dundee lost the junior lightweight title to Steve Sullivan in June of 1924 and then relinquished the featherweight crown two months later because he was having trouble making weight—fight fans still considered him the unsanctioned champion. Regardless of what the commissions believed, if Canzoneri defeated Dundee in New York at 126 pounds, few could deny him the crown. However, one of the few could be Benny Bass, who defeated Red Chapman in Philadelphia on September 12, 1927, for the vacant NBA featherweight championship of the world.

Tony Canzoneri opened the indoor season at the Broadway Arena on October 3. Matchmaker Andy Niederreiter inked the fighter to meet Tommy Ryan, aka Charles Marino, who hailed from McKeesport, Pennsylvania. A dangerous veteran battler, Ryan claimed he had never been knocked out or even floored. Both fighters, finding it difficult to meet the bantam limit, battled as featherweights.

Scaling at 125½, Tony Canzoneri took a points victory over veteran Tommy Ryan, who tipped at 124½.[10] The seasoned Ryan, who was floored for a nine count and saved by the bell in the fourth frame, would not back down. Canzoneri, knowing he had his opposer in trouble after the fourth, tried unsuccessfully to finish him off. The Buffalo boxer took an unmerciful beating from the fifth round until the conclusion of the battle. Ironically, Canzoneri—who had in his corner Sammy Goldman, legend Pete Herman, and Izzy "The Painter"—was booed for his inability to knock out his opposition.

"Little Bar of Iron," Giuseppe Curreri–Johnny Dundee

It was confirmed during the second week of October that Tony Canzoneri would meet veteran Johnny Dundee over 15 rounds at Madison Square Garden on October 24. Since Dundee had no championship status in New York State, it would not be a title fight—the state boxing commission would not recognize it. However, the

winner would likely be considered the world's featherweight champion regardless of any designation. Dundee, the old master, didn't believe Benny Bass, who recently defeated Red Chapman, was the champion. He reiterated that he had never been beaten for his NBA title.[11]

When Tony Canzoneri, 18, met living legend Johnny Dundee, 33, at Madison Square Garden, both found the situation hard to believe. Canzoneri, who had boxed the veteran in the gym, had picked up a few tricks from Dundee such as how to tie up an opponent. The teenager never thought he would formally meet "Little Bar of Iron" in a boxing ring, and certainly not inside such a prestigious venue.

You could hear a pin drop in the Garden dressing

Giuseppe Curreri, aka Johnny Dundee, shown here in the 1910s, won the junior lightweight and featherweight titles. His loss to Tony Canzoneri in 1927 was his last significant bout.

room before the bout. None of Canzoneri's seconds said a word to their fighter, by order of Sammy Goldman. The fight manager didn't want his fighter to overthink the affair, nor did he want him to view Dundee as the champion. Finally entering the ring, Canzoneri, a 6–5 favorite, was sitting on his stool when Goldman whispered in his ear that he wanted him to knock Dundee down, then pick him back up. Although Canzoneri felt the request was peculiar, he did not argue. He spent 15 rounds trying to knock down Dundee. While he failed at the mission, he won the war.

Tony Canzoneri, who scaled at 124, defeated Johnny Dundee, who tipped at 125½, via a 15-round points victory. The lackluster fight had no exciting moments, only a smattering of interesting exchanges that reminded fans whom they were watching. It was Dundee, the old Italian master, who prevented the more than 8,800 Garden fans from booing both fighters from the ring. Not overthinking the task, Canzoneri dominated the battle. Hats off to Sammy Goldman, who kept his fighter's head in the game. In the wake of the bout, the press was critical of Canzoneri for appearing to pull his punches. Since Dundee had a year's layoff and there were no damaging punches, many, including the Associated Press, questioned the integrity of the battle. Sammy Goldman, who always spoke on behalf of his fighter, refused to acknowledge the absurd statement.

After the bout, Eddie Long, Bud Taylor's manager, announced that he had accepted an offer of $20,000 from Tex Rickard for his fighter to meet Tony Canzoneri on December 5 in Madison Square Garden. As Rickard wanted the bout as a featherweight championship match, Taylor would be stepping out of the bantam division.

Getting out of town in the wake of the Dundee bout, Sammy Goldman wanted to protect his fighter from additional criticism. It was off to Philadelphia for a battle against Billy Henry on November 7. Tipping at 126, Tony Canzoneri knocked out punching bag Henry, who scaled four pounds heavier. It happened during the second round of a scheduled 10-round contest at the Arena. Had the bell not rung as the referee reached the count of four, the result would have been a first-round kayo. Having delivered a hard right into the side of Canzoneri, Henry let his guard down and caught a stunning right to the jaw that dropped him to his back. Miraculously, he was able to come out of his corner for the second round, but he wasn't vertical for long. A Canzoneri combination, a left hook followed by a right uppercut, quickly sent his adversary horizontal. He was hit so hard that it took five minutes to bring Henry back to earth so he could leave the ring.

To stay sharp, Goldman booked his fighter into the Olympia Athletic Club, in Harlem, on November 22. Wasting little time, Tony Canzoneri grabbed a first-round technical knockout victory over club fighter Vincent DiLeo. It was a bit of a surprise as DiLeo was being hailed as a talented prospect by New Jersey newspapers such as the *Morning Call*.

Ignacio Fernandez was not Bud Taylor, but since the latter drew a suspension courtesy of an injured hand, the former greeted Tony Canzoneri in Madison Square Garden on December 1. It wasn't a friendly welcome. Canzoneri began in typical form, then ramped up his intensity as if to immediately deliver Fernandez. But instead of the Filipino backing down, Fernandez countered with speed and intensity, much to the surprise of Canzoneri. This forced the Brooklyn fighter to opt for chipping away rounds one by one, in hopes of earning a victory. Canzoneri nearly had Fernandez out in the seventh round but punched himself out. This left the door open for Fernandez to take command in the eighth frame. Bounced around the ring like a child in a rumble seat, Canzoneri protected himself from a severe beating thanks to timely combinations. Rooting for the underdog, the crowd wanted a knockout, but Fernandez couldn't comply. When Canzoneri picked up the 10-round verdict, many felt Fernandez had been robbed. Were the judges influenced by Canzoneri meeting Taylor in the Garden at the end of the month? Nobody was positive, but what was certain was Rickard's desire to preserve his title gate.

Canzoneri v. Taylor, III

On the eve of his bout against Bud Taylor, Tony Canzoneri was a 7–5 favorite. The odds were a surprise considering Canzoneri had lost twice to his rival. Taylor's NBA bantamweight title was not on the line.

Tony Canzoneri, scaling at 125½, captured a unanimous decision victory over Bud Taylor, who tipped at 121.[12] Referee Patsy Haley, along with judges Charles F. Mathison and Stuart Douglas, all saw it Canzoneri. The furious battle was conducted in front of 14,000 Garden spectators who enjoyed every minute. Ringside believed Canzoneri edged out seven rounds, Taylor took two, and one round was even. Others saw it much closer with Canzoneri taking four rounds, Taylor three, and three even.

Taylor scored repeatedly with his vicious left hooks, and Canzoneri countered them with solid rights. "The Blonde Terror of Terre Haute" had his opposer in trouble in the first and seventh terms, but his rival recovered. When it was over, many believed the opening round, in which Canzoneri suffered a slight cut, was the highlight of the fight. While Taylor was given the edge in Round One, Canzoneri bounded back in the second. He used a vicious right cross that struck Taylor so hard it knocked his mouthpiece across the ring. Taylor slowed enough in the fourth to allow Canzoneri to take the momentum. A festering

Prolific and hard-hitting, Benny Bass (shown here in the 1920s) won the vacant NBA featherweight championship in 1927 and the junior lightweight title in 1929.

behavior that wasn't born in this fight but had intensified for months was Canzoneri's condescending actions when he had an opponent in trouble. He would stop fighting, plant a humiliating smile on his face, then drop his guard. While the cocksure attitude perturbed spectators, it proved to energize Taylor. As soon as he saw it, he rammed a heavy body punch, nearly dropping Canzoneri face-first to the canvas. A left hook to the jaw of Canzoneri in the seventh round dazed the fighter and gave the round to Taylor. But by the end of the bout, it was clear that Taylor had been outpunched. Scoring with flurries that rattled the Indiana pugilist, Canzoneri had enough power to win rounds even if he lacked the strength to knock out his rival. The verdict was met with approval.

The New York State Athletic Commission recognized Canzoneri as the featherweight champion despite the Pennsylvania commission still claiming the title belonged to Benny Bass of Philadelphia. Not surprisingly, a match between Canzoneri and Bass to settle the dispute was in the works.

Participating in 20 bouts in 1927, Canzoneri posted a record of 15–2–3. His trilogy against elite pugilist Bud Taylor was the highlight. It garnered him his first major recognition: featherweight champion of the world as viewed by the New York State Athletic Commission (NYSAC). Although the designation was appreciated, Canzoneri knew it meant little until he defeated Benny Bass. Of all his career battles, the one he always talked about was his bout against Johnny Dundee. Having fought many an elite pugilist, including Benny Leonard nine times, Dundee appeared in more than 300 professional fights. Raised on Manhattan's West Side, Giuseppe Curreri, aka Johnny Dundee, began his professional boxing career in 1910. Canzoneri heard stories about Dundee when he was a child growing up and never dreamed of meeting him, yet alone inside a boxing ring. And the pair would become good friends.

FOUR

Confirmation, 1928–1929

"Don't ever forget two things I'm going to tell you. One, don't believe
everything that is written about you. Two, don't pick up too many
checks."—Babe Ruth

1928

Progress was in the city air as Central Park West was widened to 100 feet to
match Fifth and Sixth avenues, land values surged—up nearly 75 percent for the
decade—and the city's first classified telephone directory was issued by New York
Telephone Company. Many believed the population of New York City could reach
seven million by 1930—the most populated borough being Brooklyn.

Hosting its fair share of ring battles, New York City was a pugilist's delight in
1928: On January 6 at Madison Square Garden, Tommy Loughran hit the deck twice
in the opening round before battling his way back to a 15-round unanimous decision over Leo Lomski; Jack Sharkey, a 3–1 favorite, knocked out Jack Delaney at the
1:13 mark of the opening round in a bout held at the Garden on April 30; in their
first meeting, on May 21 at the Polo Grounds, Sammy Mandell dominated an almost
blinded Jimmy McLarnin to take a 15-round unanimous decision; at Yankee Stadium on July 26, Gene Tunney brilliantly defended his world heavyweight championship against Tom Heeney by way of an 11th-round technical knockout, then retired
five days later; and "Cinderella Man" James J. Braddock dropped Tuffy Griffiths four
times in the second round to capture a technical knockout victory at Madison Square
Garden on November 30.

A quick look at the dominant boxers in each weight class in 1928: Heavy-
weights—Gene Tunney; Light Heavyweights—Tommy Loughran; Middleweights—
Mickey Walker; Welterweights—Joe Dundee; Junior Welterweights—Ruby Goldstein;
Lightweights—Sammy Mandell; Junior Lightweights—Tod Morgan; Feather-
weights—Tony Canzoneri; Bantamweights—Bud Taylor; and Flyweights—Corporal
Izzy Schwartz. Canzoneri hoped his first championship bout would be against Benny
Bass to unify the title, but he wasn't certain. Other division contenders included Joey
Sangor, Andy Martin, and Red Chapman.

Jess McMahon, matchmaker for Madison Square Garden, wanted the fight
between Tony Canzoneri and Benny Bass to happen under his roof as soon as possible. He hoped it would be considered a title fight, as Bass received a championship (National Boxing Association, NBA) rating in Philadelphia after defeating Red

48

Chapman, and Canzoneri was recognized by the local boxing commission as having the best claim of any fighter. As fate had it, McMahon initially inked the fight for January 27 at the Garden, and both the NBA and the New York State Athletic Commission (NYSAC) agreed to recognize the winner as the world's champion. And there was more: Both Bass and Canzoneri would battle for 25 percent of the receipts.

Unfortunately, Benny Bass came down with an illness, forcing a postponement of the bout. It was rescheduled for February 10. Not buying what they saw as an excuse by the Philadelphia pugilist, NYSAC suspended fight manager Phil Glassman and his entire stable of fighters, which included Benny Bass. It was a costly mistake.

Realizing his fighter needed a warm-up battle, Sammy Goldman spoke with Ben Feinberg at the Philadelphia Arena and inked Canzoneri to a bout with Pete Nebo. It appeared like a good fit as Nebo was a competitive boxer. Born in Cuba and living in Key West, the pugilist recently took Benny Bass the distance in a split-decision loss.

On January 30, Tony Canzoneri, who scaled at 120, fought Pete Nebo, who tipped seven pounds heavier, to a 10-round draw. Fast and furious, the bout left the crowd of 10,000 fight fans satisfied despite the verdict. Judge Frank Knarsborough ruled in favor of Canzoneri and Judge Al Voice saw it for Nebo, leaving Referee Frank Floyd to declare it a draw. Most ringside observers agreed. While Nebo surprised many with his speed, accuracy, and durability, it was his fluid movement that made Canzoneri look foolish—the latter was missing his punches. Many who witnessed the Key West fighter's bout against Bass believed he fought even better against Canzoneri.

Benny Bass

Benjamin Baruch J. Bass, aka "Little Fish," was born in Kiev, Ukraine.[1] His family emigrated to the United States in 1906 and settled in Philadelphia. Compact and muscular, Bass, who stood five feet, two inches, was a product of good genetics. As a newsboy on the streets of Philadelphia, he quickly learned to stake his ground and defend it against all comers. Honing his skills as a prolific amateur pugilist, Bass qualified for the Olympic trials in the flyweight class in 1920. Ironically, losing a decision to future gold medal winner Frankie Genaro convinced him he was ready to turn professional. Bass won the Pennsylvania state featherweight championship in 1927 and the inaugural NBA featherweight title the same year. Prior to meeting Tony Canzoneri, he held victories over Mike Ballerino, Red Chapman, and Joe Glick.

Tony Canzoneri v. Benny Bass, NBA and NYSAC World Featherweight Title

"Pre-battle opinion is evenly divided. Both lads have a host of followers who are backing up their statements with coin from the mint. This contest figures to outdraw any battle between little fellows in years.

It is no secret that the fighters hold each other in contempt. This is a poor spirit and may prove the deciding factor before the fight has gone many rounds. On class, Canzoneri figures to win. He has traveled the long route several times and proved his ability to go along at a fast pace. If Tony will only forget to show off before the home folks until the business at hand is over, he has a glorious chance of coming out a winner."—*Evening Star*, Washington, D.C.[2]

Before a Garden crowd of 14,000, Tony Canzoneri, an 8–5 favorite, was confident entering the ring against Benny Bass. Granted, a two-inch edge in height, along with a two-and-one-half-inch reach advantage was part of the reason, but the remainder was proper preparation. He was ready.

Scaling at 125, Tony Canzoneri was awarded a split decision victory over Benny Bass, who tipped a pound heavier. Bass sustained a broken right collarbone after a vicious third round attack sent him crashing to the canvas. A Canzoneri left to the jaw sent him off balance against the ropes, then onto the ring floor; consequently, the bell saved him at the count of eight. Taking considerable criticism for not tearing into Bass in the fourth and finishing him off, Canzoneri fought his fight, opting to accumulate points. Having no understanding of the extent of his opponent's injury, he made the proper decision. Yet it was not a simple task as the Brooklyn boxer was the recipient of considerable body punishment. Bass grew frustrated as the fight wore on and was twice warned by referee Arthur Donovan for punches below the belt. For his efforts, Canzoneri became the legitimate successor to the championship vacated by Louis "Kid" Kaplan years earlier.[3]

At the age of 19 years, three months, and four days, excluding the end date, Tony Canzoneri was the featherweight champion of the world. Even as a teenager he promised himself he would be a fighting champion—there would be no hiding in the bushes.

Later, Canzoneri admitted he loved the money and liked the title, but honestly he wanted to add a lightweight crown to his portfolio. As he saw it, only the lightweight and heavyweight titles were worth holding. After all, what fighter drew better than Benny Leonard or Jack Dempsey?

Thrilled by the victory, the entire Canzoneri family had their picture taken surrounding the new champion, and the photograph ran in newspapers across the country. Although the fight offers poured into Goldman's office, Canzoneri wasn't scheduled to box again until February 23. He would battle against Pete Passafiume in one of many four-round matches being staged at the Broadway Arena. The evening was a testimonial (thus the short distance) to former ring gladiator and arbiter Joe Bernstein. The former featherweight was ill in an upstate sanatorium.

Taking a four-round victory over Pete Passafiume, Tony Canzoneri, scaling four pounds lighter at 129, appeared every bit a champion. Conducting a brilliant exhibition that pleased the audience, he was impressive. Abstaining from heavy ordnance—he didn't need it—Canzoneri used light air cover to dance to victory. Unfortunately, after the match, the featherweight champion learned that he was suffering from tonsillitis. Convalescing at a private hospital on East 62nd Street, it wasn't long after the removal of his tonsils that Canzoneri exhibited signs of pneumonia—the illness proved to be the grippe instead. To say he wasn't thrilled by the setback would be an understatement.

Word hit the press the first week of April that Tony Canzoneri was slowly regaining his health at home in Marlboro, and he would meet Harry Blitman in May or June—it turned out to be June 27. His mother's care and a little of her chicken soup, aka the cure-all, would have him back on his feet in no time. The name Benny Bass was being thrown around as a possible opponent for a title defense, but nothing was firm. The healing process picked up momentum when the entire Canzoneri clan learned they were heading back to southeastern Louisiana.

Meantime, two foreign boxing champions—Kid Frances, bantamweight champion of Europe, and André Routis, the European featherweight champion—were making noise on American soil. Frances hoped to meet Bud Taylor, the NBA bantam champion, while Routis had his eyes on Canzoneri. Both had to be patient, even if it wasn't easy.

Heading to New Orleans in early May gave Canzoneri plenty of time to prepare for his fight at the Coliseum Arena against Claude Wilson on May 17. Later, the bout was postponed until May 28 because of Canzoneri's illness.

While convalescing, Canzoneri planned to visit with family and friends and even drop by the old neighborhood. The champion hoped to visit all his old haunts, from the Palmyra Street grocery store where he ran errands for the owner, to the Gayaso Athletic Club where he worked with John Galway and Basil Galiano. The New Orleans promotion was handled by Frank Walker, and while he intended on filling the 9,000-seat venue, he understood that a successful contest depended on a healthy Tony Canzoneri. In this no-decision bout (that is, when, by law or prior agreement, if both fighters were still standing at the end of a bout and there was no knockout, no decision was made and neither boxer was named the winner) both fighters were required to make the featherweight limit of 126 pounds. For Wilson, the pride of Birmingham, Alabama, it was an incredible opportunity. The youngster, far from a tomato can, had an impressive amateur career and as a professional recently defeated Ignacio Fernandez. But Fernandez wasn't Canzoneri.

In a brilliant display, Tony Canzoneri took less than two minutes of the opening round to floor Claude Wilson with machine-gun combinations.[4] Trying hard to land the plane, Wilson arose at the count of nine, in time to take a precision left hook, followed by a right jab. Referee Red Dolan, amidst cries to stop the fight, stepped in and waved it off. The crowd of 7,000-plus enthusiastic fight fans were enraptured by "their Tony's" presentation.

Delighted by his performance, not to mention inspired by his New Orleans visit, Tony Canzoneri was in good spirits. Finally on the road to recovery, his trademark grin was back. Witnessing this, Sammy Goldman hoped to ink his fighter for two or three fights during the month of June.

To kick off the month, Sammy Goldman signed Canzoneri to his first international bout. It would take place in Canada. Jake Carey, who hailed from Rochester, New York, was the former promoter at the Genesee Valley Athletic Club. Having retired for a couple of years, Carey sought to get back into the fight game in a big way. He hooked up with the Stadium Athletic Club in Canada and was conducting his first large promotion in Montreal on June 13. Goldman, familiar with Carey, agreed to sign Canzoneri to meet veteran Vic Foley. Holding victories over Bud Taylor, Frankie Klick, and California Joe Lynch, Foley was a talented boxer who won four times as many battles as he lost. The bout was fought at catchweight.

Capturing a 10-round decision victory over Vic Foley, Canzoneri was impressive. Both fighters scaled at 127 pounds. The non-title fight was held at the Montreal Baseball Stadium. Canzoneri conducted an early exposition as he danced around Foley like he was standing still. In the fourth round, the champion opened a cut over his opposer's eye that hampered the Vancouver pugilist throughout the contest. Taking the fifth round, Canzoneri went inside in the sixth term to land heavy blasts—taking two punches for every shot he landed at close quarters, he was satisfied with the assault. Turning up the heat during the final frames, Canzoneri fired at will against a fatigued Vic Foley. Though the decision victory didn't come easy for the champion, few expressed any objection to the verdict.

Sammy Goldman had hoped to match Canzoneri with feather contender Joey Sangor, out in Chicago, the third week of June. But the bout fell through. Desiring to keep his fighter sharp, Goldman turned to Max "Boo" Hoff, who handled boxer Harry Blitman—the fight managers had discussed a match earlier in the year. It was a fight that didn't feel right from the outset. Nevertheless, Sammy Goldman agreed to allow his fighter to meet the undefeated Harry Blitman. The fight was scheduled for June 27 at the Baker Bowl in Philadelphia. More machine than man, or so it appeared, Blitman was strictly regimented when it came to fight preparation. Disposing of sparring partners like ice cold water on a hot summer day, he had every intention of dismantling Tony Canzoneri punch by punch. His sessions at Max Hoff's training camp in Springfield, Delaware County, drew more than 2,000 onlookers. Meanwhile, Canzoneri, who began his training at Pompton Lakes, was finishing his preparation outdoors at Jimmy Dougherty's in Leiperville.[5]

Scaling at 127, Harry Blitman captured all 10 rounds as he drove his adversary, who tipped two pounds heavier, like a trail boss over a head of cattle. Taking a terrible beating, Tony Canzoneri lost every round. The champion was out on his feet in the fifth frame, when he was saved by the bell. Sliced and bleeding over both eyes, his lips swollen to twice the normal size, the champion took the verdict in front of 15,000 screaming fight fans. Then he thanked his lucky stars it wasn't a title bout. The abuse delivered by Blitman didn't need to happen, and the person responsible was Sammy Goldman. Hoff, who could sell ice to an Eskimo, had sold Sammy a block.

No sooner had the fight ended than Max "Boo" Hoff, Blitman's manager, posted a $5,000 forfeit with the commission as a

Southpaw Harry Blitman (shown here in 1928) claimed his 1928 battle against Tony Canzoneri was the highlight of his career.

title fight challenge to Tony Canzoneri. Honestly, there wasn't a chance in hell Blitman was going to get a title shot at Canzoneri. It was amazing how quickly Blitman moved Canzoneri off many sports pages, but this was the case thanks to Max "Boo" Hoff, who spoke for his fighter to anybody who would listen.

Using both newspapers and radio, Hoff threw endless challenges to Canzoneri with hopes of shaming the champion into a confrontation. Thankfully, the Canzoneri camp didn't bite. Had they done so, Canzoneri would have been sorry. Hoff, who was as straight as a hairpin, had his dirty hands in boxing, bootlegging, hijacking, and gambling. Without Blitman's knowledge, the fighter was matched with Canzoneri only if Hoff promised Goldman his champion wouldn't get hurt.[6] This was why Hoff discouraged Blitman from knocking out his adversary.

The second week of August, Sammy Goldman signed his featherweight champion to a 15-round title defense against an unnamed opponent—it would prove to be André Routis. The bout would be held at Madison Square Garden on September 28. A week later, it was noted that NBA bantamweight champion Bud Taylor had voluntarily resigned his title to pursue Tony Canzoneri in the 126-pound division—it was no surprise as Taylor was having trouble making the 118-pound limit. Goldman knew Canzoneri needed a confidence-builder after his recent loss, so he matched him against veteran Bobby Garcia. Nearing the end of a good career, Garcia needed a paycheck more than a victory.

Scoring an impressive knockout of Bobby Garcia brought Tony Canzoneri back on track. Both fighters scaled slightly over 127 pounds for the fight, scheduled for 10 rounds in the Newark Velodrome. Garcia was quickly dropped twice before being counted out by referee Danny Savage at the 1:07 mark of the opening round. It was a deadly right hook to the jaw that dazed Garcia before a follow-up blow dropped him to the canvas. Though he was up at the count of nine, a volley of machine-gun combinations followed by a right to the chin finished the job. A season-record 14,000 spectators turned out for the event.

André Routis

Born in Bordeaux, France, on July 16, 1900, André Routis made his professional boxing debut as a teenager in 1919. He picked up the French bantamweight title in January 1924 by beating his nemesis, Charles Ledoux—it was the third time the pair met and the first victory in the trilogy for Routis.

Struggling the following year, Routis failed in his third attempt at the EBU (European Boxing Union) title, so he began looking elsewhere. After two disappointing losses to future world champion Jack Kid Berg in London, Routis turned to the United States in 1926. During his first visit to America, he compiled a record of 9–5–1, with victories over Cowboy Eddie Anderson (three), Petey Mack and Tommy Crowley. Losses to Joe Glick (two) and Tony Canzoneri he viewed as nothing more than learning experiences. Back in the United States in March 1928, Routis continued to exhibit improvement, especially regarding his defensive skills. Using a protective style featuring crouching, weaving, and wrapping his gloves around his head as he aggressively pushed to close quarters, he confused many an opponent. After victories over Sammy Dorfman (two), Ignacio Fernandez, Carl Duane, and Vic Burrone, it was time for André Routis to face Tony Canzoneri, the featherweight champion of the world.

André Routis v. Tony Canzoneri,
World Featherweight Championship

Tony Canzoneri, a 2–1 favorite to lick Frenchman André Routis, was confident entering Madison Square Garden on September 28. Having whipped his adversary about a year before, the champion had history on his side. But that was the Routis of old, a less experienced and acquiescent fighter who was unfamiliar with the American ring. Routis had honed his skills in Europe, then polished them through experience. Having suffered only one career knockout, back in 1922, his defensive deftness had dramatically improved. Following in the footsteps of Eugene Criqui, who was the first Frenchman to win the crown back in 1923 when he defeated Johnny Kilbane at the Polo Grounds, Routis felt destined. He fought comparable to a champion.

The first bad sign came before the bout even began: Canzoneri weighed in at 127½ at 2 p.m. Thankfully, he was given time to reduce to 125¾. Nobody was certain what impact, if any, it would have on the champion. As usual, rumors flew before the battle, most stating that Canzoneri, the favorite, had the "mill in the bag"; consequently, his odds jumped to 3–1. After the first round, which Canzoneri effortlessly won, it looked as if victory was inevitable. Dropping his rival to a no count, Canzoneri utilized straight lefts and precision rights to do the damage. Routis countered in the second round by beginning a relentless body attack that would gradually take its toll on the champion. It was only when this body assault slowed in the fifth round that Canzoneri began landing combinations. Delivering a right uppercut that saved him from losing the round, Routis nearly decapitated the champion.

In the sixth and seventh frames, Canzoneri composed himself and focused on the task at hand. He even managed to send Routis to the canvas again for a no count— it wasn't via a clean punch, but more of a push that left Routis off balance. Mounting an offensive over the next three rounds enabled the Frenchman to pick up the points he needed. Weakened by the body assaults, Canzoneri drew the 11th round before losing the next three sessions. When the 15th and final round ended even, the champion was concerned. When announcer Joe Humphries gave Canzoneri an unfamiliar glance, he knew the verdict was close. Sure enough, the split decision went to André Routis, the new featherweight champion. Of the 10,000 fight fans in attendance, no one disputed the verdict.[7]

After holding the world featherweight championship for 322 days (not including the end date), Canzoneri was definitively beaten. Sammy Goldman, the fighter's manager, took the blame for not understanding how weakened his fighter was by his required weight loss. Also, he had not given his fighter the right kind, or amount, of work he needed to remain on top of his game. That said, the courage, endurance and persistence of André Routis were remarkable.

Keeping with the French theme, Tony Canzoneri, following a month of rest, took a 10-round points victory over Parisian Gaston Charles at the Broadway Arena on October 29. Both fighters scaled at 130 pounds. Canzoneri once again faced a European-trained boxer who was skilled at covering and blocking. Charles was a talented pugilist who held victories over good boxers such as Al Tripoli and Mickey Goldberg and stood his ground in losing efforts against contenders like Pete Nebo, California Joe Lynch, and Billy Petrolle. Although Canzoneri took command early and outpointed his opposer, he paid the price in cuts and bruises.

Covered with gore at the end of the battle, the former feather champion had a split lower lip and was bleeding from under his right eye. Ringside critics felt Canzoneri hadn't gained all his strength back from his recent illnesses and injuries. His punches lacked power—his best round was his last, when a weakened Charles was nothing more than a punching bag.

Convinced that he needed to take a break from the ring to catch up on the healing process, Canzoneri did just that. In addition to all the facial damage incurred against Charles, Canzoneri's right arm was bothering him from the Routis battle. With the holidays approaching, it was a good time to head north to Marlboro for rest and relaxation.

Invigorated, Canzoneri traveled to the Olympia Athletic Club, at 135 Street and 8th Avenue, in Harlem on December 8. Scaling at 130, Canzoneri knocked out veteran Chick Suggs, who tipped three pounds lighter, in the sixth term of a 10-round feature. Although the former champion took command of the fight early, Suggs, to his credit, held his ground for five rounds. The New England fighter was quicker than Canzoneri had anticipated, forcing him to bore in on Suggs to score points. The evasive Suggs, a veteran of more than 150 bouts, avoided Canzoneri early in the sixth round, but after a clash in the middle of the ring, the former champion was able to unleash a targeted left hook that caught his opposer squarely on the jaw and sent him flat.

There was no denying that New York City was the place to be during the holiday season.

Unable to resist taking advantage of shopping in Manhattan, Canzoneri was in a festive mood. He loved walking down Fifth Avenue and admiring all the window displays. Always in style, he was impeccably dressed. Under his long gray overcoat, he wore a brown suit, a red necktie, and a pair of spats buttoned under his splay-bottomed trousers. He looked every bit a champion or like somebody who was somebody. He loved to be noticed, to be stopped for an autograph or a quick conversation. Knowing his father needed a watch, Canzoneri slipped into a shop and bought him a Glycine Swiss timepiece. Understanding his father would say it was too expensive ($45), he wanted to get him something to commemorate the year. It had a very masculine rectangular 14K white gold-filled case with a jeweled movement. As the watch featured a silver dial and detachable strap and buckle, the former champion couldn't resist.

Scheduled to meet Al Singer at Madison Square Garden on December 14, Canzoneri was eager to finish out the year.

Abraham "Al" Singer, "The Bronx Beauty"

Born in a tenement on Broome Street in New York's Lower East Side on September 6, 1909, Al Singer grew up in a middle-class Jewish American family. One of five children, he excelled at athletics. Ten bouts into an amateur boxing career, he caught the eyes of boxing trainers Harry Drucker and Hymie Caplan. A student of the ring, Singer won the Metropolitan AAU featherweight title thanks to superb punching power. He idolized the great Benny Leonard, studied his ring skills, and hoped one day to have an opportunity to fight for the lightweight championship. Turning professional in 1927, he fought primarily out of Ridgewood Grove—remind you of anyone? Moving quickly up the competitive ladder, he held recent victories over Pete Zivic, Chick Suggs, Vic Burrone, and Tony Pellegrino. In his fourth appearance at Madison Square Garden, Singer would take a record of 31–4–1 into the ring to greet Tony Canzoneri.

In front of 20,000-plus spectators, Tony Canzoneri battled to a 10-round draw against Al Singer. Every inch of Madison Square Garden was occupied as attendees wanted to watch these two popular Ridgewood Grove graduates go head to head. Desperate for admittance, a crush of fight fans on 50th Street kicked in a ventilator window, and it sent glass falling to the dressing room below. The fragments just missed Canzoneri as he prepared for his clash. Both fighters entered the ring at 128 pounds.

Canzoneri opened strong and took rounds one, four and five. Scoring both inside and out, the former champion was successful at moving Singer about the ring. Canzoneri's go-to punch this evening was a targeted right that landed multiple times on Singer's jaw.

Nervous, Singer took rounds three and four. He slowed Canzoneri in the second round with a powerful right hand to the chest. A solid right to the jaw in the fourth sent Canzoneri to the ropes. Later in the frame, Canzoneri landed an accurate right of his own that shook Singer.

Accurate combinations and solid body punches were responsible for Canzoneri winning rounds five and six. The four rounds that followed were close and hard to call.

Settling in, Singer looked strong in rounds eight and nine. Scoring with his right, Singer took Canzoneri inside when he could and went to the body. He was also able to score in the ninth, as his opponent had slowed.

Rounds seven and 10 most saw as even. Singer's straight lefts kept Canzoneri from scoring. Canzoneri landed one solid right to his adversary's jaw in the 10th round, but Singer countered enough to even the round.

To Al Singer's credit, he took Canzoneri's best blows and went the distance with the former featherweight champion.

Taking 11 fights in 1928, Tony Canzoneri won seven bouts, lost two and drew two. He unified the featherweight title with a splendid performance over Benny Bass, then lost the championship to André Routis. Weakened by weight reduction, he began questioning his ability to compete as a featherweight. Illness took a toll on his health, as he never appeared to regain his strength. Canzoneri fought outside the United Sates for the first and only time in his career. Returning to New Orleans was a thrill for the family, and an opening-round knockout at the Coliseum Arena added to the excitement.

1929

The Roaring Twenties, or the decade that followed World War I, was a time of wealth, excess, overconfidence, and speculation. It was too much of a good thing, and everyone knew it. The first sign of economic trouble, at least to many in New York City, was when the Federal Reserve warned of excess speculation on March 25, 1929. A quick sell-off exposed the weakness in the market's foundation. Some, such as Charles E. Mitchell from the National City Bank, managed to slow the decline but not the delicate underpinnings. The nine-year bull market was slowly concluding. On September 20, 1929, the London Stock Exchange crashed, then came "Black Thursday" on October 24 and "Black Monday" on October 28, followed by "Black Tuesday" on October 29.[8]

Besides the fighting on Wall Street, New York City hosted boxing: Max Schmeling used his powerful right hand to drop Johnny Risko three times before putting out his lights in the ninth round on February 1 at Madison Square Garden; Philadelphia boxer Tommy Loughran sailed through the first two rounds of a heavyweight title fight at Yankee Stadium, only to catch a powerful right hand from Jack Sharkey that ended his night at the 0:27 mark of the third round; and Ruby Goldstein, dropped in the opening round and sent through the ropes in the second term, was flattened by the crushing right hand of Jimmy McLarnin late in the second session to end his night at Madison Square Garden. As all the participants understood, nobody was paid by the round.

During the first part of the year, Sammy Goldman hooked up with promoter Jim Mullen and signed Tony Canzoneri to a few Midwest bouts, the first three taking place in Chicago. Mullen was competing against Paddy Harmon and later Mique Malloy for the fistic promotional supremacy of Chicago. Goldman, with Canzoneri in his hands, felt he could create a bidding war for his fighter.

On January 19, the former featherweight champion, scaling at 129 pounds, knocked out Cuban Armando Santiago, who tipped a pound lighter, at the 1:42 mark of the fifth round. It was the feature bout of Mullen's all-star show at the Chicago Coliseum.[9] However, victory didn't come easy, as Canzoneri was viciously attacked in the opening round and dropped to a seven count. Regaining his composure, the Brooklyn boxer opted for a four-round body assault that led to his victory. As he relentlessly pounded his opposer into submission, a right uppercut found its mark in the fifth round and dropped Santiago to the canvas. Since Santiago had defeated Joey Sangor last December, fight fans weren't surprised by the intensity of the battle. Speaking of Sangor, he was scheduled to meet Canzoneri, over 10 rounds, on February 6.[10] After the battle, James C. Mullen succeeded in signing Bud Taylor to meet the winner of the Canzoneri-Sangor bout.

Tony Canzoneri, a 6–5 favorite, arrived late in Chicago owing to a family sickness. Meanwhile, his opposer, who had recently upset Tod Morgan, had been in town for days. By February 2, the bout sold out (11,000 seats) the Chicago Coliseum and was the largest crowd ever to attend an indoor boxing show in the city.

It was Tony Canzoneri's left hook against Joey Sangor's straight punches, or at least that was how some resolved the contest. It was a former champion, far better than folks gave him credit for being, convincing a Milwaukee pugilist that his recent strong performance over Tod Morgan was a fluke.

Scaling at 127½, Canzoneri was confident, as was Sangor, who tipped a pound lighter. Late in the second round, the former champion, having had his way with his opposer, dropped Sangor to the floor with combinations. Out cold, Sangor was saved by the bell. Partially revived, or so it appeared, the Wisconsin boxer was once again hit so hard that only the rope held him up. Again, he was saved by the bell.

While he made it through the fourth, fifth and sixth terms, the fuel tank was almost empty. Coming out for the seventh round, Sangor's enervation was evident.

Canzoneri, locked and loaded, fired two thunderbolt lefts to his opponent's face, followed by a right to the jaw. Yet a courageous Joey Sangor stood and even attempted to counter. Two minutes and 16 seconds into the round, Canzoneri fired a right cross to the jaw of his antagonist, finally turning out his lights.[11]

Remaining in Chicago, Canzoneri next saw the familiar face of Ignacio Fernandez on February 26—Goldman had tried to book his fighter in Cleveland against Bill Wallace, but it fell through. As some recalled, Canzoneri took a decision over the Filipino fighter about a year earlier in New York. It was one of those bouts that tested the patience of the former champion; moreover, he delivered multiple volleys with little effect on the concrete chin of Fernandez. Although Canzoneri failed to put away the Filipino gamecock, he tried. Tony Canzoneri outpointed Ignacio Fernandez over the 10-round journey. For his efforts, Fernandez received a hand from the crowd of more than 10,000 spectators. Nearly everyone ringside saw it nine rounds for Canzoneri, with one even.

Seldom, at least at this stage of his career, did Tony Canzoneri venture into the spotlight and speak for himself. That job fell into the hands of Sammy Goldman, who was wise enough to lead the press to water and make them drink. As March began, Canzoneri stated to the press that he expected to win three titles the following year. Feeling he had earned the opportunity, he hoped to meet André Routis for the featherweight crown, Tod Morgan for the junior lightweight championship, and Sammy Mandell for the lightweight title. Much of his confidence was thanks to promoters Jim Mullen and Paddy Harmon, who used the Chicago market as a springboard for the youngster's career. The former champion believed his ideal weight was 127 pounds, and he was compromising his skills at 126, the featherweight limit.

On March 8, at Olympic Stadium in Detroit, Tony Canzoneri, who scaled at 128, took a 10-round points victory over Cecil Payne, who scaled a pound lighter. Canzoneri's short right hands were timely, accurate and responsible for considerable damage. It was that punch to the chin that sent Payne to the floor twice for nine counts in the third round and once in the fourth frame. Though Payne never recovered, he was able to finish. Canzoneri danced over the last three sessions.[12]

A Spring Run

It was off to Milwaukee on April 9 to meet veteran pugilist Cowboy Eddie Anderson at the Auditorium. Anderson, like Canzoneri, was working his way through weight classes, trying to find a comfort zone. Having given André Routis, present featherweight champion, 10 furious rounds of confrontation, Anderson planned to slug it out with Canzoneri. That he did. However, at the end of 10 rounds, the newspaper decision went to Tony Canzoneri. It was as close as many had anticipated, yet not one person of the 9,000 in attendance at the Milwaukee Auditorium seemed to mind. Anderson, who scaled at 131, was on his game, as he blocked magnificently and frequently countered his opponent's assaults. But Canzoneri, who tipped at 129¾, was aggressive from the opening bell and frequently scored with an accurate right cross—he also never slowed. As for a damage assessment, Canzoneri had a cut opened under his right eye in the eighth term. It was a close fight; moreover, ringside saw it five rounds for Canzoneri, four for Anderson, and one even.

Having not fought in New York since December of last year, it was good for Canzoneri to return home. Not only did he miss his friends and family, but he also wanted to share with them the success he had on his Midwest trip. He had signed to a Garden battle against Sammy Dorfman on April 26, and there was no time to rest. Dorfman's last loss came at the hands of André Routis back in May, and he had six consecutive victories. While he hoped to add Canzoneri's name to that list, his opposer was a 2–1 favorite—the day of the bout, the odds shifted to 13–5. Canzoneri's punching power had improved. Thus, Dorfman, who could jab and move, would have to move even quicker to avoid damage.

Scaling at 130 pounds or a half-pound advantage, Tony Canzoneri took a listless, 10-round points victory over Sammy Dorfman. Nearly 9,000 fight fans watched and waited for Canzoneri to deliver Dorfman, but he never did. After he dropped Dorfman to a nine count in the opening round, not a soul inside Madison Square Garden believed it would go the distance, but they were wrong. Taking nine out of 10 rounds, Canzoneri knew he had the fight after the first five sessions and began showboating. After connecting to the jaw of his opposer and tilting him to one side, Canzoneri would back off and let him live another round. Viewing the humiliation firsthand, Dorfman retaliated with four punches south of the border and was warned each time. Canzoneri countered by dropping Dorfman to the canvas three times. Though Canzoneri was victorious, his display was incongruous for the time.

Promoter Paddy Harmon signed Tony Canzoneri to a fight against André Routis on May 10 at Chicago Stadium. It was the feature bout of three 10-round matches. Having built a considerable following in the Windy City, Canzoneri was excited about the opportunity—his last three Chicago fights were sell-outs. However, the Frenchman, who won the featherweight title from Canzoneri seven months earlier, refused to put his title on the line.

A record indoor boxing crowd of 24,500 spectators witnessed a close battle that saw Tony Canzoneri, a 6–5 favorite the day before the bout, awarded a unanimous verdict over André Routis. Both men fought brilliantly, and of those in attendance, few could pick a winner. It was a razor-thin victory. When the verdict was read, a chorus of boos and hisses was heard over cheers. Canzoneri opted to keep his distance and chip away with left hands to the head and body, while Routis went inside to inflict what damage he could with combinations. Canzoneri would not remain stationary, nor would he attempt to stop any aggressive assault by Routis. Instead, he retreated or bolted away. The crowd was on their feet in the third session, when both boxers went toe to toe for nearly the entire round. The eighth round saw Canzoneri at his best, as he sent Routis into the ropes with a hard right to the jaw before pounding hard rights to his chest. Though Routis successfully used a two-fisted body attack to force his rival to retreat, the judges were more impressed by Canzoneri's boxing prowess. Afterward, Team Canzoneri headed back to New York.

Matchmaker Al Weil, working his magic over at Queensboro Stadium, signed Tony Canzoneri to meet Ignacio Fernandez in the opening feature of the venue on June 4. Canzoneri, a 9–5 favorite entering the contest, was confident—and why not, as he had defeated Fernandez twice?

As for Fernandez, prior to his victory over Al Singer on May 17, he took the fight with Canzoneri. The *Evening Star* noted:

Catapulted into big money by stopping Singer, the Filipino through his manager tried to checkmate the Queensboro club's officials by claiming an injured hand. Apparently, Fernandez did not care to risk defeat at the hands of the former featherweight champion, while his star was in ascendancy and his value as a box office attraction at its peak. An examination proved the emptiness of Fernandez's claims, and he was ordered to go through with the fight under pain of suspension.[13]

In front of 12,000 persons, Tony Canzoneri, who scaled at 129¾, took a 10-round points victory over Ignacio Fernandez, who scaled at 128. The former champion won every round. Fernandez, who was game right from the start, put on a courageous exhibition. Yet, like many, he gradually wilted from Canzoneri's machine-gun blows. In the fifth term, the best for Canzoneri, he nearly had Fernandez out with a series of hard rights to the face, but the fighter somehow managed to stay vertical at the bell. However, from that point forward, Fernandez had nothing left. Dancing around his adversary as if the latter were in quicksand, Canzoneri unloaded the chambers—nearly every punch was unanswered. From a ringside broadcast over WHSG, with Sam Taub over the mic, to ringside introductions—on hand were Davey Abad, Jack Kid Berg, Mushy Callahan, Tony Caragliano, and Cannonball Eddie Martin—it was an outstanding evening of boxing.

One aspect of Canzoneri's ring behavior wasn't working: Once he believed a fight was won, he liked to show off, and it wasn't going over well. Granted, Canzoneri was young, and he was winning, but there was no need for those displays. The Brooklyn boxer was still fighting the field, as he was first to say, because he believed if you beat the field, you wouldn't have to ask for a match with the champion. Outwardly claiming titles didn't mean much, because he had made more money without one, Canzoneri nevertheless didn't hide his desire for the lightweight championship.

After the Fernandez battle, Canzoneri headed back to the farm in Marlboro to recuperate and enjoy some time off. Working the farm kept him strong, and his mind stayed off the fight game. He took a break the third week of June to head over to Hoosick Falls, New York, to watch Paulino Uzcudun train for his Yankee Stadium battle against Max Schmeling. He was not impressed by the Spanish heavyweight.

Marching to Mandell

By the end of June, promoter Paddy Harmon had signed Tony Canzoneri to meet Sammy Mandell, world's lightweight champion, at Chicago Stadium on July 18. They ended up meeting on August 2. Mandell, who hailed from Rockford, Illinois, headed to Chicago the last week of June to select a training camp. Up in weight—reports had him above 140 pounds—he was confident in his ability to reduce without sacrificing his strength. Mandell eventually selected Washington Park Racetrack for his camp. Canzoneri, who planned to finish his training in Chicago, hoped to arrive before July 15.[14] Having worked his weight up, he hoped to scale close to the 135-pound limit set for the lightweight division. Team Canzoneri knew their fighter needed a tune-up battle, so they matched him with Phil McGraw on July 9 at the Queensboro Arena.

McGraw, who was born in Greece and now lived in Detroit, was a seasoned boxer who held victories over Basil Galiano, Johnny Rocco, and Tod Morgan. Despite his comments claiming Canzoneri was "highly overrated," he knew better.[15]

Before 6,000 spectators, Tony Canzoneri, who scaled at 134, captured a 10-round points victory over Phil McGraw, who tipped at 132. However, it cost him. In the sixth round, Canzoneri sustained a severe cut over his right eye—it was an old cut opened by a headbutt. Through the four succeeding rounds, it bothered the fighter. Noting the injury, McGraw targeted the gash with wild swings, and as he did, Canzoneri's temperature began to rise. The former champion retaliated by battering McGraw in the seventh, eighth and ninth rounds. He took out every ounce of aggression he had on the countenance of his opposer. Remarkably, McGraw was able to remain upright. The Detroit pugilist fought a sloppy battle, as he was warned twice in the early rounds about fouling, was staggered multiple times from rounds three through five, and was responsible for the head-on collision in the sixth.

Afterward, Canzoneri's management was criticized for allowing their fighter to take

Among the callers at the White House to see President Coolidge in 1925 were Sammy Mandell (right), new lightweight champion of the United States, and his manager Eddie Kane, who also managed Tommy Gibbons (Library of Congress).

the bout against McGraw. It was justified. Canzoneri needed a clean tune-up fight, not a battle against a pugilist who had nothing to lose. Casting logic to the wind, McGraw fired wild left hooks—not to mention the numerous shots south of the border—and it was a matter of time before one was going to find a target. A boxing manager prepares and protects his fighter; he does not get him injured prior to a championship battle.

The *New York Daily News* featured a photograph of Miss Violet Clifford, who, like many boxing fans, enjoyed visiting the training camps of popular boxers. The smiling fighter featured next to her was none other than the handsome Tony Canzoneri.

Sammy Mandell

Be it the "Rockford Flash" for his speed, or the "Rockford Sheik" for his good looks, Salvatore Mandala, aka Sammy Mandell, transformed his 105-pound frame into one of the best lightweight boxers ever. He did it in Rockford, Illinois. Too young and underweight to join the army, the southpaw turned professional at the age of 15.

Progressing through the ranks—he defeated Memphis Pal Moore at 17, Joe Burman at 18, and Babe Herman at 19—Mandell exhibited tremendous skills. Trained by the legendary Jack Blackburn, he defeated Rocky Kansas on July 3, 1926, to win the NYSAC, NBA and *The Ring* lightweight titles. Mandell's first four battles in 1928 were all victories; moreover, he defeated Billy Petrolle (newspaper decision), Jackie Fields (UD), Eddie Wagner (PTS), and Jimmy McLarnin (UD). His first six battles of 1929 were all victories and led him to Tony Canzoneri.

A Dark Cloud—Sammy Mandell v. Tony Canzoneri, World Lightweight Championship

Under police protection, Sammy Mandell was sneaked in and out of his training camp, where he was making final preparations for his defense of the world lightweight championship. The action was a result of daily threats delivered to his camp—they were believed to be originating from a gambling group trying to stage a betting coup. How this would impact his date with Canzoneri, at Chicago Stadium on August 2, remained to be seen.

As the odds mounted steadily in Mandell's favor and improved as the fight drew closer, Mandell's concern increased. Quartered in his hotel room with a bodyguard, the Illinois pugilist was in fear of even answering the phone. An additional concern was weight: Canzoneri, a natural 133-pounder, would be at full strength, while Mandell struggled to reduce to 135.

Those who knew boxing felt Canzoneri lacked the power, ring generalship, and killer instinct of Mandell. However, age (he was younger than his rival), a snappy punch, and infighting skills could work to his advantage. It also seemed that Mandell was at the pinnacle of his pugilistic proficiency, while Canzoneri had yet to reach his. Later, it appeared these observations were correct.

Mandell, who was four years, nine months, and one day older, two pounds heavier, and an inch taller, brought more than a one-inch reach advantage into the ring. Canzoneri, who had a bigger waist, biceps, thighs, and calves, hoped to work inside to negate the impact of Mandell's arsenal. If he did not, it was going to be a long evening of punishment. Let the battle begin.

Canzoneri was effective the first two rounds because he rushed Mandell and did not let him settle in. He was even successful backing him into the ropes. However, Mandell turned up the heat in the third round and began outpunching his opponent. By the fourth round, Canzoneri had lost his mark and began missing punches. Mandell also effectively countered his rival's body assaults by keeping him out of range. Missing punches in rounds seven, eight and nine, Canzoneri could not find his target. In the final round, he went back to rushing Mandell and began hitting his mark, but it was too late.

Sammy Mandell, who scaled at 135, defeated Tony Canzoneri, who tipped at 132½, over 10 stirring rounds of pugilism at Chicago Stadium. Speed and sheer ability garnered Mandell the win, as he found a groove by the third round and rode it to victory. After losing the first two sessions, Mandell called on his long left hands and choppy rights to chip away the rounds from Canzoneri. When it was over, referee Dave Barry cast his vote for Canzoneri, while both judges, Ed Klein and Phil Collins, saw it for Mandell. More than 24,000 witnessed the split decision victory for Mandell, but few saw it differently.[16]

The gross receipts were given at $165,000, of which Mandell received 40 percent, while Canzoneri pocketed 20 percent. Eddie Kane, Mandell's manager, believed his fighter had an off night, and even Mandell admitted he couldn't get his engine started. The comment spoke volumes to the skills of Sammy Mandell.

No sooner had Canzoneri picked up his paycheck than promoter Paddy Harmon signed him to a 10-round engagement with Tod Morgan, junior lightweight champion. Harmon hoped to close the match for September 6 but hadn't worked out the details. Once it appeared the Morgan bout wasn't going to happen, Sammy Goldman matched his fighter with Eddie Kid Wolfe of Memphis. The fight was scheduled for Heinemann Park in New Orleans on September 20.

Tony Canzoneri planned to train in Marlboro before heading south a week before the bout. Meanwhile Eddie Wolfe, his young opponent, was in Mandeville, Louisiana, preparing for what would be the second-most significant bout of his career. A 10-round victory over elite pugilist Johnny Dundee, back in April, was all the confidence he needed to face Tony Canzoneri. Having begun his career in 1927, Wolfe had only lost one decision in New Orleans, and that was on a foul to Joe Cook.

On September 20, Tony Canzoneri, a 3–1 favorite, took a 10-round points victory over Eddie "Kid" Wolfe. Both fighters scaled at 133 pounds. The former champion dominated his adversary. Pounding Wolfe continuously with combinations, Canzoneri sent him to the canvas twice for nine counts. By the sixth round, Wolfe was tired and was forced to go on the defensive for a remainder of the contest. Despite being dominated by his opponent, Wolfe never stopped battling. Not a soul in attendance disputed the decision by referee Jimmy Moran.

Say It Ain't So

Afterward, Frankie Edwards, promoter of the bout, disappeared with $20,000 in gate receipts. Everyone from ushers to the principal fighters waited for hours at the payoff window, hoping for his return. When he did not appear, the group took their case to the Louisiana Boxing Commission, who then turned it over to the district attorney. Before he vanished, Edwards did manage payment to some of the preliminary fighters and even left behind money to apply to the amusement tax. Edwards was last seen by his wife, having stopped home for a cup of coffee before disappearing into the night. Edwards owed Canzoneri $8,000 and Wolfe $5,300. The former champion departed for Chicago, leaving behind Sammy Goldman and his father to figure things out.

That same day, Canzoneri learned he had been signed to a battle against veteran Eddie Mack of Denver. The pair would meet at 130 pounds at Chicago Stadium on September 27. Mack, who brought over 70 fights' worth of experience to the ring, held victories over Al Corbett, Goldie Hess, Tod Morgan, and Dock Snell. Whereas he had lost only five fights, it would soon be six.

Scoring a technical knockout over Eddie Mack in the eighth round of a contest scheduled for 10, Tony Canzoneri was elated. A packed house witnessed both box-ers fighting an even battle until the point of the knockout. Canzoneri telegraphed a monster left hook, and Mack, while attempting to evade it, slipped off balance and right into the line of fire—Mack, having sprained his right ankle in the first round, was unstable. The punch was a direct hit to the jaw. Dazed, Mack was up without a count, but referee Phil Collins realized Mack was in no condition to continue, and the fighter agreed. A negative turned into a positive; the unforeseen loss proved to ignite Mack's career, and the Denver fighter won his next 12 battles.

Returning to New York, Garden matchmaker Tom McArdle inked Canzoneri to meet Johnny Farr over 10 rounds on October 18. Farr was an ambitious young fighter whose impressive list of victims included Jimmy McLarnin, Ray Miller, Joey Sanger, and Bud Taylor. The last time he was in the Garden, he was badly beaten by Benny Bass. Farr trained at Stillman's, while Canzoneri worked out at Pioneer Gym. The Friday evening event featured three 10-round bouts: Canzoneri versus Farr, George Hoffman versus Ad Warren, and Pal Silvers versus Nick Testo. The card also included one six-round bout and one four-round preliminary. Tickets were scaled at $1.05 (general admission), $2.10, $3.15, $4.60, and $5.74.

Scaling at 133¼, Tony Canzoneri, a 3–1 favorite, took a decision victory over Johnny Farr, who tipped at 131½. In front of more than 8,000 enthusiastic Garden fight fans, Canzoneri scored with combinations, while his left jab kept his adversary at bay. Turning to right hooks for the bulk of the damage, Farr mixed assaults with an occasional left hook to the jaw. By the fourth round, the Cleveland pugilist had cuts over both eyes and was bleeding from his nose. The damage, along with his inability to catch Canzoneri, cost Farr the fight.

It started in September and ended in October, and it was known as the Great Crash. It was primarily associated with October 24, 1929, called Black Thursday, the day of the largest stock sell-off in U.S. history. Five days later came Black Tuesday, when investors traded some 16 million shares on the New York Stock Exchange in a single day. With the crash signaling the beginning of the Great Depression, the "Roaring Twenties" hit a brick wall. How such a devastating financial event would impact boxing was anybody's guess.

Ending the month in Chicago, Canzoneri was inked to a match against Stanis-laus Loayza at an event promoted by Jack Dempsey. The heavyweight legend hoped to match the winner against Sammy Mandell. However, the economics of the fight game would soon change.

Scaling at 133, Tony Canzoneri won a unanimous decision over Stanislaus Loayza, who tipped three pounds heavier, on October 30. Nearly 8,000 spectators jammed the Coliseum for the event that saw Canzoneri get the best of his oppo-nent. However, when his hand was raised in victory, the crowd voiced its displeasure. Though Canzoneri had the victory, Loayza had the hearts of fans who admired his courage in defeat. Ringside saw it seven rounds for Canzoneri, two for Loayza, and one even. With his mauling style, the Chilean tried hard to draw Canzoneri to close quarters but was unsuccessful.[17]

Scheduled to meet Jack Kid Berg in Madison Square Garden on November 15, a bruised Tony Canzoneri had little choice but to cancel. Matchmaker Tom McAr-dle signed Maxie Rosenbloom to battle James J. Braddock instead. He then moved the Canzoneri versus Berg battle to January 17, 1930.

It took time, but word finally leaked: Tony Canzoneri turned 21 years old on November 6. A reminder: In New York, no one was permitted to fight more than six rounds unless they were 21. Let's say the state athletic commission was not thrilled by Canzoneri's admission.

Feeling the disdain for his concealment, Tony Canzoneri sought a sunnier alternative. The pugilist headed to Miami Beach for a hard-earned 11-week vacation. This left Sammy Goldman to smooth matters out with NYSAC. Despite the loss to Mandell, it was a successful year for the boxer, who posted a record of 12–1–0 with one no-decision. Sammy Goldman's strategy of establishing a relationship with competing Midwest promoters was successful at inflating the value of his fighter, while returning him to the spotlight. Had he stayed in New York, that might not have happened. Every boxer Canzoneri faced had a winning record, and many were on top of their game. There were the usual difficult victories—over Sammy Dorfman, Andre Routis, and Eddie Mack—but they were oh so sweet. "The Roaring Twenties" had drawn to a conclusion, but for Tony Canzoneri, his legendary career had only begun.

FIVE

The Depression, 1930

"The test of our progress is not whether we add more to the abundance of those who have much; it is whether we provide enough for those who have too little."—Franklin D. Roosevelt

The Chrysler Building, 77 stories tall, opened on May 27 at the northeast corner of Lexington Avenue and 42nd Street; New York's most notorious gambler, Arnold Rothstein, was shot and killed during a poker game at the Park Central Hotel in Manhattan; and Cole Porter composed "I Happen to Like New York." Meanwhile, more than 1,300 banks closed during the year, as the Great Depression, deceptive as it could appear at times, began working its way down the food chain.

Despite the economic conditions, New York City managed to host its fair share of ring anomalies. All eyes turned to Yankee Stadium in June to witness Max Schmeling's acquisition of the heavyweight championship—vacated by Gene Tunney's retirement—by way of a foul over Jack Sharkey. A low left hook, south of the border, sent a grimacing Schmeling to the canvas. With Schmeling eventually carried to his corner, nobody watching was certain what had taken place. In another shocker, Sammy Mandell, who reigned supreme over the lightweight division, was knocked out in the opening round of a July battle at Yankee Stadium. For his 106 seconds worth of humiliation (he was knocked down three times before he was kayoed), Mandell pocketed more than $45,000, while his belt, along with more than $19,000, departed with Al Singer.

Jack Kid Berg, "The Whitechapel Windmill"

Born in London's East End on June 28, 1909, Judah Bergman, aka Jack Kid Berg, was an ambitious, strong, and athletic youth. As one of nine children, he had to quit school early to earn a living to help feed the family. He apprenticed as a lather boy in a barber shop, and his adolescence was filled with fascinating stories about the great British pugilists of the past. Intrigued and inspired by the art of self-defense, he began training at the Oxford and St. George's clubs. Berg's professional debut, a victory over Johnnie Gordon, took place on June 8, 1924, at Premierland in Whitechapel.[1] He was 14 years of age. Many East End boxers, especially the talented Jewish fighters such as Berg, honed their skills there. Fighting out of the venue until February 11, 1926, the prolific and successful fighter soon found himself inside Royal Albert Hall in Kensington. Taking his first significant loss, to veteran Harry Corbett, didn't dissuade Berg. He defeated André Routis in his next fight—this bout too was held at the distinctive venue.

Turning to America in 1928, Berg won his first four battles before enduring a pair of hard-hitting bouts courtesy of Billy Petrolle—the first contest a draw, the second a loss. Catching the eye of many, including trainer Ray Arcel, Berg moved to the United States to take advantage of the opportunities. At this point in his career, he was undeniable in the ring, rolling over opponents such as Alf Mancini, Bruce Flowers, Mushy Callahan, and Spug Myers.

He was in perpetual motion inside a boxing ring. Jack Kid Berg's piston-shooting style of boxing excited fans. The more he fought, the more his American fan base grew. Training hard in Orangeburg, New York, he wasn't taking Tony Canzoneri, an opponent with a similar style, for granted.

Meanwhile, at his home in Marlboro, Tony Canzoneri was preparing for what he realized would be a challenging contest. The dailies believed Canzoneri, a 7–5 favorite, would stop Berg thanks to his punching power and ring generalship. Besides, it was pointed out, Berg was overdue for a loss. Others felt differently; moreover, they repeated the criticism that Canzoneri didn't finish off an opponent once he had an opportunity. They added that he was a slower puncher than Berg.

What was certain: Canzoneri fought best at his own pace, therefore he was not going to allow Berg to take control. Departing his comfort zone, he understood even at this stage of his young career, left him vulnerable.

The Friday evening show, on January 17 at Madison Square Garden, saw three competitive 10-round battles: Tony Canzoneri versus Jackie Berg, Sammy Dorfman versus Harry Carlton, and Herman Perlick versus Jake Zeramby. It also included one six-round and one four-round preliminary. Those who arrived early could still feel the chill in the air left behind from the previous evening's hockey game.[2] Tickets were scaled at $5.74, $4.60, $3.15, $2.10, with general admission at $1.05. The ambiance of the Garden alone was worth the price of admission.

Scaling at 134, Jack Kid Berg captured a 10-round split decision over Tony Canzoneri, who tipped a pound lighter. For those 18,800 spectators who viewed the opening term, it was like watching two different bouts—an antithesis of fighting strategies. Canzoneri dominated his opponent and won the first round by a wide margin. Had the fight ended at this point, it would have been a sensational victory for Tony Canzoneri. It did not.

From the second round onward, the Englishman swarmed his rival and carved him up like a Thanksgiving turkey—it was one of the worst beatings the seasoned Brooklyn boxer had experienced. Deep gashes over both eyes, small cuts on his cheeks, and lips swollen to twice the normal size made Canzoneri looked like he fell through a plate glass window.[3] In contrast, Berg sustained only a small forehead cut.

In the end, referee Mike Hylis saw the bout for Canzoneri, while both judges, George Patrick and George LeCron, saw it for Berg. How on Earth Hylis saw it Canzoneri was beyond belief, yet he was the third man in the ring. With the victory, Berg hoped to match with Al Singer, followed by Sammy Mandell, but not until he returned to America in the spring. For Canzoneri, it was time to reassess his skills.

The press, especially local scribe Frank Casale of the *Standard Union*, hit

Canzoneri with both barrels of his literary shotgun, claiming he was "slipping rapidly" and his pounding by Berg "sealed his doom."[4] Outboxed, Canzoneri had little choice but to endure Berg's intense punishment. Twice he took two shots after the bell, not to mention being thumbed and heeled, as Berg roughed him up good. Countering, Canzoneri sent several shots south of the border, hoping to slow "the Whitechapel Windmill," but they did little.

Scheduled to meet Steve Smith in Wilkes-Barre on January 29, Sammy Goldman's fighter was in no condition. Thus, the Pennsylvania commission suspended the fighter—New York State followed suit—on February 4. Goldman felt bad and informed Smith's handlers. He also canceled a battle against Goldie Hess, scheduled for February 7 in Chicago. As for Canzoneri, he would convalesce at home in Marlboro. Later, he planned to assist his stablemates while riding out his short suspension. For example, he assisted Tony Abruzzi's corner during their fighter's battle against Georgie Keen. The third week of February, Garden matchmaker Tom McArdle signed Canzoneri for a 10-round main event against Stanislaus Loayza. Understanding that his fighter needed a warm-up bout before meeting Loayza, Goldman contacted Tony Martello at the Broadway Arena and committed him to a Tuesday, March 3, feature bout against Brownsville boxer Solly Ritz.

Canzoneri, somewhat agitated by the comments made by Frank Casale, trained hard at the Pioneer Gym. He planned on using Solly Ritz to send a clear message to everyone that his skills weren't slipping. Pushed for an alibi regarding his loss to Berg, Canzoneri blamed his extended Florida vacation. As for Ritz, who was training at Libby's Gym, he hoped to emerge from obscurity with a victory over Canzoneri.

In front of 3,500 fight fans, Solly Ritz lasted 56 seconds in the ring against Tony Canzoneri. Sporting that deer in the headlights look, Ritz, who tipped at 135, walked out of his corner and took a left hook by Canzoneri, who scaled at 131¾. It nearly floored the novice pugilist. A quick volley of machine-gun combinations, followed by an accurate left hand, propelled Ritz to the canvas for a two count. Once vertical, a dazed Ritz was easy prey. After Ritz took blow after blow from Canzoneri, without a return, referee Art Donovan caught Ritz before he fell face-first to the canvas. It was over. Donovan carried Ritz to his corner, where it took five minutes for Ritz to re-enter the atmosphere. For his first start since losing to Berg, or "putting out the Ritz," Canzoneri walked away with $1,800 in his pocket. As for the media, not everyone was convinced; Frank Casale refused to retract his remarks until Canzoneri defeated a more experienced foe.

Back in October 1929, Tony Canzoneri took a 10-round victory, while enduring a solid beating from Stanislaus Loayza; conversely, ringside felt the aggressive Chilean deserved the decision. In Canzoneri's mind, only a rematch—which was set for March 14 at Madison Square Garden—could prove who was the better fighter. Whereas Loayza was initially considered a 6–5 favorite, by the day of the fight, the odds had shifted in the opposite direction: 2–1 in favor of Canzoneri.

For two rounds, the crouching Loayza displayed the aggressiveness that had become his trademark. Unfortunately, that was the extent of his offense. By the third frame, Canzoneri found his range and was scoring from both sides with a variety of blows. In the fifth round, Canzoneri caught his opposer with a right hook to the chin that stunned Loayza. However, the Chilean managed to fight his way out of trouble.

It wasn't until the final frame that both exhausted pugilists fought toe to toe. Firing simultaneous missing right hands, the pair landed on the canvas seconds before the final bell—the action a clear indication of the energy expelled by both. Scaling at 131 or to a four-pound deficit, Tony Canzoneri was awarded a unanimous decision over Stanislaus Loayza. In the end, it was Canzoneri's speedy footwork that made his rival look reckless.

It was hard to believe a fighter as prolific as Tony Canzoneri had never fought in the nearby state of Connecticut, but that would soon change. The former champion would face Steve Smith, a durable pugilist who hailed from Bridgeport, in a make-up bout. Ethnic pride ran deep in the Nutmeg State, and though most fight fans had never witnessed one of Canzoneri's bouts, they had read about him in the newspapers—this explained why advance ticket sales were brisk. Promoter Denny McMahon believed the fight would draw the largest crowd of the season to the New Haven Arena on April 1. In a fight scheduled for 10 rounds, Canzoneri, who scaled at 131½, would need seven. He defeated Steve Smith, who tipped at 130, by way of a seventh-round technical knockout. A Canzoneri swift left hook caught his opposer's temple and opened a deep gash. The referee had little choice but to stop the contest. The positive reaction of the crowd led promoter McMahon to offer Canzoneri a standing invitation to return to New Haven.

Back at the Broadway Arena, Tony Canzoneri was slated to meet Frankie LaFay on April 8. A seasoned veteran, LaFay, who hailed from Troy, New York, held a decision over Joe Glick and was closing out a good ring career while instructing at Rensselaer Polytechnic Institute (RPI). As a 2–1 favorite, Canzoneri didn't think the fight would make the 10-round distance, and he was correct. Dropped on five occasions in the opening round, LaFay refused to capitulate. Finally, flattened for the sixth time, LaFay failed to reach his feet before the count of 10. Tipping at 131 or to a six-pound deficit, Canzoneri had no intention of making it a long evening. The capacity crowd of 3,500-plus was given two minutes and 54 seconds to evaluate the fighting prowess of the former featherweight champion. As skillful as Canzoneri appeared, spectators were impressed by the courage displayed by LaFay.

Sammy Goldman, hoping to keep his fighter sharp, signed Canzoneri to a May 5 battle against Harry Carlton at St. Nicholas Arena. Despite posting an impressive 9–1–1 record in 1929, Carlton's career was fading fast. The competitive New Jersey lightweight, who had lost four of his last five fights, was good target practice and not a high-risk fighter.

Scaling at 130½, Tony Canzoneri outpointed Harry Carlton, who tipped at 135, over 10 rounds. Uncharacteristically, the former featherweight champion decided to slug it out with Carlton. To the credit of his opposer, the Jersey City fighter took it. It was clear by the early rounds that Canzoneri wasn't going to drop his opposition—scoring well with rights to the jaw, he had rocked Carlton on multiple occasions. Slowed by a cut left eye, the former champion rode out most of the last few tiring terms. He nearly floored his opposer with a succession of rights to the jaw in the final round. Despite an admirable performance, critics felt Canzoneri looked out of shape. Honestly, the bout was what the doctor, aka Sammy Goldman, ordered.

In another goodwill gesture, Goldman granted matchmaker Denny McMahon another wish and booked his fighter into the New Haven Arena on May 14 to face

Johnny Farr—Canzoneri, some recalled, had defeated Farr at Madison Square Garden the previous October. Since the Cleveland fighting machine had given Connecticut ring legend Louis Kid Kaplan a feisty battle in March, McMahon hoped Farr would do the same with Canzoneri. Incidentally, the aggressive Connecticut promoter was also pushing Goldman hard to match Canzoneri with Kaplan, but the fight manager strategically refused by jacking up the price of his fighter. Goldman believed that if McMahon wanted Canzoneri that bad, it should cost him. In a slow and lackluster affair, Tony Canzoneri, scaling at 131½, outpointed Johnny Farr, heavier by a pound.

Summer meant the outdoor season and big money bouts. Goldman agreed to have Tony Canzoneri meet Joe Glick over 10 rounds at Ebbets Field. Pete Reilly and Jess McMahon were handling the promotion. It was the June 4 feature of an exciting evening of boxing at the ballpark—three 10-rounders, a six and a four—in Brooklyn. How could the promoters go wrong with two Williamsburg boxers in the feature event?

Joe Glick, who began his career in 1921 and by the mid–1920s was considered one of the top boxers in the junior-lightweight division, was a Brooklyn boxing legend. Knocking out the great Johnny Dundee (at the end of his career) was no doubt a factor in the designation. Glick had fought Benny Bass three times and Jimmy McLarnin twice.

In front of a crowd of 10,000 spectators, Tony Canzoneri pounded veteran Joe

This ticket was for the Tony Canzoneri v. Joe Glick bout. The event was conducted by the Ebbets-McKeever Exhibition Company on June 4, 1930, at Ebbets Field.

Glick over 10 rounds to pick up a points victory. Glick, who hit the deck twice in the sixth round, by some means managed to stay on end despite taking a heavy beating. Slicing a deep gash over Glick's eye in the seventh, Canzoneri took advantage of his blinded opposer by freely knocking him around the ring.

Next up for Tony Canzoneri: a battle against Omaha boxer Tommy Grogan at the Queensboro Arena on June 24. This would prove to be a tune-up bout for Canzoneri's proposed battle against Benny Bass. Although an 8–5 favorite, the former feather champion knew he had to be on his guard against the hard-hitting Grogan. Sure enough, the free-for-all went the distance.

The Omaha scrapper came out swinging and dropped his opposer in the second frame to a nine count—Canzoneri immediately recognized his mistake, as a left hand came up short and left him open for a Grogan hard right to the chin. Unhurt but embarrassed, the Brooklyn boxer fought his way back over the proceeding rounds. In the eighth frame, Canzoneri sent an unforgiving combination that dropped his adversary. Visibly hurt, Grogan instinctively bounded to his feet without a count. Witnessing the helpless countenance of his rival, the Brooklynite gladly pounded Grogan over the remainder of the round. After enduring at least three blows below the belt, Canzoneri, who never claimed foul, was happy to take out his aggression on his opposer. For the record: Canzoneri always pledged never to claim a fight on a foul. In the end, it was Tony Canzoneri, who scaled at 131¼, capturing a 10-round unanimous decision over Tommy Grogan, who tipped at 135¼.

Back to Bass

Back on February 10, 1928, Benny Bass lost the world featherweight title to Tony Canzoneri in a 15-round split decision. Even though both boxers had since outgrown the division, he remained bitter. Bass wanted another shot at Canzoneri to redeem himself. But by the time both parties could arrange a meeting, Canzoneri had lost the title to André Routis.

Turning his attention next to the junior lightweight championship, Benny Bass sought that title even

Born and raised in Brooklyn, Joe Glick (shown here in the 1920s) was a prolific pugilist and contender who fought professionally from 1921 until 1934. He was managed by Benny Ford.

though it wasn't universally recognized. He won the 130-pound crown by defeating a tough opponent in Tod Morgan. Despite his new title, Bass always contended that had he not dislocated his collarbone, he would have retained the feather crown. Speaking of designations, when Bass finally signed to re-enter the ring against Canzoneri, his junior lightweight title would not be at stake, as his management insisted that both participants weigh 131 pounds, or a pound over the junior lightweight limit. They also insisted that the rematch be held in Philadelphia.

Meanwhile, Tony Canzoneri, who was training at home, shot over to Orangeburg, New York, to watch Sammy Mandell, lightweight champion, train for his fight against Al Singer at Yankee Stadium. He wasn't alone. In attendance were Victorio

Campolo and Jack Kid Berg. It was no secret that Canzoneri sought the lightweight title and believed a decisive victory over Bass would take him one step closer. But just in case, he also planned to issue a formal challenge to the winner of the Mandell versus Singer contest. That provocation would go to Al Singer.

Philly promoters Herman Taylor and Robert Gunnis announced on July 1 that the bout between Tony Canzoneri and Benny "Little Fish" Bass, originally scheduled for July 28 at the Phillies' ballpark, was moved up to July 21. This was due to a previous commitment by Canzoneri.

Even though fouls had always been a part of the fight game, the Pennsylvania State Athletic Commission felt obligated to take a stand on the issue, and adopted a foul clause as part of a fight contract. Thus, Phil Glassman, manager of Benny Bass, and Sammy Goldman, manager of Tony Canzoneri, signed contracts that included a clause stating neither boxer would be paid until a second meeting, if their first meeting ended by a foul blow. Foul coupons entitled ticket holders to witness a return bout. Although fans thought it was an interesting twist, few thought it would last.

The rousing 10-round affair had no title attached, simply pride. And pride ran deep for both Tony Canzoneri and Benny Bass. The 12,000 in attendance in Baker Bowl could attest to that.[5] Ringing up his second victory over Bass, Tony Canzoneri, who scaled initially at 129¾, refused to back down. In the end, ringside saw it five rounds for Canzoneri, two—or at most three—for Bass and two even. Because of contract stipulations, Canzoneri had to gain weight following the weigh-in—he managed to take his weight to 131¼ pounds prior to the contest.

Finally realizing he was running out of time, Benny Bass captured the sixth round for his best round of the fight. Why he didn't start the engines sooner was because of Canzoneri's incessant assaults. The former feather champion, who happened to plant a noticeable shiner on Bass, smothered his adversary throughout the contest with combinations. Overwhelmed by a much stronger opposer, Bass had few options. Yet it was hard to believe this was the same Benny Bass who was bitter about losing his initial battle with Canzoneri. Would Bass have fought harder if his title was on the line? Probably, but so too would Canzoneri.

During the second week of August, Hymie Caplin, Al Singer's manager, contacted the New York State Athletic Commission to get permission for his fighter, who was the lightweight champion, to meet Jimmy McLarnin in a non-title bout before the end of the outdoor season and to discuss a title defense. He also met with Sammy Goldman and agreed to terms—the negotiated range was an unimpressive 10 to 12½ percent—for a title defense against Tony Canzoneri.[6] Goldman wanted the fight and made it clear to every party involved. He wanted it because his fighter had always wanted it; both believed defeat was inevitable for Al Singer. Goldman even mentioned that his fighter would fight for nothing to prove it—a taboo for any fight manager.

On August 26, at Queensboro Stadium on Long Island, Tony Canzoneri, who tipped at 132, captured a 10-round points victory over Goldie Hess, who scaled to a four-pound advantage. The Los Angeles boxer, holder of the California lightweight title, absorbed a vicious body attack by Canzoneri, who was a 13–5 favorite. Ringside gave all but one round to the former featherweight champion. There were no knockdowns. The bout was a form of consolation for Hess, who was originally scheduled to meet Canzoneri in Chicago back in February.

Hoping to keep his fighter in prime condition for a battle against Al

Singer—Canzoneri was under contract to meet the lightweight champion in November—Sammy Goldman signed him to a Chicago promotion to benefit Patricia Harmon, widow of Paddy Harmon. The promoter and creator of the stadium was killed in an automobile accident in July. Canzoneri's opponent, on September 11 at Chicago Stadium, was Billy "Fargo Express" Petrolle. Holding a knockout victory over Jack Kid Berg and a decision over former champion Sammy Mandell, the hard-hitting Petrolle was on the comeback trail following a nine-month layoff. For their efforts, Canzoneri would take home 25 percent of the gate, while Petrolle would grab 15 percent.

Drawing a disappointing crowd of 13,260 (a bit more than half capacity), the benefit failed to meet monetary expectations. However, it compensated for the downfall by providing fight fans with an evening of action. Petrolle tore into Canzoneri like a hungry tiger over a freshly killed water buffalo. Blasting Canzoneri with left hooks to the head and body, Petrolle soon had Canzoneri bleeding from a large gash over his right eye, nose, and mouth. He also quickly accumulated the number of rounds needed to garner a victory. Canzoneri's best round was the second, when he managed to send his rival to the ropes thanks to two left hooks. Although he rallied in the sixth and seventh rounds to gain a level of respectability from the loss, it was clear his timing was off. Nevertheless, his participation was appreciated.

All eyes turned to Al Singer's first defense of the world's lightweight championship.

Al Singer

Early in his career, Al "the Bronx Beauty" Singer honed his skills at Ridgewood Grove. Picking up $10 a round on a good night, he was one of the boys. In 1927, Singer picked up his first professional victory over Jim Reilly and his first loss to Joe Barbara, both battles conducted at the Grove. His convincing style, as 30 victories could attest to, quickly caught the attention of area promoters. Drawing with Tony Canzoneri in Madison Square Garden on December 14, 1928, propelled him into the spotlight, and back-to-back victories over Bud Taylor in 1929 kept him there. Singer's impressive first-round knockout of Sammy Mandell ended the "Rockford Sheik's" four-year reign at the 1:46 mark. Less than two months later, Singer suffered a third-round knockout, in a non-title fight, to Jimmy McLarnin. Needing to recommit himself to his profession, he did just that. A month before his defense against Tony Canzoneri, Singer captured a 10-round unanimous decision over Eddie Mack.

Tony Canzoneri, stereotypically labeled a Brooklyn Italian by the New York press, was selected as Singer's opponent for his first defense. The pair were scheduled to battle over 15 rounds at Madison Square Garden on November 14. It was the venue's first title bout of the season, and tickets were scaled from $2.10 to $10.40. If Canzoneri won the lightweight title from Singer, he would become the seventh modern boxer to win two championships and join Bob Fitzsimmons (the only boxer to win three), Terry McGovern, Harry Greb, Gene Tunney, Mickey Walker, and Johnny Dundee.

Two things didn't help the Garden promotion: Al Singer's third-round loss to Jimmy McLarnin back in September and Canzoneri's recent embarrassment against Billy Petrolle. Matchmaker Tom McArdle was justifiably concerned.

Everybody in and around the sport had an opinion.

Those backing Al Singer insisted the fighter never would have taken the defense against Canzoneri if he wasn't certain of victory. They were convinced that the Al Singer who met Canzoneri as a featherweight years ago was not the same fighter. He was stronger, smarter, and quicker. Besides, Canzoneri's best days were behind him. The championship distance of 15 rounds also favored Singer. Canzoneri was a 10-round fighter, plain and simple.

Those supporting Canzoneri saw a fighter with integrity, a rarity. His ring record stood with the best and he was proud of it. Canzoneri too had improved, and he was finally healthy after all his setbacks. This was a title he had desired for years, and he was not going to let the opportunity slip away.

Over at Gus Wilson's camp in Orangeburg, New York, Canzoneri was training harder than he ever had for a bout. Assisted by trainer Leo Fink, along with Jack DiSantis, Bobby Risdon, and Walter Salmon, he looked sharp. As for Singer, he was over at Stillman's but not impressing onlookers. But the champ was the champ for a reason. While his pre-fight swagger was one thing, his ring performance would be another.

Tony Canzoneri v. Al Singer, World Lightweight Championship

It took Tony Canzoneri one minute and six seconds after the opening bell to add another title to his resume. A left hook to the chin dropped Al Singer face forward and onto the canvas. By the count of eight, Singer brought himself to his knees, but fell backward, nearly through the ropes at "ten and out." It was Canzoneri's seconds who prevented Singer from falling to the floor. Singer, scaling two pounds heavier at 134, managed to toss two early left hands without a return. But the champion overextended his reach, and Canzoneri caught him with a left hook to the head. Instinctively returning fire, the champion looked up as Canzoneri stepped back and delivered another left hook, this time to the side of his jaw. For Singer, a 12–5 favorite entering the ring, it was lights out.

Afterward, Canzoneri admitted he was shocked by the knockout. The 14,500-plus fight fans in attendance agreed.

Tony Canzoneri, who posted a record of 11–2, began the year with a disappointing loss to Jack Kid Berg

Following his reign at featherweight, Tony Canzoneri (shown here in the 1920s) was ranked the top contender at lightweight by *The Ring* **from October 1929 until July 1930.**

and ended it as the world lightweight champion. Ironically, he had once told Singer they both would one day fight for the title. Every fighter he faced in 1930 had a winning record, and three of them (Glick, Bass and Petrolle) had more than 100 career victories.

Six

Undeniable, 1931

"Success is not final, failure is not fatal: it is the courage to continue that counts."—Winston S. Churchill

Movie theaters were turning to double features with hopes of bolstering revenues, the 11-story Brill Building opened at 1619 Broadway and quickly became home to Tin Pan Alley music publishers and bandleaders, and construction workers, in a holiday twist, put up a Christmas tree at Rockefeller Center. Even though many Americans were struggling, the human spirit still existed in New York City.

Suffering from the Great Depression, Gotham managed to host some memorable bouts: Bat Battalino retained his world featherweight title with a 10-round decision over Fidel LaBarba and Maxie Rosenbloom retained his world Light-Heavyweight title with a 15-round decision over former world champion Jimmy Slattery. But the year belonged to one man, Tony Canzoneri, who became the second man to win world titles in three divisions and the first since the great Bob Fitzsimmons in the 19th century.

At 22 years of age and strikingly handsome, Tony Canzoneri began the year on top of the world. You couldn't pick up a city newspaper that didn't include his name and predictions about his future. Word was the lightweight champion would likely engage in several overweight bouts before defending his title. But defend he would, as Canzoneri wanted to be the people's champion. The title also allowed him to lend a helping hand whenever and wherever he could; moreover, he didn't want to forget the altruism attached to it. The designation appeared to fit him like a tailored suit, and he enjoyed the benefits of being introduced as the lightweight champion.[1]

As usual, the beginning of the year included retrospective newspaper articles noting the champion's looming opposition. Pugilists such as Justo Suarez, a respected South American fighter, Jack Kid Berg, the popular Englishman, and Billy Petrolle, conqueror of Jimmy McLarnin, were noted. Then there were the rising stars, such as Jack Portney, a southpaw out of Baltimore who exhibited promise. Predictions were common and noted but seldom accurate. For example, critics predicted the lightweight champion's reign would not last much longer than Al Singer's 120 days. Tony Canzoneri disagreed.

Returning to New Orleans as the lightweight champion was a dream come true for Tony Canzoneri. He planned on meeting Cleveland fighter Johnny Farr over 10 rounds at the Coliseum Arena on January 26. Technically Canzoneri's lightweight championship would be on the line, as all Farr had to do was knock him out—as though such an action was routine. This was because all Louisiana bouts were no-decision affairs. This would complete the pair's trilogy.

Wasting little time, the champion went right to work winning rounds, four to be exact. Farr picked up the pace in the fifth term because he had to—he was running out of opportunities. Ringside saw the 10-round contest 5–2–3 in favor of Canzoneri. Jack Dempsey, who was the third man in the ring, didn't disagree. There were no knockdowns, only frustration due to the lack of engagement. Even Dempsey's warnings to speed up the bout failed. Nevertheless, it went into the record books as a no-decision. Unofficially, it was a newspaper decision in favor of Canzoneri. Both fighters tipped at 132 pounds.

Scheduled for a 10-round non-title bout in Chicago against Goldie Hess on February 3, Canzoneri, days before the battle, learned that his opponent was ill. While matchmaker Nate Lewis scrambled to find a substitute, it proved pointless. During the process, Canzoneri was forced to withdraw due to a sinus infection.[2] Seeking rest, the champion left the city for his farm in Marlboro. While convalescing, the champion learned he would battle Joey Kaufman at the Hollywood Arena in Jersey City on February 25. The veteran New York boxer had turned punching bag a few years back to collect a paycheck and posed little threat to Canzoneri but could make distance. Or so it was believed.

Tipping at 131, Tony Canzoneri gained a technical knockout over Joey Kaufman, who scaled six-and-a-half pounds heavier. It happened at two minutes and one second of the opening round. Kaufman hit the canvas multiple times before the referee stepped in to stop the massacre.[3] As one of five champions crowned last year in the ring—the others being Max Schmeling (heavyweight), Maxie Rosenbloom (light heavyweight), Tommy Freeman (welterweight), and Jack Berg (junior welterweight)—Canzoneri had yet to be challenged this year. But that was about to change.

Sabino Ferullo, aka Sammy Fuller (shown here in the 1920s), was born and raised in Boston. Fighting professionally from 1924 until 1943, he compiled a successful career by winning three times as many bouts as he lost.

Sabino Ferullo, aka Sammy Fuller, was an experienced 24-year-old boxer who fought out of Boston. When he was signed to meet Tony Canzoneri over 10 rounds at Boston Garden, nobody gave him much of chance to live through the ordeal, let alone compete. But those who knew him felt Fuller's recent performances were impressive—his bouts with Andy Callahan and Bruce Flowers often referenced—and he could go the distance on March 6. Understanding this could be the most important bout in his career, Fuller trained hard at Arthur's Gym. Meanwhile, Canzoneri, who arrived a few days before the contest, was training at Jim Tolland's Gym.

In a fistic upset, Sammy Fuller, who scaled at 135½, won a 10-round unanimous decision over Tony Canzoneri, who tipped two pounds lighter. Thankfully for Canzoneri, his lightweight title was not on the line—Fuller was forced to enter the ring over the lightweight limit (135 pounds). A two-handed body attack, accompanied by a solid left, penetrated Canzoneri's inefficacious defense and was responsible for carrying Fuller to victory. More than 10,000 spectators watched their hometown hopeful draw Canzoneri to close quarters before executing a sound body offensive. Capturing six rounds and an undisputed verdict, Fuller never gave up. Simply put: Canzoneri's performance was abysmal. The level of intensity he had summoned to become champion needed to be there each time he entered a ring, even when the title was not on the line.[4]

"The Western Whirlwind," (Clarence) Tommy Grogan (shown here in the 1920s) fought professionally from 1924 until 1950. Not only did he win over twice as many battles as he lost, but he favored knocking out his opponents.

Canzoneri had hoped to match with Billy Petrolle in his first lightweight defense but could not get NYSAC approval.[5] He turned his attention to Nebraska fighter Tommy Grogan. They were inked to a battle at the Arena in Philadelphia on March 23. Since this was a non-title bout, the Nebraskan pugilist agreed to enter the ring four pounds overweight. Grogan, as some recalled, had been defeated by Canzoneri last June. His last start saw him victorious over Herman Perlick in Madison Square Garden. Meanwhile, NYSAC, knowing Canzoneri's grace period was running out, offered the names of Sammy Fuller of Boston or Jack Berg of England as opponents for the champion's first defense. In the end it would be Berg, in Chicago, on April 24. Anyone surprised?

Tony Canzoneri, scaling at 132, took a 10-round points victory over Tommy Grogan, who tipped at 139. It happened inside the Philadelphia Arena. To Grogan's credit, he was the aggressor throughout the contest. His go-to punch was his powerful right hand, which Canzoneri wisely avoided with his speed. By the time Grogan caught up to Canzoneri, the champion had already banked enough rounds to guarantee a decision. Canzoneri's most memorable shot came at the end of the opening round when he sent Grogan flailing across the ring and through the ropes as the bell sounded.

Al Singer v. Hymie Caplin

A sweeping right hand by boxer Al Singer struck Hymie Caplin, his fight manager, in the neck while he was sitting down. Caplin, having thrust his chin inward, missed getting knocked out by inches. Singer turned his anger to Joe (Yussel) Levy, who trained many Caplin fighters. He struck him in the face with such intensity it split his lip and spewed blood in every direction. Levy countered with a kick to Singer's leg that sent him against a partition in matchmaker Tom McArdle's office. Caplin, having shaken the fog that rolled in, stood up and smashed Singer in the face. That's when Louis Singer, who accompanied his brother to Madison Square Garden, started firing volleys. Al Singer, noting the lack of power behind his punches, began hurling furniture and even a spittoon at his management. McArdle stepped in to slow the hostilities, and following a few offensive words, the Singer boys departed.

The bitterness began on November 14, when Singer hit the Garden canvas courtesy a powder-puff punch—or at least it was viewed by some that way—by Tony Canzoneri. Caplin's handling of Singer was the rub.

As Caplin saw it, Singer quit, gave up. Caplin was furious because he, along with his friends, wagered heavily on Singer. Afterward, the fight manager gave his fighter all the money he felt he deserved, and not a penny more.

As Singer saw it, he was robbed. Caplin failed to pay the fighter his $21,700.27 from the fight purse. The boxer was also upset that Caplin refused to release him from his contract at a fair price ($12,500). Caplin laughed and demanded a *slightly* higher figure ($20,000). For the record, Caplin eventually agreed to $15,000, and Singer turned to his brother for management.

The incident took place on March 24. No word if McArdle signed the group to a rematch—hey, it's boxing.

Tony Canzoneri v. Jack "Kid" Berg, NBA World Lightweight Title and NBA World Junior Welterweight Title

"The shot heard 'round the world" has always been a phrase that referred to the opening shot of the battles of Lexington and Concord on April 19, 1775, but it could easily be applied to the Canzoneri-Berg lightweight championship bout. The New York Commission was attempting to steal the bout from Chicago, or the National Boxing Association.

As the *Evening Star* noted:

Canzoneri will be called before the Boxing Commission tomorrow [March 20, 1931] and requested to sign for a bout with Jack Kid Berg of England. If he refuses the plan is to match Berg with Sammy Fuller of Boston in the Garden on May 1 and declare the winner champion in place of Canzoneri. The official communique issued by the commission after yesterday's session merely stated that Berg and Fuller had challenged the champion.[6]

It was all about politics and greed: New York had first call on Canzoneri's defense, and the champion agreed to fight Billy Petrolle in Madison Square Garden. However, NYSAC refused to approve the bout; they did approve Jack Berg or Sammy Fuller. Matchmaker Tom McArdle wanted Jack Berg strictly for an outdoor show (Sammy Fuller couldn't take the bout), so he ended negotiations. Canzoneri looked west and agreed to terms with Chicago Stadium to fight Berg. NYSAC was furious and called both managers to dangle a bigger New York carrot. The rub was the financial arrangements: New York State restricted champions to 37½ percent, with 12½ percent to the challenger, yet NYSAC desired the bout as a *charity fundraiser* and wanted Berg to accept 5 percent. Chicago agreed to 50 percent for Canzoneri and 10 percent for Berg. The NBA stated that they would suspend both fighters (preventing them from fighting in Illinois and affiliated states) if they didn't go through with their bout. The fight would take place in Chicago.

All eyes turned to Chicago Stadium on April 24, 1931, as Jack Kid Berg, owner of the junior welterweight crown, put his title on the line against Tony Canzoneri, the lightweight champion, who did the same with his designation. It was the tale of two titles, with Berg a 7–5 favorite on the day of the clash. Canzoneri's title was drawn into consideration when Berg made the lightweight limit of 135 pounds. While it was true that most saw the bout as Berg's to lose, Canzoneri countered by claiming the Britisher had weakened in order to reach the weight limit. Thus, he could deliver his rival by way of knockout within five rounds. When Berg heard the prediction, he grinned. Mind the smile.

With tickets scaling from $2 to $10.80, those involved with the promotion were hoping for a large gate. However, the presale figures were off the mark, and a gate about half the size of Canzoneri's last title fight against Sammy Mandell appeared more realistic.

Canzoneri's key to a victory was an early knockout, while Berg, a notable slow starter, hoped to warm up quick before picking his opposition apart piece by piece. Berg, at 24, was older, taller, and had a greater reach. He also had a bigger neck and thighs. Canzoneri had bigger biceps, calves, and ankles. Berg was considered unstoppable—his

British-born Judah Bergman, aka Jack Kid Berg (shown here in the 1920s), came to America in 1931 and was trained by the legendary Ray Arcel.

last loss was way back in 1928, when he took a beating from Billy Petrolle, and that was more than 30 fights ago.[7] Canzoneri, so critics believed, was washed up following his feather title loss to André Routis, and his legs were gone—his loss to Berg last January was proof.

Working in his trademark windmill fashion, Berg constantly drove to close quarters against the lightweight champion. But his open style made him a good target. Canzoneri methodically took the first two rounds, scoring with rights to the body, left hooks to the head, and overhand rights to the face. In the third frame, while both were in a neutral corner firing away, Canzoneri stepped back and released two sharp rights to the head of Berg. Sure enough, Berg looked up in time to catch one of the punches on the chin. Dropping to the canvas like a block of ice, the Brit rolled over and attempted to rise. Using the assistance of the ropes, he was partially up at seven but fell back to the floor. The knockout came at the 2:23 mark of the third round.[8]

Canzoneri, typically cool and composed, jumped around the ring like a kernel of corn in a hot frying pan. As the tears of joy poured from his eyes, he rushed over to Berg's corner to shake his hand. Once in the dressing room, the grin on his face appeared permanent. By his side was his father, who kept mumbling in disbelief, "Three world titles." To Canzoneri's credit, he never doubted for an instant that he could knock out Berg. As for Berg, his comment, or excuse, if you will, was that Canzoneri got to him before he warmed up. Translation: Canzoneri's sagacious and strategic offensive was successful because it was superbly timed.

As for the take, well, it wasn't as much as most had hoped. Canzoneri's 50 percent yielded between $20,000 and $25,000, while Berg left without a belt and about $5,000 in his pocket. By the way, Sammy Goldman intended to give Berg a return fight.

Taking time to indulge, Canzoneri planned on shopping in New York City. Still trading time between the Bensonhurst section of Brooklyn and Marlboro provided him a variety of entertainment options. He was thinking about an exhibition tour of the Midwest and West. Meanwhile, Sammy Goldman was busy charting his course over the next few months. The first title defense, though a date hadn't been set, was signed before the end of the month. Canzoneri would face Kid Chocolate. Madison Square Garden would be the place, and the champion's end would be 37½ percent.

Not So Fast

After the match was made between Canzoneri and Berg, Nate Lewis, the Chicago matchmaker, realized this was the first time in boxing history that two titles had been at stake at the same time. Granted, champions had met before, but never with two titles on the line. It was his understanding, as both men entered the ring under the 140-pound limit, that the junior welterweight title was on the line.

Some, including Harry Lenny, a fight manager, disagreed. It was Lenny's belief that unless it was in the contract, he could not lose his title. The Canzoneri-Berg fight contract said nothing about the junior welterweight title. It was assumed that if Berg was trying to meet the lightweight limit, it didn't prevent him from losing the 140-pound crown. Nevertheless, General John V. Cinnin, National Boxing

Association president, ruled that Canzoneri rightfully won the title. Canzoneri took his place next to Robert Fitzsimmons, who also held three titles. As for Harry Lenny, who was a renegade at heart, he was welcome to believe what he wanted to believe.

Returning to work in June, Canzoneri was back in Orangeburg, New Jersey, training for a 10-round non-title feature against Herman Perlick. The fight was scheduled for June 25 at the White City Stadium in New Haven. Matchmaker Al Weil was behind the promotion that brought the champion to the Constitution State.

Awarded nine of 10 rounds, Tony Canzoneri, who scaled at 134, took a points victory over Herman Perlick, who tipped at 140. The champion was on display and knew it. Thus, he went to work chipping away rounds. Perlick, who had been in the ring with some good fighters, including Wesley Ramey, Tommy Grogan, and Jack Kid Berg, fought a cautious yet respectable bout.

Why did Goldman take this fight? Matchmaker Al Weil enticed both feature fighters by putting Maxie Pink, Canzoneri's sparring partner, and Perlick's brother Henry on the undercard. Later, Henry Perlick had to withdraw because of an eye injury and was replaced by Babe Herman.

Tony Canzoneri v. Cecil Payne, World Junior Welterweight Title

As far as Cecil Payne was concerned, his two-knockdown loss to Tony Canzoneri back in 1929 was a fluke. The free-swinging Kentuckian had improved and was training hard on Soper's Ranch just north of Los Angeles. Although his opponent was favored at 2–1 in the pair's title bout, Payne didn't give it thought. Having recently beaten Tod Morgan, former junior lightweight champion, Payne was sanguine about his skills. He figured Canzoneri would fall prey to one of his roundhouse rights, or at least a sneaky left, during their 10-round battle. It was, in his opinion, a matter of time. Agreeing to weigh 136 pounds or more so that Canzoneri's lightweight title wasn't also on the line suited him just fine. As he viewed the event, it was all about the opportunity. The title fight was scheduled for July 13 at Wrigley Field in Los Angeles.[9]

In front of more than 20,000 spectators, Cecil Payne caught a blistering right hand to the jaw that sent him to the canvas one minute into the opening round. It looked like it was going to be a short night for the Kentucky challenger. But as it turned out, it was a challenging evening for both pugilists. While staying out of range, Canzoneri picked away at the early rounds but he gradually got tired. He began drifting into Payne's sight and caught a few of his opposer's trademark looping punches. As the pace slowed in later rounds, the crowd's screams for action prompted referee Abe Roth to tell both fighters to step it up. Canzoneri, who took at least six rounds, defeated Payne, who won three at best, to successfully defend his synthetic title, as some pugilistic pundits still labeled it. Some reviews gave the champion all ten rounds. Canzoneri scaled at 132½ pounds, while Payne tipped at 136.

Jack Dempsey, no stranger to a big payday, met with Sammy Goldman in Reno, Nevada, on July 17. The former heavyweight legend saw dollar signs in Sammy's eyes. Using Dempsey's Rickardesque charm, the pair announced that Tony Canzoneri was willing to meet Jimmy McLarnin, or Young Jack Thompson, welterweight champion, in a 20- or 25-round prizefight. Naturally, the fight would be held in Dempsey's open-air arena in Reno on Labor Day. Goldman even stated that he would allow Canzoneri's opponent to scale at 145 pounds, while his fighter would stay at 133 pounds. If they declined, Goldman expressed interest in having Canzoneri meet Kid Chocolate, who held the junior lightweight crown (NBA world super featherweight title). Should the latter meet, it would be the first time in history that three titles rested on the outcome of a single bout. Kid Chocolate accepted the challenge.

During the third week of August, Canzoneri agreed to meet Jack Kid Berg over 15 rounds at the Polo Grounds. It would be his first defense of the lightweight title. The contest was scheduled for September 10. Goldman felt his fighter needed a tune-up fight, so he met with New Jersey promoter Lew Diamond and scheduled a battle against Herman Perlick at Bayonne Stadium. Unfortunately, the weather failed to cooperate, and the fight was indefinitely postponed.

As Tony Canzoneri's ring confidence grew, so too did his willingness to speak with the press. The reticent pugilist spoke honestly about how he wanted to continue to defend his current titles against all meaningful challengers. Canzoneri didn't enjoy hearing from the newspapers about the fighters he failed to defend his titles against. He was more than happy to meet any challenger under the proper conditions. Stating his plans, Canzoneri hoped to battle for the junior lightweight crown before trying to recapture the featherweight title. Five titles—aggressive, to say the least—was his goal. Then, and only then, would he be satisfied. As Sammy Goldman had always been Tony Canzoneri's voice, this was a rare occasion. Granted, he had made some one-off remarks to a few publications, including *The Ring*, but the young fighter was seldom out of the shadow of his manager.[10]

Tony Canzoneri v. Jack "Kid" Berg, NBA World Lightweight Title and NBA World Junior Welterweight Title

In the champion's mind, he wondered how much had changed. A mere 140 days, or four months and 18 days, had passed since Tony Canzoneri last met Jack Kid Berg. In the interim, Canzoneri had taken two bouts and won both, while Berg had fought six times without a defeat.

With the best seats in the house priced at $5, the Polo Grounds anticipated a crowd of about 30,000 to witness the rubber match between Canzoneri, who was favored 8–5, and Berg. The word on the street was that Berg had fought himself out and was nothing more than an easy target.

Scaling at 131¾, Tony Canzoneri handed Jack Kid Berg, who tipped at 134½, a merciless beating and defeat over 15 rounds. Twice floored for counts of nine, the Londoner was covered with gore as he awaited the verdict.[11] Looking as if he were auditioning for a horror movie, Berg wasn't surprised when he heard the unanimous verdict for Canzoneri. To the 17,000 in attendance, Canzoneri lost only one round. The champion had dropped Berg with a low left hook in the eighth, and it cost him.

The low blow, or eighth round foul, ignited the point: If the bout had been staged in London, as originally hoped, the championship would have changed hands. Under

NYSAC rules, a fighter cannot win or lose on a foul. Granted, it was peculiar watching referee Patsy Haley counting over the pained figure of Berg, an action that didn't sit well with some spectators. Nevertheless, a rule was a rule, and the action cost Canzoneri the round. To Berg's credit, he made distance.

Keys to Canzoneri's victory: conserving energy, delivering his devastating lefts to Berg's midsection, and altering his attack from body to face repeatedly rather than multiple strikes to the body. This strategy worked as his opposer was unprepared for the offensive. Berg's slow start hurt him and, surprisingly, his corner was unable to alter his actions.

Afterward, challenges poured into the office of Sammy Goldman. As always, it would take time to determine which offers were best for the champion. Hungry for news, the media turned to hearsay. Each day brought another rumor, from Louis Kid Kaplan to Tommy Grogan; another match was always in the final stages. By the middle of October, only one match was certain: Tony Canzoneri would clash with Kid Chocolate in a 15-round championship bout in Madison Square Garden on November 20. The question was what titles they would be fighting for. If Canzoneri should make 130 pounds, Chocolate would be defending his junior lightweight crown. If not, both of Canzoneri's belts would be on the line. Goldman believed Canzoneri would scale anywhere from 130 to 133, while Louis Gutierrez, Chocolate's fight manager, believed his

This Polo Grounds ticket was for the Tony Canzoneri v. Jack Kid Berg bout. The bout was conducted by the Outdoor Sporting Club, Incorporated, on September 10, 1931.

fighter would tip at 131. As a few pointed out, this would be the first time a White and Black boxer would meet for the lightweight title since Gans fought Nelson 20 years ago. Word from Garden guru James J. Johnston was that Canzoneri signed for the champ's 37½ percent, while the challenger inked for 12½ percent. Ironically, Canzoneri's warm-up for his battle against Chocolate was a junior welterweight championship defense against Philly Griffin, pride of Newark's 14th Ward.[12]

Tony Canzoneri v. Philly Griffin, World Junior Welterweight Title

Tony Canzoneri, who tipped at 132, took a 10-round unanimous decision victory over Philly Griffin (aka Phillip DeLuca), who scaled at 138¾. It happened on

October 29, in the Newark Armory. About 3,200 fight fans watched as Tony Canzoneri glided to an easy victory and a successful defense of his world junior welterweight crown. The inconsistent display saw the champion perform brilliantly in rounds one through four, satisfactorily in rounds five and six, then impressively from round seven until the end of the bout. While Griffin was noticeably beat up—the Newark boxer was cut on his mouth in the seventh—he was never dropped to the canvas. Frankly speaking, he could have been. Since the Newark Armory seldom hosted a champion the caliber of Canzoneri, let alone against a hometown boxer, the vibe was far more exciting than the fight.

Kid Chocolate

This Newark Armory ticket was for the Tony Canzoneri v. Phil Griffin junior welterweight championship bout. The event was conducted under the auspices of the 113th Infantry Athletic Association on October 29, 1931.

Born on January 6, 1910, Eligio Sardinias Montalvo was proud to call Cuba his home. Although his family lived in a once-thriving area of the island, the municipality was in a gradual state of decline. It was a newsboy in Havana who first introduced Eligio to the art of self-defense; moreover, he knew the economic value of his corner and was willing to defend it. It was through a newspaper, *La Noche*, that the youngster won his first notable amateur boxing tournament. Impressed with Montalvo's performance, Luis Guiterrez, the newspaper's sports editor, offered to guide the youngster.

Compiling an impressive amateur career, Montalvo turned professional in the fall of 1927.[13] By the summer of 1928, Guiterrez had him in New York, where he felt the youngster belonged. Posting a record of 55–0–1, Chocolate entered the Polo Grounds on August 7, 1930, and took his first loss against Jack Kid Berg. Rebounding with two quick wins, he lost back-to-back unanimous decisions to conclude the year—he was defeated first by Fidel LaBarba and next by Battling Battalino. Following a few months off, he won 10 consecutive battles, including victories over Benny Bass, Steve Smith, and Lew Feldman. By defeating Bass, by way of a seventh-round technical knockout, he won the NBA world junior lightweight championship. This led to his battle with Tony Canzoneri.

A week before the match between Tony Canzoneri and Kid Chocolate, it was being called the greatest lightweight battle of the year. The bulk of the New York dailies were favoring Canzoneri but felt it would be close. Chocolate was a stronger and better boxer than Jack Kid Berg, but there were questions regarding his stamina. Could he make 15 rounds? If it went that far. Noted as the best pound-for-pound pugilist in the fight game, Canzoneri certainly wasn't intimidated by his opposer's impressive record. The betting men agreed and had Canzoneri favored at 2–1.

Kid Chocolate began his preparation at the St. Nicholas Gymnasium before heading to Madam Bey's Training Camp in Summit, New Jersey. Tony Canzoneri preferred to train at Gus Wilson's place at Orangeburg, New York.

If Tony Canzoneri made 130 pounds for this bout and won, he would become the first four-division champion in boxing history—he would pick up Kid Chocolate's junior lightweight title. It was only, according to most, a matter of two pounds. But he couldn't do it.

Tony Canzoneri v. Kid Chocolate, NBA World Lightweight Title and NBA World Junior Welterweight Title

It would be hailed as one of, if not the, greatest lightweight championship battles in Madison Square Garden history. It would also be known as one of the loudest and most boisterous post-fight displays ever witnessed at the venue. Tony Canzoneri, scaling at 132, defeated Kid Chocolate, who tipped at 127, by a 15-round split decision. Many of the 19,000-plus spectators never sat down due to the unceasing action. It was so close a fight nobody wanted to make a prediction. In the end, judge Charles F. Mathison gave the verdict to Chocolate, while judge Joe Agnello and referee Willie Lewis saw it for Canzoneri. Ringside had it eight rounds for Canzoneri, five for Chocolate, and the remainder (first and eighth rounds) even.

Canzoneri's ability to take command and force the fight earned him the decision. He went to the body early with hopes of slowing Chocolate, but the Cuban took the assault in stride. True to form, Canzoneri included a showboating act for a beautiful woman ringside. It nearly got him knocked out in the fifth frame, but that young lady would soon become Mrs. Canzoneri. Chocolate gradually began to slow from the sustained beating. Turning on the afterburners in round 10, Canzoneri was impressive. It gave him the slight edge he needed to take the contest.

A portion of the crowd stayed for 10 minutes after the verdict to voice their dissatisfaction. It wasn't pretty, as the abusive remarks could not be contained. The action wasn't unexpected in such a close and important contest.

Chocolate, having taken a record of 67–3–1 into the bout, wept after the verdict, while his manager swore his fighter was framed. Unquestionably, the Canzoneri-Chocolate feud was not over—thankfully for the many fans who enjoyed this rivalry.

Coming more and more out of his shell, Tony Canzoneri spoke to the media afterward about how surprised he was that Chocolate kept on backing up. He also criticized the Cuban for fighting only the first two minutes of each round. In other words, he left Canzoneri to dominate the last minute of each frame.

This event was also a battle between the two of the best-dressed champions ever. Stating the outcome in a different way: A stylish, spare-no-expense charismatic champion from Brooklyn defeated a flashy Cuban Keed, who changed suits three or four times a day to rotate his impressive wardrobe, and it happened in the fashion capital of the world.

A few days later, Gutierrez met with NYSAC to offer Canzoneri a $25,000 flat guarantee to battle Chocolate at Tropical Stadium in Havana (one source stated $35,000). Hey, you can't blame him for trying. While Canzoneri wanted to fight in December, he took three stitches to the eye and was told to stay out of the ring for six weeks.

Another Leonard?

Promoters do it, as do fight managers and beat writers: they take a fighter and compare them to a legendary figure of the past, fair or not. No sooner had Canzoneri picked up his third world title than out came the name Benjamin Leiner, aka Benny Leonard. Practicing the "art of self-defense," Leonard combined mental strength with accuracy, attentiveness, power, speed, and technique to build a better fighter—better, some believed, than Young Griffo, James J. Corbett, and even Gene Tunney. "The Ghetto Wizard," who stole the nickname from an entertainer because no Jewish fighter fought under his own name, made victory look easy. He was a student of the fight game because he understood that style and technique evolved, and to be successful as a fighter, he had to change with them.

Benny Leonard began his professional career in 1911, before Tony Canzoneri turned the age of three. While their careers overlapped (1925–1932), they were from different eras and approached the fight game differently. Leonard was smooth, smart, and powerful, while Canzoneri was quick, durable, and tenacious. Leonard established himself as an international force when he finally defeated Freddy Welsh (arguably one of the greatest ever). Canzoneri made his mark on the international scene by defeating Jack Kid Berg in three rounds. While it was quicker than the years it took Leonard, his competition wasn't a living legend—that said, the durable "Whitechapel Express," aka Jack Kid Berg, had never been wrecked until his recent match with Canzoneri. A double title holder, Canzoneri had the honor of being a three-time champion. Leonard—who would mount a comeback in October 1931—could not say the same.

Indeed, it was presumptuous on the part of every writer to compare Canzoneri with his mentor—the Brooklyn boxer cherished the lightweight legend. Leonard was 14 months younger when he began his professional career. When both fighters reached their 100th professional bout, Canzoneri (1931) had more than 10 victories and half the number of losses Leonard had.[14] But Canzoneri still had a long road ahead, or so it was hoped, and he never looked better.

Taking 10 bouts and one exhibition, Tony Canzoneri, voted the greatest fighter for his weight and inches in the world in the annual boxing poll of the *Evening Sun*, posted a record of 8–1, with one no-decision. Half the battles he participated in were championship bouts.

Seven

Bring It, 1932

"Whether you think you can, or you think you can't, you're right."—
Henry Ford

The Great Depression continued to show no mercy as the average weekly wage fell from $28 in 1929 to $17 in 1932. Meanwhile, Radio City Music Hall opened in December at 160 Sixth Avenue at Rockefeller Center, and famed bank robber William Francis "Willie the Actor" Sutton, who was born in Brooklyn, escaped from prison. "Say it isn't so," as Irving Berlin would croon, but it was.

Boxing still thrived in "the city that never sleeps," as hard-hitting Billy Petrolle pounded Battling Battalino into submission by scoring a knockout in the 12th round on March 24, Max Schmeling was robbed by way of a split decision against Jack Sharkey on Long Island on June 21, and legendary lightweight Benny Leonard, who was mounting a comeback, was sent into retirement for good by a much stronger Jimmy McLarnin on October 7.

Dressing to the Nines

A champion must look like a champion, Tony Canzoneri believed. Hitting Manhattan to add to his wardrobe, the pugilist enjoyed the strong masculine presence created by a suit; moreover, the wide shoulders, narrow waist and full legs enhanced his form. They made the lightweight look far bigger and stronger than he was—maybe it was the padded shoulders and wide lapels. Single- or double-breasted didn't matter, he enjoyed and wore both styles. Maybe he favored the double-breasted more, but it depended on the event. For example, if he was going to the Garden to attend a fight where he was going to be introduced, he liked the freedom of a single-breasted suit. The pants always fit well because they bulged over Canzoneri's large thighs. While most of his suits came with matching six-button vests, he could take them or leave them. Tans and shades of gray were popular summer colors, and he would switch to navy blue and browns during the fall and winter. Regarding patterns, Canzoneri had a weakness for pinstripes because they made him look taller. As far as shoes were concerned, he favored the current style, and despite standing five feet, four inches tall, he did not favor a higher heel. Hats were imperative, and that meant a fedora or a hat with a soft brim and indented crown. The color depended on his mood or suit. When Tony Canzoneri became involved in a clothing business with Sammy Goldman, it surprised few, as both men always dressed for the occasion.

Before the first month of the year ended, Tony Canzoneri agreed to meet Johnny Jadick in a battle for the junior lightweight championship. The bout was scheduled for January 18 at the Arena in Philadelphia. Jadick, a veteran Philadelphia pugilist, had been streaky of late, but to his credit he always fought the best competition possible. In the 10 fights leading up to Canzoneri, he posted a record of 5–4–1, with victories over Davey Abad, Tony Herrera, and Lew Massey. A dangerous boxer, Jadick was always competitive.

There was no need for Canzoneri to begin the year with a title defense—he hadn't fought in 60 days. Not against a fighter as talented as Johnny Jadick. And not in Philadelphia, where a close battle wasn't going to fall Canzoneri's way.

Johnny Jadick

Born on June 16, 1908, in Philadelphia, "Gentleman" Johnny Jadick resided in the area most of his life. Tall for a lightweight, five feet, eight inches, the youngster patterned his style after Tommy Loughran, a local light heavyweight champion. Beginning his professional career in 1923 at the young age of 15 (one month and eight days), he battled primarily out of the Cambria Athletic Club—and more than a year earlier than when Tony Canzoneri turned professional. It wasn't until about 50 fights into his professional career that he began increasing the level of competition. Trying hard to pull himself into the rankings, he took some difficult losses to Benny Bass, Ray Miller, Wesley Ramey, and Sammy Dorfman. Yet for Jadick, defeat wasn't an act of losing but of learning. It was his competitive nature, not to mention a great left jab, that got him signed to a hometown title bout against the world junior

The talented John Jadich, aka Johnny Jadick (shown here in the 1930s), who never failed to get the best of Tony Canzoneri, won the world junior welterweight championship.

lightweight champion. Thrilled by the opportunity, he couldn't wait for the event.

Johnny Jadick v. Tony Canzoneri I, NBA World Junior Welterweight Title

A 3–1 choice to retain his junior welterweight title in Philadelphia, Tony Canzoneri nevertheless knew he had his hands full with Johnny Jadick. The 10-round bout would be the first championship booked in Pennsylvania for the year but not the last if Jadick had his way. Understanding it was his time to shine, the Philadelphia pugilist had no intention of disappointing his fans. He wouldn't if he learned how to avoid Canzoneri's sweeping left hooks and powerful overhand rights.

As for the champion, he had never seen Jadick fight. However, Sammy Goldman had seen the pugilist at work and believed that if Canzoneri got a fair shot, he should have nothing to worry about. Knowing Jadick was a slow starter, Canzoneri needed to take the early rounds. During the process, if he could inflict enough damage to slow his opposer, he might be able to send Jadick into a steady retreat as Benny Bass did back in 1930.

All the smart money had Canzoneri to win. But the smart money was wrong. Johnny Jadick, who scaled at 136½, rode his left jab the distance to win a unanimous decision victory over Tony Canzoneri, who tipped four pounds lighter. With the victory, Jadick took ownership of the world junior lightweight championship that Canzoneri had grabbed from Jack Kid Berg back on April 24, 1931. Thankfully, Canzoneri's lightweight title was not on the line; furthermore, Jadick was over the lightweight limit of 135 pounds.

Jadick almost lost the fight in the opening round when a Canzoneri crushing left hook caught him on the jaw and sent him halfway across the ring. Although dazed, he managed to make it through the term. Jadick was still gathering his marbles at the start of the second when Canzoneri sent his adversary to the canvas for the count of four thanks to a hard left to the jaw. Again, Jadick was able to shake it off. Staggering his opposer in the sixth frame with a volley of right and left hooks, Canzoneri wobbled Jadick but didn't put him down.

Meantime, Jadick stuck to the jab and kept on scoring points, as Canzoneri's face puffed like a marshmallow over a hot fire. Backing off his opponent after the sixth round, Jadick was content to stay out of range. Sensing the champion was behind, Canzoneri's corner told him to go all-out and unload the arsenal in the 10th round. And the champion complied. Both fighters went toe to toe until they could barely stand.

The verdict, among the more than 7,000 in attendance, was met with mixed emotions. Judge Coles scored it 6–4, Judge Volce 4–3–3, and Referee Leo Houck saw it 5–4–1, all for Johnny Jadick. It was close but not close enough for a draw. Canzoneri thought he had won or at worst fought to a draw. He may have taken defeat in stride, as he did all his fights, but no champion ever enjoyed losing. In retrospect, the decision to take this fight, on this date, in this city, was bad judgment on the part of Sammy Goldman. Granted, the lightweight title was worth more to Canzoneri than a synthetic title, but there were times when he was no less proud.

Catching the entertainment bug, Tony Canzoneri was making cinema shorts that explained the art of the sweet science. He had struck up a friendship with sports reporter Ted Husing. Working at the CBS Radio Network, Husing was coming into his own as a sportscaster, and adding Canzoneri's million-dollar smile to a broadcast didn't hurt.[1]

Reflecting on his career thus far, Canzoneri recalled his battle against Harry Blitman on June 27, 1928, as one of his toughest. It was difficult because he took his opponent for granted. Blitman hadn't defeated any outstanding opponents, not to mention that Canzoneri was heavily favored entering the battle. Once the opening bell sounded, Blitman went at Canzoneri like an uncaged lion. The southpaw pounded the Brooklyn fighter, who appeared helpless. Canzoneri also recalled the contest as the first time he lost control in the ring—he went to the wrong corner at the end of a round. Had Canzoneri similarly underestimated Jadick? It appeared that way.

The first week of February, Sammy Goldman signed his fighter to another bout in Philadelphia, and at the same venue. Canzoneri would meet Lew Massey, aka Louis Massucci, a contentious fighter, in the Arena on February 15. However, the boxer Canzoneri was hoping to meet was Billy Petrolle. Canzoneri had agreed to meeting "the Fargo Express" in Madison Square Garden on February 26, but Petrolle turned it down. Knowing a lightweight championship defense would draw twice as much outdoors, Petrolle preferred to postpone the match until summer.

Lew Massey, who typically won twice as many battles as he lost, was viewed as another veteran fighter who had nothing to lose. He had won three of his last seven fights; his losses were at the hands of Al Singer, Johnny Jadick, and Tony Herrera. As a seasoned fighter, he understood a shot at the champion, even in a non-title contest, was worth its weight in gold. Having witnessed Canzoneri's excruciating body punches against Kid Chocolate, Massey knew what was on the menu, as they say, and he was ready for it. Putting his faith in one good punch, he intended on going all-out against his opposer.[2]

George Canzoneri, Tony's father, made the trek south to Philadelphia. He wanted to watch his son do battle for the first time as 135-pound champion. Seeing the familiar countenance ringside motivated the champion; consequently, his presence did not bode well for Lew Massey. Hoping to impress his father, even if Philadelphia hadn't always been kind to the champion, Tony was hell-bent on giving a quality performance. Going to the combinations early, he battered Massey. But to the credit of the hometown fighter, Massey battled back even after being dropped in the second round. Coming on strong in the third and fourth rounds, Massey began scoring with crisp right hands to Canzoneri's jaw. Yet the champion was the champion for a reason; he rebounded in the sixth and seventh frames and took command. Sending his opposer at will across the ring with his powerful right hand, Canzoneri was amazed that Massey remained upright. Scaling at 133½, Canzoneri took the unanimous 10-round victory over Lew Massey, who scaled four pounds heavier. Loaded with action, it was an outstanding evening of boxing.[3] And yes, George Canzoneri, as always, was proud.

The lightweight division was driving interest in the sport thanks to the names Tony Canzoneri, Bat Battalino, Jackie Berg, Sammy Fuller, and Billy Petrolle. Garden matchmaker Jimmy Johnston, who was pushed and pulled from every direction for matches, was overwhelmed. He had hoped to match Fuller with Canzoneri, but Sammy Goldman wanted to wait and see who would end up on top of the Petrolle-Battalino contest on March 11. For the time being, Canzoneri returned home.[4]

By the middle of March, Tony Canzoneri decided to head south to New Orleans and face Ray Kiser in a 10-round non-title fight at the Coliseum Arena. Martin Burke was behind the promotion in the Crescent City. Needing to stay confident and sharp, Canzoneri felt New Orleans was the perfect place. Meanwhile, Sammy Goldman was setting a course toward a title defense. Billy Petrolle, who sliced up Bat Battalino on the way to a knockout victory in March, appeared to be the first choice.

On April 4, Tony Canzoneri, who tipped at 133, defeated Ray Kiser, who scaled at 137, in a unanimous 10-round decision. Goldman had instructed Kiser that he was to enter the ring at an eight-pound advantage, but the Louisiana Boxing Commission had a five-pound limit on weight advantages. More than 4,000 fight fans attended the non-title bout. Canzoneri started slow but hit his stride from the second through the fifth rounds. Kiser, whose strongest performance was the middle rounds, staggered Canzoneri in the sixth term with a right hand to the chin. Resetting the chess board, Canzoneri battered Kiser's optics until his left eye was closed in the ninth round. Nevertheless, Kiser managed to finish the fight. For his troubles, Canzoneri pocketed $5,000 plus expenses, while Kiser put $1,250 in his pocket.

Always with one eye open to opportunity, Sammy Goldman picked up the management of Ruby Goldstein. "The Jewel of the Ghetto" had developed a large fan base in New York City thanks to an astounding knockout percentage. Following a humiliating knockout loss to Jimmy McLarnin in December 1929, Goldstein's career appeared to be over. Goldman disagreed, believing there was plenty of fight left in Goldstein and perhaps even a welterweight title. The fight manager planned to reestablish his confidence and bring him back to his winning ways.

Despite the never-ending newspaper articles previewing a Tony Canzoneri versus Billy Petrolle match—a bout that had yet to be scheduled—the champion's main concern was staying in shape. Therefore, Sammy Goldman booked him for a fight at Meyers Bowl in North Braddock, Pennsylvania (outside Pittsburgh). On May 23, Canzoneri would meet fighter Battling Gizzy, aka Mike Urilli, of Donora, Pennsylvania. A windmill-style fighter, Gizzy held victories over Cowboy Eddie Anderson, Sammy Dorfman and Harry Forbes. However, he was also coming off a 10-round decision loss to the talented Wesley Ramey. Canzoneri planned to do the bulk of his training at his home in Marlboro. Following his battle against Gizzy, the champion was scheduled to meet Harry Dublinsky in an outdoor 10-round, non-title bout in Chicago. It would be the first show of the newly-licensed West Side Boxing Club. This year Dublinsky, who was from Chicago, had already beaten Jackie Davis, Prince Saunders (newspaper decision), Johnny Jadick, and Tommy Grogan (newspaper decision).

Eager to meet Battling Gizzy in a non-title feature, Tony Canzoneri looked and felt good. It was the opening boxing show of the outdoor season in Allegheny County, and it appeared as if every area boxing fan was in attendance.[5] Sitting on the stool in his corner, Canzoneri took a few seconds to enjoy the stunning panorama. Since 1929, Meyers Bowl had become a popular summer fight venue.[6] It was the champion's first battle in the Steel City, the location an eastern suburb of Pittsburgh, and he was impressed.

From the opening gong, Canzoneri took command and never looked back. He waged a severe body attack on his opponent, and Gizzy had little choice but constant retreat. When the fighter did manage a wild shot at Canzoneri, it was off its mark and made him look foolish. In the fifth round, Canzoneri spun his adversary so hard out of a clinch that he fell out of the ring—into the laps of newspapermen ringside—and onto the floor. From his horizontal position, he began moaning about his back. Referee Red Robinson tried to assist him back into the ring, but Gizzy refused. After being counted out, he slowly and cautiously returned to the ring. The end came at one minute and 53 seconds of round five.[7]

Tony Canzoneri was forced to postpone an engagement with Eddie Cool, scheduled for June 6 at the Arena Stadium in Philadelphia, due to an injured shoulder. It happened during the battle with Gizzy and seemed to get progressively worse as the days passed. Goldman was afraid the injury might not heal in time for Canzoneri to go through with his fight against Harry Dublinsky.

Canzoneri, who enjoyed the limelight, wasn't thrilled when his personal life entered the public domain. However, when you are a handsome, flashy pugilist with a million-dollar smile, it is tough to stay out of gossip columns. Walter Winchell's syndicated feature "On Broadway" noted in one of his May columns that a woman by the name of Sonia Mitchell had taken a fancy to the 23-year-old pugilist. Since we are talking about the Great White Way, Paramount actor George Raft, a former professional boxer, had been making personal appearances in New York City and invited his boxing friends to drop by. Both Tony Canzoneri and Paolino Uzcudun took the popular actor up on his invitation. Canzoneri couldn't resist asking the actor about his current film, *Scarface.* Like many, the pugilist was impressed by Raft's performance. His character's frequent flipping of a coin (a nickel) became an iconic trope in gangster films. For some reason the act captivated folks, including Canzoneri. Naturally, he had to ask the actor about it. Ironically, almost a decade later, a young future featherweight champion from Hartford, Connecticut, tracked down Raft in Hollywood, California, and asked him the same thing. His name was Willie Pep.

During the first week of June, Johnny Jadick, junior welterweight champion, inked a contract to defend his title against Tony Canzoneri at Baker Bowl in Philadelphia. The promoter of the event was none other than lightweight great Lew Tendler. Canzoneri's lightweight title would not be on the line.

As for Canzoneri, he was training at Pompton Lakes, New Jersey. The lightweight champion was working out with Vince Dundee, uncrowned middleweight champion, and Steve Hamas, Penn State star athlete. Canzoneri would move to Trafton's Gym and Arcade Gym upon his arrival in Chicago.

All eyes turned to Sparta Stadium on June 16 to see how Tony Canzoneri, a 7–5 favorite, would fare against Harry Dublinsky. Although the 10-round duel didn't have a title involved, the ramifications for both fighters were enormous. Contenders for Canzoneri's crown were looking for opportunities and even holes in the champion's armor, while Dublinsky was hoping a sound performance would bounce him into a title shot. Fight analysts believed that Canzoneri, who viewed this as a tune-up for a title defense, would have to have a bad night for Dublinsky to win, and Dublinsky would have to conduct one of his finer performances to upset the champion. Canzoneri could be beaten in an overweight match, but the stars needed to align properly, and that wasn't probable.

Scaling at 134, Tony Canzoneri took a close, 10-round split decision over Harry Dublinsky, who tipped at 136½. It wasn't impressive, but it was a victory. For Canzoneri, he was lucky Dublinsky waited far too long to engage. The Chicago pugilist depended on his pesky left jab to score early, but it wasn't enough. In the sixth round, Dublinsky, over his nerves, got serious. He began going to close quarters and scoring. But by that time, his right eye was swollen shut and he was running out of rounds.[8]

Sammy Goldman, looking for a lightweight defense in New York, believed area promoters were dragging their feet. They were more concerned about bleeding the opportunity for every cent rather than signing his fighter. Canzoneri was familiar with contingency bouts. For example, if a division hopeful took a match with a certain boxer and won, a promoter might be able to land him a fight with the division champion. It wasn't until Goldman threatened to take his lightweight defense elsewhere that he finally signed with Jimmy Johnston, Madison Square Garden matchmaker, for a defense against Billy Petrolle on August 8.

Although most New York City fight fans had their minds on the lightweight division, all the eyes in Philadelphia were focused on the junior welterweight title held by Johnny Jadick. Their hometown fighter, under manager Tommy White, was sportsman enough to give Tony Canzoneri a rematch on July 18, even if he didn't have to. Jadick could have pressured Canzoneri to put his lightweight belt on the line, but he didn't. Yet Canzoneri, also a gentleman, promised Jadick a second look at the lightweight crown in the future, and that appeared to pacify his opposer—until Canzoneri signed to meet Billy Petrolle in a lightweight title defense. Jadick was furious. Once the junior welterweight champion calmed down, cooler heads prevailed; moreover, both fighters understood that each could draw their fair share of fans to Baker Bowl and take home an impressive paycheck.

Johnny Jadick v. Tony Canzoneri II, NBA World Junior Welterweight Title

Promoter Lew Tendler assembled an outstanding outdoor fight card at Baker Bowl, known formally as National League Park. Veteran Buster Brown grabbed a decision over Young Patsy Wallace, lightweight Lew Massey took a points victory over veteran Young Joe Firpo, and super lightweight Eddie Cool, having won five of his last six battles, came off the canvas in the opening round to defeat rising star Joey Costa, a Canzoneri stablemate. But most were in attendance to cheer on Johnny Jadick, "the Kensington Stringbean," in his rematch against Tony Canzoneri.

When the verdict was read following the feature event, it created a chorus of boos that could be heard all the way to Lancaster County. In a split 10-round decision, Johnny Jadick retained his world junior lightweight title. Shocked and disappointed, spectators began hurling objects in the direction of the ring. Quickly, the crowd got out of control. The referee, Joe McGuigan, and one judge, Tom Walsh, gave Jadick the victory, while the other judge, Stewart Robinson, saw it for Canzoneri. How close was close, you ask? When you total the rounds, a single point separated the pair. Too close, as many experts believed, to involve a title change rather than a draw. Appalled by the actions of those around them, security could do little to control the crowd. Even Canzoneri was struck by a flying cushion.

As the aggressor during the battle, Canzoneri, who scaled at 133, danced brilliantly around Jadick, who tipped at 135¼, and even landed solid blows to his jaw and midsection. But Jadick's crafty left jab abruptly stopped many of Canzoneri's assaults. It was that success that no doubt contributed to the scoring. The lightweight champion scored the only knockdown of the bout when he sent Jadick to the canvas in the tenth frame.

Both fighters had embarrassing moments. In the eighth round, Canzoneri, following a blistering two-handed body assault to Jadick, lost his balance and fell through the ropes onto the press table. Jadick suffered a horrible nosebleed that began early in the bout and lasted throughout the fight. By the final bell, crimson gore covered the face of the hometown fighter.

Exhausted after the fight, Tony Canzoneri planned on a bit of rest before hitting the gym to prepare for Billy Petrolle. While he did head to Dr. Bier's in Pompton Lakes, the first few days were about healing, not working. Meanwhile, Billy Petrolle was busy working out of the Pioneer Gym.

Tony Canzoneri v. Billy Petrolle, World Lightweight Title

Back on September 11, 1930, Billy Petrolle gave Tony Canzoneri a 10-round beating in Chicago few could forget. Immediately, the beat writers put Canzoneri out to pasture. Even those who had never seen the fighter in action before figured the Brooklyn boxer was on borrowed time. It wasn't fair, but it was part of the fight game.

Things had changed: Tony Canzoneri was a tireless battler, terrific puncher, aggressive warrior, and crafty defensive boxer. His ring generalship was not questioned. He possessed a powerful left hook and deadly straight right, and no element of his game could be taken for granted by any foe. Trainer Lou Fink, who had quietly prepared his fighter over the last four years, believed his fighter was in the best condition ever.

Word came on August 2 that Billy Petrolle had sustained a broken left elbow while sparring with Prince Saunders in the Pioneer Gym. Thus, the lightweight championship scheduled for August 8 in Madison Square Garden was called off. Petrolle, having sustained numerous injuries over the years, believed this injury originated the previous winter. Petrolle was released from the hospital after a week that included an elbow operation. The postponed lightweight championship was rescheduled for October 12, then moved to November 4.

Needing to get his fighter back into the ring, Sammy Goldman signed Canzoneri to a 10-round overweight match with Lew Kirsch. The battle took place at Queensboro Stadium on September 29, the boxers wearing five-ounce gloves. Hailing from New York's Lower East Side, Kirsch began boxing in 1925. Fighting out of the Pioneer Sporting Club, he pushed his record to 32–0–1 before he took his first loss to Tommy Grogan—this fight was on the Canzoneri versus Singer undercard. Following the loss, he was involved in an automobile accident. He fought once in 1929 before hanging up the gloves. But the economic conditions soon changed, and Kirsch was back in the ring. In

This Madison Square Garden Bowl ticket was for the Tony Canzoneri v. Billy Petrolle world's lightweight championship bout. The bout, scheduled to take place on Monday evening, August 8, 1932, was canceled.

his last three battles, he defeated Tony Caragliano, Joey Costa, and Tony Scarpati. Unknown outside the city, Kirsch wasn't a tomato can, but he wasn't Billy Petrolle. Benny Leonard was added to Kirsch's team as an advisor—the association wasn't a surprise as Leonard had been using Kirsch as a sparring partner during his comeback. Was the fight a favor? Distinctly possible, but should Kirsch get any ideas, Goldman added a $5,000 weight forfeit to the contract.

Originally scheduled for September 13, the battle between Canzoneri and Kirsch was postponed until September 27, then to September 29. It was Kirsch who requested the postponement due to an infected nose.

All the attention given to Lew Kirsch, who had a pile of offers sitting in his manager's office should he defeat Tony Canzoneri, faded in three rounds. Following months of training, Canzoneri went right to work, blasting rights to the jaw of his opposer. Kirsch, who scaled at 136¼, looked confused as he had no luck reaching his adversary, who tipped three pounds lighter. Seconds after the start of round three, Canzoneri fired a lightning right to the chin that thrust Kirsch into the ropes. Sensing the kill, he locked on Kirsch and fired multiple volleys into his body before moving north to the head. Noting that Kirsch couldn't keep the boat afloat, referee Willie Lewis stepped in and waved it off. The end came at 1:29 of round three. Canzoneri looked every bit like a champion, and once again the ringside press had crow for dinner.

Afterward, Canzoneri rushed back to Dr. Bier's camp at Pompton Lakes to continue his training for a battle against Chicago southpaw Ray Miller on October 5. That non-title fight was scheduled for 10 rounds on the Masonic camps' relief fund card at Ebbets Field. Promoter Humbert J. Fugazy had expressed concern regarding the recovery time for the fighter, even taking insurance out on the pugilist. Yet Sammy Goldman's biggest concern was not about the condition of his fighter but the weight of his opponent. Goldman signed for an overweight match, which meant Miller had to come into the battle over 135 pounds. But by October 4, it no longer mattered as Miller was forced out of the match due to an injured nose. Fate intervened, as Frankie Petrolle, Billy's brother, substituted for Ray Miller.[9] Frankie was best known as the pugilist who beat Bat Battalino twice. Canzoneri wasn't thrilled at the thought of tackling a scrapper the caliber of Frankie Petrolle, but Goldman talked him into it. After all, it was a benefit program. Was there a psychological element to the bout? Sammy Goldman believed there was, and it could work in favor of his fighter.

After concluding his training session for Frankie Petrolle, Canzoneri spoke to the press in a cocksure manner. He believed that following decisive victories over the Petrolle family, it was time for him to pursue the welterweight title. Certain he could defeat Jackie Fields, Canzoneri was asking himself "why not?" After all, other quality fighters had gone after multiple titles. Bring on Frankie Petrolle.

The end came at the 1:10 mark of the third round. If the lightweight champion of the world wanted to make a statement regarding his boxing prowess, he managed to do so at Ebbets Field on October 12. Tony Canzoneri, scaling at 132½, defeated Frankie Petrolle, who tipped at 140¼, by way of a knockout.

When Frankie Petrolle came out in round one, he looked tired and was; he had defeated Mike Sarko via a TKO in Albany two evenings earlier. Canzoneri, observing his opposer's crouching style, immediately sized him up and mounted an impressive offensive, using right uppercuts along with precision rights. Petrolle, who was told to go to the body of Canzoneri, was blocked by his opposer.

Petrolle used the left hook early in the second session, while Canzoneri opted for precision lefts and rights. As Petrolle targeted his opponent's body, he was taking a beating above the shoulders. Canzoneri's combinations quickly drew gore from the face and nose of his opponent. At one point, a dazed Petrolle managed to fire a Hail Mary overhand right to the face of Canzoneri that wobbled the fighter. It was his best punch of the evening.

By the third round, Petrolle, still fighting out of a crouch, was vulnerable. Taking a couple of solid rights, "the Fargo Flyer" missed with a counter. That was when Canzoneri fired a series of machine-gun lefts, followed by a short right that dropped his opposer in the center of the ring. Referee Jack Dorman, standing over the motionless carcass of the fighter, counted him out. As the crowd of 9,000-plus cheered, Canzoneri basked in the adulation. He had delivered a clear message to the Petrolle family.

The Rub on Billy Petrolle

Billy Petrolle needed a title like an artist required a masterpiece, and his magnum opus needed to be the lightweight championship. If he took it from Tony Canzoneri, even better. That was because Canzoneri was talented and favorably regarded. Fans of "the Fargo Express," and there were many, didn't want their hard-hitting pugilist to enter the record books without one. It wasn't fair to them or to Billy.

The biggest concern everybody shared was Petrolle's pounds: He fought best at 140 to 142 pounds, too big to be at his best as a lightweight and too light to handle a welterweight. Everybody, even the dumbest trainers, understood it was better to give away a few pounds than to weaken yourself making an unnatural weight. If a fighter isn't at his natural weight, it shows.

As any good fighter who leaves the fight game without a title will tell you: Not only was it hard to accept, but it also bothered them for years. It was like a sore that never healed. Nobody wanted to see Billy Petrolle slip into obscurity, and a title was the only way to guarantee he wouldn't.

Leading up to the battle between lightweight champion Tony Canzoneri and Billy Petrolle, the biggest concerns were how tight Madison Square Garden ushers could pack spectators into the venue, and Billy Petrolle's ability to come into the battle under 135 pounds. Most agreed that both concerns were a challenge. Jack Hurley, Petrolle's manager, insisted that not only would his fighter make weight, but he fought his best at that level.

Favored 6–5 three days out, Tony Canzoneri was disposing of sparring partners like tissues. He felt great and looked spectacular. The odds moved to 2–1 in favor of Canzoneri the day before the fight, due to a concern that Petrolle's weight loss had weakened the fighter. Then the odds shifted 9–5 in favor of Canzoneri the day of the battle. A capacity crowd of about 20,000, which could gross a $90,000 gate, was anticipated for the 15-round affair. The media was positioning the fight as a throwback to the old days, when fighters were concerned about making sure folks got their money's worth of action. As it would prove, it was—not a customer was disappointed.

10c OFFICIAL PROGRAM 10c

FIRE NOTICE

Look around now and choose the nearest exit to your seat. In case of fire, walk (NOT RUN) to that exit. Do not try to beat your neighbor to the street. JOHN J. DORMAN, Fire Commissioner.

MADISON SQUARE GARDEN
49th and 50th Streets, at Eighth Avenue

FRIDAY, NOVEMBER 4th, 1932, 8:15 P. M.

TONY CANZONERI   VS.   **BILLY PETROLLE**
CHAMPION   *CHALLENGER*

WORLD LIGHTWEIGHT CHAMPIONSHIP

Program from the world lightweight championship between Tony Canzoneri and Billy Petrolle held at Madison Square Garden on Friday, November 4, 1932.

After 10 rounds, Billy Petrolle had a slight edge. That was when Canzoneri, sensing the fatigue in his opponent, turned on the auxiliary engines and began fighting at a torrid pace. Driving Petrolle around the ring, the champion battered his rival until Petrolle had little choice but to clinch.

Canzoneri never slowed as the rounds ticked off in his favor. Petrolle, with both eyes nearly closed and bleeding from the nose and mouth, endured a severe beating. The best he could muster was a few short-lived flurries to prove he was conscious. In the 14th round, Petrolle, barely standing in his corner, took numerous unanswered volleys from Canzoneri as the crowd cheered for a knockout. Taking the bulk of the punishment, Petrolle covered. Occasionally firing a left jab to prove his gameness, Petrolle was nearly out on his feet due to fatigue. Beaten as he stepped out for the 15th and final round, Petrolle slipped to the floor following a miss. Once Petrolle was vertical, Canzoneri gave his adversary 30 seconds of free fire. Then the champion waded in and emptied the arsenal. How Petrolle managed to stay erect was anybody's guess.

Afterward, Petrolle gave no excuses. Although he felt fine before the fight, his legs began to tire near the end, and he lost power behind his punches. Petrolle acknowledged the skills of the champion and appeared satisfied he had performed at his best.

Canzoneri looked physically fit and outpunched and outboxed Petrolle. The champion began strong and finished strong—his conditioning was superb. Anticipating a body attack, Canzoneri did an outstanding job blocking punches with his arms and was prepared to counter. As he turned 24 years old on November 6, the victory over Billy Petrolle was the perfect present.

The champion planned to enjoy his title in the months ahead. From ring introductions and mentoring fighters to radio shows and store openings, life was good for Tony Canzoneri. Promoter Jimmy Johnston wanted to match "Canzy," or "Canzi," as many were now calling him, in January against Sammy Fuller, if, and it was a big if, Fuller defeated Jimmy McLarnin. He did not. In the second annual poll of sportswriters conducted by the Associated Press, the only boxer to make the top 10 list of the year's outstanding sports performer was Tony Canzoneri (#10).

Tony Canzoneri turned his attention to the stage at Prospect Theater, in the heart of South Brooklyn, on December 30. Always a lover of music, he couldn't resist an opportunity to lead a band. Other great fighters, such as Willie Ritchie and James J. Corbett, had graced the stage at the theater, so why not Canzy?

For Tony Canzoneri, 1932 brought nine fights, seven victories and two losses to add to his impressive resume. Granted, Johnny Jadick got his goat by handing Canzy two losses, both during world junior welterweight championships, but his impressive lightweight title defense against Billy Petrolle silenced the critics. Among his opponents, Lew Kirsch was the boxer he defeated with the fewest losses, while Billy Petrolle was the pugilist with the most victories (119) to lose to the champion. Every boxer he faced had a winning record and at least 25 victories. In retrospect, Canzoneri's victory over Petrolle was not only his best battle of 1933, but it was also one of the finest performances of his career.

EIGHT

A Rocky Road, 1933

"When you come to the end of your rope, tie a knot and hang on."—
Franklin D. Roosevelt

President Franklin D. Roosevelt took office on March 4, Wall Street's Dow Jones Industrial Average closed the year at 99.90, up from 59.93 at the end of 1932, former heavyweight legend James J. Corbett died at Bayside, Queens, at age 66, and Prohibition, which began in 1920, came to an end, leaving many a bootlegger facing a career change.

New York City hosted more than its fair share of unbelievable bouts, and fight fans there watched as 7–5 underdog Max Baer shocked the boxing world by knocking out Max Schmeling in the 10th round of their June 8 battle at Yankee Stadium. Before the month ended, Primo Carnera, who scaled at 261, knocked out Jack Sharkey, who tipped at 201, in the sixth round at the Madison Square Garden Bowl, Long Island City. Sharkey, who had won by a 15-round decision at Ebbets Field in their first battle, was dropped by a powerful right uppercut that struck his chin with such force many believed he had been killed. When referee Art Donovan finished the count of 10 at two minutes and 27 seconds of the sixth round, the Gob remained motionless. Ringside scribe Grantland Rice compared Sharkey to a frozen herring.

Opening the year by conducting his 12-piece jazz orchestra about town, the lightweight champion had found a new stage that appeared as satisfying. Booked to a two-week engagement at the Academy of Music, 14th Street and Broadway on January 4, Canzoneri was elated. On the same bill were vaudeville acts Collins and Peterson, Nick Lucas, and Hilton and Goron. Ben Roberts, who conducted the Palace orchestra for years, was behind Canzoneri's instrumentalists, and Johnny Hall, of RKO Theaters, was handling Canzoneri's stage management.[1] Could it be that the pugilist's majesty on a ring canvas had been translated to a conductor's stand? It appeared that way.

Despite talk of landing Tony Canzoneri a date with Jimmy McLarnin in February, Sammy Goldman couldn't seal the agreement at 142 pounds. Pop Foster, McLarnin's manager, held out for 144 pounds. Goldman, understanding that no lightweight could give away weight to McLarnin and expect to win, turned away. However, he did sign his fighter to meet Pete Nebo. It was Nebo, some recalled, who fought Canzoneri to a draw back on January 20, 1928.

While Jimmy Johnston was working New York dates for Canzoneri against opponents like Benny Bass, Sammy Fuller, and Chicago youngster Barney Ross, matchmaker Nate Lewis of the Chicago Stadium was focusing strictly on a match between Tony Canzoneri and Barney Ross. As a benefactor of the competition between promoters, Sammy Goldman wanted what was best for his fighter. If that meant a substantial payday from a large summer stadium event, he would have his fighter prepared.

The Schuyler House—Dr. Joseph Bier Training Camp, Pompton Lakes, New Jersey

Dr. Joseph Bier (December 5, 1886–February 12, 1952) was a talented ear, nose and throat specialist who happened to possess a successful treatment for cauliflower ears. Consequently, it came as little surprise that professional boxers sought his services. Upon their arrival in the Garden State, many pugs were impressed by the beauty and tranquility of the region. It would be the perfect place to prepare for a prizefight.

In operation since 1923, Bier's Training Camp attracted the finest in the fight game including Jack Kid Berg, Lou Brouillard, Primo Carnera, Harry Greb, Ace Hudkins, Benny Leonard, Jimmy McLarnin, Pancho Villa, and Tony Canzoneri.

The epicenter of the training camp was the Schuyler House, a Dutch Colonial later remodeled in the Second Empire style. Built in 1715, the house featured a mansard roof with arched dormers and two chimneys. It served as the headquarters for the Continental Army in 1781–1782, and the rich history of the home was enhanced by its future owners, including Dr. Bier. (It would be here where the great heavyweight Joe Louis would find solace in 1935 and put the town of 3,000 on the map.)[2]

Canzoneri planned to head to Pompton Lakes to train for his battle against Pete Nebo on February 23.[3] As Nebo was no walk in the park, Sammy Goldman believed his orchestra conductor needed a tune-up bout, so he booked him—with NYSAC's approval—to an overweight battle against either Ray Miller, Johnny Jadick, or Billy Townsend at Madison Square Garden on February 3. To get approval for the bout, Canzoneri understood he would defend his title, against a suitable opponent, during the month of March in New York. That opponent appeared to be Barney Ross, a talented Chicago Golden Glover.

Billy "Blond Tiger" Townsend, a talented Canadian welterweight, would be Canzoneri's conclusive test for his welterweight ambitions. Could the lightweight champion pack on the pounds without being slowed up? If so, Goldman believed he could target Jimmy McLarnin before challenging Jackie Fields for the title.

Canzoneri Charisma

When Canzoneri entered the Garden ring against Billy Townsend on February 3, it had a different vibe. The venue was testing a new $3 ticket ceiling for fights. As the *Evening Star* reported:

> These are different times to be sure, but Canzoneri is a different champion. Though it is customary to refer to the holder of the heavyweight title as the champion of champions, that honor just now belongs to Canzoneri.... The main reason for Canzoneri's popularity, with press and public alike, is not hard to discover. Tony knows how to fight and never fails

to give the boys a show. He bars nobody at his weight or above it either, in so far as the boxing commission will permit him to take on heavier boys.[4]

If Canzoneri couldn't sell out the Garden, could anyone? A million-dollar smile, complemented by incomparable talent and charm, seemed the perfect recipe. Regardless
of weight, Canzoneri was the best fighter in the game.[5]

Despite being outweighed by about 10 pounds, Tony Canzoneri was a 3–1 favorite entering his match against Billy Townsend. Confident of his ability, the champion felt the weight differential wasn't an issue. His Canadian opposer, who enjoyed
mixing it up with his competition, wasn't concerned about odds because he understood all it took was one lucky punch. For those attentive to the physical edge each
boxer possessed, Canzoneri was older, wiser, lighter, and shorter by two inches.
Townsend was younger, taller, and had a seven-inch reach advantage. From the waist
up, the measurements were about even, but Townsend's frame was supported by
larger legs.

Scaling at 132¾, Tony Canzoneri, without even messing up his hair, knocked
out Billy Townsend, who tipped at 141, in 65 seconds. For his efforts, he pocketed
around $5,000.[6] Exhibiting his impressive physique, Canzoneri exited his corner
and immediately conducted a quick range check using a light jab. As Townsend
blocked the jab, he caught a hard left to the ribs, followed by a stiff right to the jaw.
As he instinctively covered up, Canzoneri drove him around the ring with combinations. The sheer extent of the attack dropped the Canadian to the canvas. After rolling to his back, Townsend made no effort to stand. The crowd of more than 14,000
fight fans booed—more out of frustration than anything else, as many never made it
back to their seats from the concession stands.[7] Following the announcement, Canzoneri quickly left the ring. As for Townsend, he remained in his corner and was still
being assisted by his seconds. The following day, Jimmy Johnston announced that
he had reached an agreement with Sammy Goldman to give Madison Square Garden
exclusive rights to the services of Tony Canzoneri for as long as he held the lightweight title.

Canzoneri planned to head to Miami by train on February 13. His training
quarters, for his battle against Pete Nebo, would be Roman Pools. In 1928, Nebo
was ranked by *The Ring* as the #5 featherweight in the world, and a year later was
ranked as the #5 junior lightweight in the world. One reason: He defeated Sid Terris in back-to-back battles in 1930. Nebo also held victories over Frankie Carlton,
Young Joe Firpo, and Jackie Davis, but he had won only three of his last five bouts. As
a streaky yet dangerous fighter, he was not taken for granted by Canzoneri. Tickets
for the event were scaled at $1.10, $3.30, and $5.50.[8]

Satisfied he was ready, Tony Canzoneri took it easy the day before the fight. He
was the guest of honor at Frolics, a cabaret located at 13th Street and Causeway in
Miami. The evening's entertainment featured Sally Rand in her seductive fan dance.
Delineator of blues Etta Reed also performed. Hey, there were times when a guy just
had to be a guy, and besides, Dave Harmon, conductor of the orchestra at the club,
even planned to surrender his baton to Canzoneri.

More than 10,000 fight fans turned out at Miami's Madison Square Garden
Arena to watch Tony Canzoneri, who scaled at 133, capture a 10-round points victory
over Pete Nebo, who scaled at 136½. It was an interesting bout, as Nebo fought to the

finish—most had predicted an early knockout. Despite the fortitude exhibited by the Key West boxer, there was no doubt who was the superior fighter, as Canzoneri hooked and sliced with efficiency. Yet each time the champion had his opposer in trouble, Nebo would cover and wait until the fog lifted. Canzoneri was held off during the first three rounds before pulling back and opting to score with long-range ordnance. Catching Nebo with a targeted left hook in the seventh round, Canzoneri had his prey in trouble but couldn't deliver him. He paid the price for trying to knock out his opponent, as he broke his right thumb. All but one of the rounds belonged to Canzoneri.[9]

Sidelined for a couple of months with his injury, Canzoneri was seen all over New York City trying to pass the time. Finally, by the first week of April, his schedule was

Pedro Nebot, aka Pete Nebo (shown here in the 1930s), was a talented boxer and ranked contender in both the featherweight and junior lightweight divisions. Born in Cuba, he resided in Key West.

starting to take shape. Sammy Goldman was working with Pete Reilly, who managed both Wesley Ramey and Freddie Miller. Although a date wasn't firm, it appeared certain that Canzoneri would meet Ramey. Also, a New Orleans date against Battling Shaw was in the works.

On April 5, word hit the press: Tony Canzoneri would defend his title against Barney Ross in Chicago during the Chicago World's Fair—A Century of Progress International Exposition held in the city in 1933–1934. Since Ross, a resident of the city, won his last fight at Chicago Stadium on March 22—he outpointed Billy Petrolle over 10 rounds—he couldn't have been happier.

Barney Ross

A New York–born fighter named Barney Ross (born Dov-Ber Rasof [Rasofsky] and called "Beryl" David Rasofsky on December 23, 1909) appeared to be the one youngster who could give Tony Canzoneri a run for his lightweight title. Compiling an astounding record—he hadn't lost a fight since March 1931—he appeared

on the national horizon following a unanimous decision victory over Bat Battalino on October 21, 1932. But those in the Midwest knew Ross through his success
with the Intercity Golden Gloves—he was the Chicago Golden Gloves champion
in 1929.

When the Rasofsky family moved from New York to Chicago, Isidore, the child's
rabbi father and grocery store owner, found a home in Chicago's Maxwell Street
neighborhood, a vibrant Jewish ghetto akin to the New York's Lower East Side of the
1920s and 1930s. While his father hoped his son would follow in his footsteps, it was
not to be. The boy's life was changed forever when his father was shot dead resisting a
robbery at his neighborhood store.

The youngster's life soon spun out of control. From his mother placing him,
along with his siblings, in an orphanage to becoming a street brawler, thief and

A classic view of the Polo Grounds from Coogan's Bluff, 1909 (Library of Congress). Wesley Ramey (bottom left), a Michigan native, fought professionally from 1929 until 1941.
Barney Ross, a Golden Gloves champion, ruled the welterweight division the first half of
the 1930s (bottom right). Both are shown here in the 1930s.

money runner—he was even employed by mobster Al Capone—Dov Rasofsky was vindictive toward everybody and everything. Little mattered because he saw no alternative to his current lifestyle. That was when he discovered the sweet science and realized boxing could be the vehicle to reform his life.

With his thumb healed, it was time for the champion's third bout of the year. Scaling at 133 pounds, Tony Canzoneri, not prepared, lost a 10-round decision to Wesley Ramey, who tipped at 136. The non-title contest happened on April 20 at the Civic Auditorium in Grand Rapids, Michigan. Not only had Canzoneri not trained with the dedication that ensured his success in previous bouts, but he suffered multiple lacerations: a cut over his left eye, a gash in his eyelid, and smaller cuts that bled for nearly six rounds.[10] Ramey, who hadn't lost a bout since December of last year, had beaten Battling Shaw, Tony Herrera, Eddie Ran, Steve Halaiko and Johnny Jadick before facing Canzoneri.[11] The perpetual flow of blood on the champion's face hampered his efficiency and created a sense of desperation during the final rounds. When the decision was read, there was no objection from the 5,500 fight fans in attendance. They had seen a terrific battle conducted by two outstanding gladiators.

Since Canzoneri had signed to defend his lightweight title against Barney Ross in June before the battle, nobody was certain how this loss would impact the champion or the gate. One thing was certain: In the weeks leading up to his title defense, Canzoneri had a full calendar of events outside the ring. Since they required a considerable amount of his time, he needed to learn how to balance these activities with his training. And he needed to do it now.

Two promoters were being considered for the show in June. It would be either Chicago Stadium or James C. Mullen. It wasn't a surprise when Chicago Stadium got the promotion, as Sammy Pian and Art Winch, managers of Barney Ross, had a strong relationship with the group. Promoter James C. Mullen would likely get the rematch—both principals signed a return bout clause within 60 days—should Ross lift the lightweight title.

Tony Canzoneri v. Battling Shaw, NBA World Junior Welterweight Title

Needing a tune-up battle before meeting Barney Ross, Canzoneri was concerned. So was Sammy Goldman, who inked his fighter to a bout against Battling Shaw, junior welterweight title holder.[12] The bout would take place at Heinemann Park in New Orleans on May 21. As you may recall, Canzoneri lost the title to Jadick in January 1932, and Shaw won it from Jadick on February 20, 1933—this was Shaw's first defense of the crown. I'll say it for you: Yes, a title battle in preparation for another title battle. Sammy Goldman felt this was what was needed to get Canzoneri's skills back on track.

Battling Shaw, aka Jose Perez Flores, was a hard-hitting, 21-year-old Mexican-born boxer who hailed from Laredo, Texas. Considered one of the greatest Mexican fighters since the days of Joe Rivers, he was excited about the opportunity to defend his newly-won junior welterweight championship against Tony Canzoneri.

Shaw would face Canzoneri on Sunday, May 21, as Louisiana allowed Sunday boxing. Promoter Marty Burke believed a gate more than $20,000 was realistic considering the participants, timing, and demand. The Southern Pacific Railroad was even running special excursions for Sunday, May 21. Travelers could pick up a $1.50 round trip ticket to New Orleans from numerous origination points.[13]

Getting down to business: Tony Canzoneri, scaling at 133, and Battling Shaw, who tipped at 136½, fought evenly during the early rounds. But as the fight progressed, Canzoneri got stronger. Igniting in the seventh round, Canzoneri dropped Shaw with a damaging right hook, then repeated the action in the eighth. In truth, Shaw was lucky to get out of the seventh round, as the bell sounded before referee Jimmy Moran could start a count—Shaw's seconds had to carry him to his corner. More than 6,000 spectators cheered for their native fighter, and Canzoneri enjoyed every minute of it. While Sammy Goldman was ecstatic about the 10-round unanimous decision in favor of his fighter, he was even happier to get the junior welterweight title back. The reason: He wanted it abolished. He wasn't alone, as other fight managers felt the same. NYSAC, which created it, abolished the designation two seasons earlier; they also ruled out the junior lightweight class.

Brooklyn's *Times Union* ran an interesting article about Canzoneri's early days. Johnny Galway, who operated Gayoso Club in New Orleans, was interviewed by a staff reporter. Galway candidly spoke about Tony's father coming into the gym and selling the talent of his 75-pound son. The club operator listened and put Tony in the ring for his first amateur bout. It would be the only loss young Tony Canzoneri ever took in New Orleans. Galway talked about grooming the fighter for the 100-pound championship. He confirmed that the day of the show, Tony's brother Joe came to him, claiming his mother refused to allow Tony to fight. Galway panicked and immediately traveled to the Canzoneri home. Confronting a weeping Mrs. Canzoneri, Galway insisted her son would not be hurt. Finally, Tony's father took control of the situation and approved of his son's bout. But the situation wasn't over. Following a pre-fight examination, a physician observed that the boy had a weak heart and should not go on. A puzzled Galway, who didn't want to explain to Mrs. Canzoneri why her son didn't fight, decided to have the youngster reexamined. Thankfully, Dr. Gomila, city commissioner, examined Tony Canzoneri and approved his participation. The youngster went on to win the 100-pound championship.

Barney Ross v. Tony Canzoneri I, World Lightweight Championship and World Junior Welterweight Title

Training in his outdoor camp in the Wisconsin woods, Barney Ross looked good and felt great. He was trimming weight and felt confident he would enter the conflict with Canzoneri prepared. Canzoneri was finishing up his training at Trafton's Gymnasium—Ross would finish his training there as well—and was confident of his chances at victory.

The press was playing the ethnic card—hey, it's boxing, and cultural pride sells tickets—as Ross, the west side Hebrew, was a slight favorite over the little New Orleans Italian. At least that was how the Chicago press framed it. Canzoneri was a made-to-order opponent for Ross. Of course, that was what was said when Canzoneri faced Bass, Berg, Chocolate, Petrolle and Singer.

Naturally, the Horatio Alger slant, that honest, hard work can overcome poverty, was applied to young Barney Ross. Four years removed from the Golden Gloves, the popular intercity featherweight champion was now facing Tony Canzoneri. Like an Alger hero, Ross faced overwhelming odds.

To win, Ross would have to ride his left hand, like a cowboy rides a horse, for 10 rounds and hope luck fell his way. Ross was leading a parade of challengers, and his career had no place to go but up, while Canzoneri, who was forever being put out to pasture, could only look down.

About a week out, Canzoneri was given 4–5 odds of repelling Ross, but it changed daily and moved to 8–5 in favor of Canzoneri before the fight. What didn't change was the loot both pugs would take home for their troubles. Ross, if the event sold out, could grab about

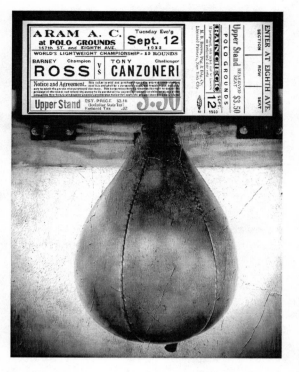

This Polo Grounds ticket was for the Barney Ross v. Tony Canzoneri bout. The event was conducted under the auspices of the Aram Athletic Club on September 12, 1933.

$18,000, while Canzoneri hoped to add twice that amount to his wallet.

A Glove Affair

Looking to take advantage of every angle, Sam Pian, Ross' co-manager, went before the Illinois commission to discuss the typical issues, such as announcements, corner selection, and choice of referee. Uncharacteristically accommodating—which should have been a clue—Pian suddenly shifted gears to the selection of boxing gloves. Of the six pairs of boxing gloves provided, Pain asked the commission to take two pairs, seal them, and then lock them into a safe. They would be brought into the ring the night of the fight.

Pian knew Canzoneri had small fists, so small that he wrapped them heavily with gauze and adhesive tape before placing them in custom-made gloves that then, and only then, fit perfectly. Since Ross had difficulty fitting into the custom gloves provided by Canzoneri, they were eliminated. The two pairs of gloves that were locked away, Ross favored for their size.

Canzoneri wore custom-made gloves when he knocked out Jack Kid Berg back in April 1931, and Pian remembered the action. After the fight, Sol Gold, Berg's manager, claimed the gloves were illegal and did not weigh the regulation six ounces. Gold had a point until it was determined that Berg's gloves were larger and heavier than the rules allowed. Despite the point backfiring on Gold, Canzoneri's gloves were an issue. If Pian needed an edge, perhaps he had found one. Only time would tell.

Only a few words could be heard, but they were enough: "The new champion...." The fight was so close at the finish, not a single person of the 11,000-plus in attendance was certain who won. Canzoneri made the most—though nobody was sure it was enough—of the first eight rounds, but Ross did a terrific job of negating that impact during the final two frames. Both judges saw it for Ross, while referee Tommy Gilmore saw it even.[14]

Stunned by what he had heard, Tony Canzoneri, standing in his corner, dropped his chin to his chest. With his eyes closed, he could feel the sweat pouring down his face. For a moment, he silenced the crowd with his mind and did his best to hold back the tears. He could not. In his mind, and in the minds of those around him, he had fought to at least a draw.

The first round could be seen in favor of either party, but the edge went to Ross in rounds three and four. This was due to an almost unstoppable left hand. Canzoneri took command in the fourth and fifth rounds and even managed to open cuts over Ross' eyes. The pace slowed over the sixth, seventh and eighth frames, as both fighters traded punches and frequently clinched. Ross did his best to keep his annoying left hand in Canzoneri's face. He turned up the heat in rounds nine and ten by relentlessly hooking to Canzoneri's head and blocking his opposer's assaults. It was more of the same in the tenth round with Ross scoring with solid rights to Canzoneri's skull. One right caught Canzoneri squarely on the jaw and came close to putting him out.

With the victory, Ross became the first Golden Gloves fighter to capture a professional title. While the fighters gave a sound performance, the gate did not meet expectations, a far cry from four years earlier, when Canzoneri and Mandell brought in more than $100,000. Because of this, Chicago Stadium believed they lost about $10,000 on the event. Regardless of the economic debasement, the fight was a classic confrontation.

On July 24, 1933, in Ed Sullivan's popular Broadway gossip column in the *Daily News*, it was noted that showgirl Rita (Goldberg) Roy had taken a fancy to Tony Canzoneri. The stunning Miss Roy, whose captivating eyes and luscious lips were difficult to ignore, was having a noticeable impact on the popular pugilist. The attractive couple were often seen at the Paradise Nightclub.

Barney Ross v. Tony Canzoneri II, World Lightweight Championship and World Junior Welterweight Title

During the first week of July, word hit that the rematch between Barney Ross and Tony Canzoneri had been booked for September 14 at the Polo Grounds—the date would be moved to September 12. Ross and co-manager Art Winch, who were on a 10-day vacation at Excelsior Springs, Missouri, were staying informed through Sam Pian. Afterward, Ross planned on training for the rematch, first at Stillman's gymnasium, then at Lake Swannanoa, New Jersey. As for Canzoneri, he headed to Pompton Lakes on August 16 to begin his preparation.

Barney Ross, who was born in New York, couldn't resist visiting his old neighborhood. The building he was born in stood at 252 Rivington Street on the Lower

East Side—his family moved to Chicago when he was two and a half. When he shifted his interest to boxing, he had two idols, Jack Dempsey, which surprised few, and, ironically, Tony Canzoneri. Admittedly nervous when he first faced Canzoneri, Ross recalled sitting ringside and watching the former champion knock out Jackie Kid Berg in 1931—he was on the undercard. Admitting he never thought he would be inside a boxing ring facing his mentor, much less in a title bout, Ross couldn't believe it.

Say it ain't so: On August 28, Tony Canzoneri was accused of sending a spy to the training camp of Barney Ross at Lake Swannanoa. It was Sam Pain and Art Winch, co-managers of Ross, who spotted the familiar face of Marty Fuller among a party of invited newspapermen. As a close friend of Canzoneri for nearly a decade, he wasn't fooling anybody. Naturally, Fuller, who claimed he was the driver of the media party, denied the charge. After Fuller was asked to leave, he waited briefly outside the facility, then drove over to Doc Bier's training camp at Pompton Lakes to relay the story to Team Canzoneri. The former champion got a good laugh out of the incident.

Speaking of training camp, Canzoneri was committed to a five-week training period—his average training camp was two weeks, and his longest previous camp was three. Routinely attracting more than 300 fans to watch him spar two rounds apiece with Johnny Bonito, George Riley, and Al Santora, he maintained a strict schedule. Knowing what to anticipate from Ross and aware of the added benefit of a couple of extra weeks of preparation, he believed the extended camp was the proper decision. It worked against Billy Petrolle, so why not Barney Ross?

A week before the battle, Barney Ross was at his training camp and in the ring sparring with Benny Leonard. The old master was teaching Ross new tricks. Meanwhile, over at Pompton Lakes, Tony Canzoneri was enjoying a day of rest before resuming training. After his routine four-mile run, Canzoneri spent the afternoon watching the New York Giants football team practice. By the way, the fighters' training camps were located a mere 20 miles apart.

Youth must be served, believed the Ross backers. They ignored the close decision Ross had over Billy Petrolle and an even closer decision over Tony Canzoneri. They continued to reiterate that Canzoneri was "washed up" while disregarding all claims to their fighter's lack of endurance or making the 15-round distance.

Experience must be acknowledged, believed the Canzoneri backers. You can't beat an experienced fighter who can change styles as fast as chameleons change colors. Canzoneri supporters were quick to point out that Ross was no longer fighting in Chicago. Canzoneri's thumb, which bothered him during the first bout, was healed. Canzoneri's speed alone should negate the Ross arsenal and keep him from enduring those pesky portside swipes.

Although Canzoneri was fighting history, as no ex-champion of the 135-pounders had ever regained the title, it appeared as if the event would draw the greatest crowd ever for lightweight boxing, even breaking the 1923 record set by the Benny Leonard–Lew Tendler second bout. The challenge associated with both these elements motivated him.

The specifics: Venue—Polo Grounds at 157th and Eighth Avenue; Time—Main Event 10:00 p.m.; Rounds—15; Purse—Ross 40 percent of gate receipts, Canzoneri 12½; Promoter—Tim Mara; Matchmaker—Al Weil; Estimated attendance—40,000; Estimated receipts—$125,000; Preliminary Bouts—Carmen Knapp v. Bobby Bruno (four rounds); Al Roth v. Nick Scalba (six); Joe Walker v. Nick Pastore (six); Billy Hogan v. Patsy Pasculli (six); Lou Ambers v. Joey Costa (six)[15]; Benefit—Free Milk Fund for Babies.

Scaling at 135, Barney Ross won a 15-round split decision over Tony Canzoneri, who tipped a pound lighter. For Ross, it was his first defense of his world lightweight title and world junior lightweight title. As in their first bout, a dispute arose over the winner as judge George Kelly saw it Canzoneri, while judge Harold (Greenpoint) Barnes, along with referee Art Donovan, voted for Ross. It was noted that Donovan discredited Canzoneri three rounds—sixth, eighth and ninth—due to unintentional low blows. There were no knockdowns. While the low blows didn't help Canzoneri's scoring, it wasn't the main cause of his loss. Canzoneri couldn't deliver his opposer when he had an opportunity, for example, when the knees of Ross buckled in the ninth round.

Ross finished so strong and with such zest it was clear how the decision would fall. Unlike their first fight, which many saw as a draw, this fight leaned toward Ross. The champion, who intended to buy his mother a house, could now walk down the street and have folks not dismiss his initial victory over Canzoneri as a "hometown decision." Minus the bruises from the low blows, Ross was unmarked. Canzoneri, on the other hand, suffered a swollen and cut mouth, a blackened left eye, and numerous welts from the body punches of Ross. Everyone in Camp Canzoneri believed their fighter won—upset at the verdict, Tony's father climbed into the ring and nearly threw a stool at one of the judges. The match drew a gross gate of almost $119,000. Ross pocketed about $36,000, while Canzoneri took home about $13,000. Paid attendance was 28,289.[16]

Rinsing Away a Label

Taking well-deserved time off, Tony Canzoneri still had to weather the common and overused expression "washed up" that surfaced regularly in the newspapers. Imagine being 24 years old, having lost back-to-back lightweight championship bouts to Barney Ross, and having to read, almost on a weekly basis, that your best days were behind you or that your career was over.[17]

Canzoneri waited for Sammy Goldman to chart his next course. The former champion continued to invest in the careers of other fighters; for example, he held a 50 percent managerial interest in heavyweight Charley Massera. Canzoneri sparred with Lew Feldman, a contender in the featherweight division, who had signed with Sammy Goldman and was now a stablemate.

On October 17 came word Tony Canzoneri would return to the Ridgewood Grove ring, on October 28, to battle Frankie Klick of California. They had been matched before, but the bout was canceled due to Canzoneri being ill. Recognized as the lightweight champion of the Pacific Coast, Klick had recently scored impressive victories over Tony Falco and Eddie Cool. Maurie Waxman, Klick's manager, claimed his fighter had more than an outsider's chance to upset Canzoneri owing to his awkward style of mauling an opponent. Yet Canzoneri was a 7–5 favorite entering the contest.

Tipping at 133½, Tony Canzoneri won a unanimous 10-round decision over Frankie Klick, who scaled at 133. A strong draw at his former venue, the Brooklynite attracted 5,000 fight fans to watch the spirited battle. Taking command early, Canzoneri tried, but without much success, to negate Klick's left jab. In the third round, Klick managed to send a powerful right that cut the bridge of Canzoneri's nose. Although the cut was one of those everlasting bleeding injuries that continuously bothered the fighter, Canzoneri was able to fight onward and capture seven of the 10 rounds. There were no knockdowns.

Free time in Brooklyn meant heading to Jimmy Kelly's Paradise on the corner of Atlantic and Fourth Avenue in Brooklyn. Canzoneri was a regular there and was always treated like a champion. Jimmy Kelly, an outstanding night club operator, knew that if he could bring a celebrity the caliber of Canzoneri into the joint, other Brooklynites would follow. And he was correct. Kelly even advertised that Broadway celebrities and radio stars could be seen at the club.

Canzoneri had hoped to squeeze in two more fights before the end of the year, then head to Europe. However, the only battle that looked certain was against Kid Chocolate in Madison Square Garden on November 24. The winner of this battle would meet Cleto Locatelli, the Italian champion.

Labeled "two slipping top notchers" by the *Times Union*, Tony Canzoneri, tipping at 133, knocked out Kid Chocolate, who scaled at 130, in a spectacular lightweight battle at Madison Square Garden.[18] A powerful, and what would prove noteworthy, right hand ended the contest after two minutes and 30 seconds of round two. More than 13,000 fight fans witnessed Kid Chocolate, in what some saw as his 100th professional ring battle, suffer his first knockout loss.

Canzoneri fired a thunderbolt of a left hand into Chocolate's stomach that folded his adversary and brought his chin into range. Locking on his target, Canzoneri planted a firm right hand onto his rival's chin and sent him face-first to the canvas. Reaching a squat as the count neared 10, Chocolate lost his balance and tipped over to his back. It was quick but far from painless. The pair had fought evenly over the first frame, testing their range while establishing their footing.

It was a magnificent Friday evening of boxing that also included two four-round bouts and four six-round battles. The latter witnessed Lew Feldman defeat Jimmy Slavin, Solly Krieger defeat Frank Fullam, Mike Belloise defeat Pet DeGrasse, and Cocoa Kid draw Joe Ghnouly. Tickets were scaled at $1.00 (general admission), $1.50, 2.50, $3.00., $4.00, and $5.50.

Afterward, Sammy Goldman accepted terms for a 10-round bout against Cleto Locatelli on December 15. The winner would be destined, they believed, for a title shot against Barney Ross. Goldman reminded Canzoneri about Cleveland's all-star Christmas fund boxing show on December 4. It was a popular and well-attended charity event. Canzoneri was scheduled to meet Cecil Payne at Public Hall. So much for the European trip.

Tipping at 134, Tony Canzoneri knocked out Cecil Payne, who scaled four pounds heavier. The end came at the 1:07 mark of round five. Canzoneri skated by his opposer during the first four rounds. In the fifth frame, a retreating Payne caught a hard left to the chest, followed by a long right to the head, then tumbled to the canvas. Payne, who had compiled 10 consecutive wins, including victories over Allen Whitlow, Mickey Cohen, and Davey Abad, hadn't lost a fight since June.

Leaving Cleveland, Canzoneri headed to Madame Bey's Training Camp in Summit, New Jersey. Knowing Locatelli, the European lightweight champion, was far from a routine bout, he felt he needed additional time to prepare. Locatelli, who happened to see Canzoneri drop Kid Chocolate at the Garden, wasn't the least bit intimidated at battling the former champion. Taking solid victories over Jack Kid Berg, Belgian Francois Sybille, and Pete Nebo, he was secure in his skills. Locatelli's manager, Kid Francis (Albertanti), affirmed that his fighter's duel with Canzoneri would be a thrilling confrontation. Three days before the battle, Canzoneri was an 8–5 favorite.

Knowing his strengths, yet understanding his weaknesses, Tony Canzoneri stated to the press that he had developed a new punch—naturally, word hit the press the day before his Madison Square Garden battle. Having kayoed his last two ring opponents, Canzoneri, or should we say Sammy Goldman, had a foundation for the fabrication. Details about the secret punch were not forthcoming.

After 10 rounds at Madison Square Garden on December 15, nobody was certain who had won the battle between Tony Canzoneri and Cleto Locatelli. Both fighters scaled at 134 pounds and fought their hearts out. The only thing certain, as evidenced by the concerned look of both fighters, was that it was razor close. Among the 10,000 spectators in attendance, views were mixed: Canzoneri, a familiar figure, fought his fight and scored. Fighting brilliantly, Locatelli, with his crafty glove magic, impressed everyone.

Both fighters got off to a slow start. The hopping style of Locatelli took time to get used to, but Canzoneri managed to bloody the nose of his opposer by the end of the opening round. The Brooklynite shook his opposition in the second session, but Locatelli did not balk. He didn't clinch but treated it as though it were a warning. Noting the withering of his opponent in the fourth and fifth terms, Canzoneri successfully went to the body and nearly dropped his prey. But he became overconfident in the fifth round; consequently, he even stood in contempt of his opposer before punching him about the ring. Having misjudged Locatelli's stamina, Canzoneri slowed in the seventh round, and his opposer took command. A Locatelli right cross caught Canzoneri near the end of the round and rocked the fighter. Momentum shifted as the eighth and ninth rounds belonged to the European. Locatelli relentlessly pounded his opposition—during one rally, Canzoneri took five unanswered shots. Rebounding in the final round, Canzoneri dazed Locatelli with a sensational left hook. Sending his opposer bouncing off the ropes with only seconds left, Canzoneri lost an opportunity to end the battle with one final blow. The 10-round unanimous decision—which caught everyone by surprise—went to Tony Canzoneri. As the crowd booed the verdict, Canzoneri slipped out of the ring.

Matchmaker Jimmy Johnston, no stranger to opportunity, promptly reacted to the fight; moreover, it was announced that Cleto Locatelli would get another crack at Tony Canzoneri at Madison Square Garden on January 12, 1934. This time the fight would be a 12-round contest.

Boxing fan and syndicated columnist Ed Sullivan, who had befriended Tony Canzoneri, couldn't resist the opportunity to acknowledge the fighter in his Broadway column. On December 18, he mentioned the flashy diamond watch that adorned the wrist of Rita Roy, courtesy of the former champion.

For the year, Canzoneri's 10 bouts, including three title fights, resulted in seven wins, three via knockout, and three losses. Even though he was on the losing end of his two outstanding title fights against elite boxer Barney Ross, the bouts would be talked about for years. Washed up? Not a chance.

NINE

A Legend Secured, 1934

"Mediocrity knows nothing higher than itself; but talent instantly recognizes genius."—Arthur Conan Doyle, *The Valley of Fear*

Ernest Hemingway stopped by Wheeler Shipbuilding in Brooklyn and purchased a fishing boat he later named *Pilar*; meanwhile, his friend F. Scott Fitzgerald was putting the final touches on his novel *Tender Is the Night*, and former *New York Times* reporter Max Perkins, working at Charles Scribner's Sons, was building an unparalleled stable of literary giants that included both authors. Talent, as Perkins understood, needs not only guidance, support, and opportunity but also faith.

New York City turned to Madison Square Garden Bowl, an outdoor arena in the borough of Queens, to host the fight game's biggest events: On May 28, Barney Ross defeated Jimmy McLarnin in the first of what would be a classic trilogy; Max Baer floored giant Primo Carnera 11 times while winning the heavyweight title on June 14; and on the undercard of that bout, veteran James J. Braddock, supposedly washed up, picked himself off the canvas to knock out heavyweight contender Corn Griffin. Pugilism, as fight fans understood, was always the orphaned son of probability.

Bringing in the new year at the Newburgh Elks Club, Tony Canzoneri led his orchestra through an entertaining evening of music. While Guy Lombardo, over at the Hotel Roosevelt Grill, didn't feel threatened by his new competitor, Canzoneri did manage to draw an impressive crowd.

Madison Square Garden planned to host the rematch between Tony Canzoneri and Cleto Locatelli on January 12. This time the rival lightweights planned to meet over the 12-round distance. As the first fight of the new year, it had all the makings of another competitive and entertaining battle. No sooner was it announced than it was abandoned due to a nose injury sustained by Canzoneri. Madison Square Garden agreed to a 10-round battle between Jack Kid Berg and Cleto Locatelli on January 12. Once Canzoneri healed, the rematch would be rescheduled. Because of the injury, Sammy Goldman was forced to postpone Canzoneri's bout against Eddie Cool in Philadelphia on January 22.

Looking ahead, the fight manager did confirm that Canzoneri had agreed to meet Baby Arizmendi, the Mexican sensation, in Los Angeles and possibly Frankie Klick in San Francisco. Both bouts would take place following Canzoneri's rescheduled bout against Locatelli. Should the Brooklyn boxer be fully healed and victorious in all these battles, Goldman planned on challenging Barney Ross once again.

A View of Canzoneri's Approach to Boxing

Speaking of Barney Ross, the champion gave an outstanding perspective to reporters on doing battle against Tony Canzoneri. Admitting he knew what to expect in the ring against the champion during their first bout, Ross was immediately struck by the fighter's ability to shift his style of fighting. Canzoneri wasn't afraid to modify his approach once he sized up his opponent's defense. During the first round, he approached Ross with a plethora of left hooks. After the session, the champion's corner offered a variety of solutions, including an effective counter-punch strategy. However, in the next round, Canzoneri dropped the left hooks in favor of straight right hands. Therefore, Ross changed his countering strategy and moved to the left jab. Canzoneri switched again to more of a hit and run approach—flipping a stiff right or left, then quickly altering his position. In stark contrast, there were rounds when Canzoneri sat back and refused to lead. Ross confirmed there was no global or universal approach to fighting the pugilist. An adversary had to know almost instinctively how to counter Canzoneri. It was an informative synopsis given by a rival elite fighter.

During the third week of January, word came that Barney Ross could no longer make the lightweight limit. After his next bout, against Billy Petrolle, the lightweight champion planned to enter the world of the welterweights. The move sent shockwaves through the division. Sammy Goldman immediately headed to NYSAC on behalf of Canzoneri, hoping to coax them into allowing his fighter's clash against Cleto Locatelli, scheduled for January 26, to become a 15-round title bout. As both were rated challengers, it made sense. Although NYSAC appreciated Goldman's concern, it was presumptuous, as the champion could change his mind.

Tony Canzoneri, who was over at Madame Bey's training camp in Summit, New Jersey, told Sammy Goldman that if he did indeed beat Locatelli, he wanted to go before NYSAC and request to be declared champion. While the fighter meant what he was saying, he understood that this job belonged to his manager. Though part of him was happy for Ross, another part was disappointed. Canzoneri was hoping for a third bout with Ross to avenge his losses. Meanwhile, Locatelli finished his training at the St. Nicholas gym before announcing that he would return home if beaten by Canzoneri. No sooner had he made the proclamation than he fell ill with influenza and was forced to withdraw from his battle. The rematch was rescheduled for February 2.

Days before his first battle of 1934, Tony Canzoneri countered by claiming he would quit boxing if he didn't beat Cleto Locatelli. One of the fighters was destined for a career change; the question was, which one?

Waltzing into Madison Square Garden a 7–5 favorite against Cleto Locatelli, Tony Canzoneri understood he had a job to do. Last year's December verdict didn't meet with everybody's approval, and it bothered him. Therefore, a decisive victory over his rival, he believed, was his only option. And a decisive victory was what Canzoneri delivered.

Outslugging and outboxing his European foe, Tony Canzoneri, who tipped at 133, performed magnificently. Twice (in the second and third rounds) he dropped his adversary to the count of one. A small crowd, about 5,000–7,000 spectators, watched as Canzoneri made Locatelli, who scaled three pounds heavier, look silly. However, when tenor Joe Humphries announced the decision a draw, people were shocked. It wasn't what they had witnessed—ringside scored the contest eight rounds for Canzoneri, three for Locatelli and one even. It had to be a mistake, and it was: The judges had tabulated the scoring incorrectly and the victory belonged to Tony Canzoneri. By the time the error was discovered, both fighters had shaken hands and left the ring. The oversight was insulting to everyone involved, especially Canzoneri, who at this point in his career deserved better. It was believed to be the first time in the history of the venue that two decisions were rendered.

During the last week of February, Canzoneri confirmed he was headed for the West Coast. Working his way across the country, his next bout was against Pete Nebo at Convention Hall in Kansas City on March 1. From there he would travel to Los Angeles to meet Baby Arizmendi on March 13 at the Olympic Auditorium. Canzoneri was looking forward to the trip for a couple of reasons: The fight against Nebo would complete a trilogy with the competitive Key West boxer, and Arizmendi, a fighter who seldom left the West Coast, was making significant waves in the division.

Pete Nebo was coming off an embarrassing loss to Barney Ross and hoped to gain ground in the rankings by defeating Canzoneri. He had met, and lost to, Tony Canzoneri last year at Madison Square Garden Stadium in Miami. Since that time, he had boxed nearly every contender in the division. Unfortunately, he was often on the losing end.

Tony Canzoneri, fighting at a five-pound deficit, soundly defeated Pete Nebo, who scaled at 135, over 12 brisk rounds.[1] Making an impression, Canzoneri defeated his opposer by even a far greater margin than Barney Ross. Nebo was down for a no-count in the second round, and it was a preview of coming attractions as the fighter was only able to win one round. While he battled evenly in the fifth and seventh rounds against Canzoneri, it wasn't enough. The event drew an enthusiastic crowd of 8,000 fight fans.[2]

While preparing for his bout with Baby Arizmendi, Canzoneri learned that Barney Ross had fought Frankie Klick to a draw. While it wasn't a loss for Ross, it indicated he was vulnerable, a fact that few believed after seeing him pound Canzoneri. The former champion, who went on record acknowledging Klick's ability before the fight, wasn't surprised by the result. Canzoneri was sticking to his strategy of continuing to defeat all logical challengers to the title held by Ross so he would be the last man standing. He would then be destined, so he believed, for a third bout with the champion. Canzoneri also wanted to get to Ross before the champion tangled with the dangerous Jimmy McLarnin.[3]

For the time being, Baby Arizmendi was far from a speed bump for Tony Canzoneri. In his last 13 bouts, Arizmendi had lost only once, and he held victories over Eddie Shea, Freddie Miller, and Tommy Paul. The Mexican-born boxer, according to some, was also one of the youngest boxers ever to turn professional—at the age of 13. With Arizmendi prone to bouts of wild swinging antics, Canzoneri would have to stay attentive the entire bout or else.

Scoring another decisive 10-round victory, Tony Canzoneri, who scaled at 131, outboxed 20-year-old Baby Arizmendi, who tipped at 128. It happened at the Olympic Auditorium on March 13.[4] Taking the early rounds as part of a sound fight strategy, Canzoneri used his targeted left jab to control the bout while turning to the right cross for the bulk of the damage. Arizmendi tossed enough quick volleys to keep the battle interesting, but most of his attempts to score were suppressed. Only in two rounds, the eighth and ninth, did Arizmendi manage to reach Canzoneri. Those ringside, along with most of the 12,000 in attendance, saw it 7–3, or 6–2–2, Canzoneri.

With the outdoor season approaching, big money was on the minds of everyone associated with the fight game. That money belonged to three individuals in the lower divisions, Barney Ross, Jimmy McLarnin, and Tony Canzoneri, because they had the drawing power. It was reported during the first week of April that Tony Canzoneri would meet Jimmy McLarnin in a world welterweight championship bout in May. The statement, which sounded more like fantasy than fact, was probably printed to entice Ross to move up and take on McLarnin. Co-managers Sam Pian and Art Winch believed it didn't make sense for Ross to spot McLarnin 10 pounds or more to step out of his class. Besides, they confidently believed, once Ross beat McLarnin, there was nobody left to fight. Another factor was Pop Foster, McLarnin's manager, who drove a hard bargain and always wanted the largest piece of the pie. While McLarnin, who last fought on May 29, 1933, wanted to battle Ross on May 28, the terms needed to be worked out—no simple task. Therefore McLarnin, world welterweight champion, looked to Canzoneri. Imagine, and Tony Canzoneri did, adding a fourth title to his resume. Ross countered by claiming he had two sound offers: The first was $35,000 to meet Frankie Klick in San Francisco, while the other was $30,000 to defend his title against Tony Canzoneri in Los Angeles. It was time to wait and see how the negotiations proceeded.

Canzoneri turned to his business ventures while he waited for word of his next battle. Not only did he have a piece of a few fighters, but he also had a piece of Coindore, an Italian eatery on West 52nd Street. Hitting all the popular nightspots, the former lightweight champion was a target for the gossip writers. For example, he was noted in establishments such as the Hickory House, and typically in the company of a beautiful lady—the future Mrs. Canzoneri?[5]

During the last week of April, it was probable that Tony Canzoneri would meet Frankie Klick over the summer. Busy matchmaking, Al Weil had his mind on three ballpark promotions. Ever aggressive, he hoped to match the winner of Canzoneri versus Klick with Barney Ross. However, that was about as easy as blowing out a candle through a pane of glass. Completing step one, Canzoneri did agree to meet Klick over 12 rounds at Ebbets Field on June 27.

On May 28, Jimmy McLarnin planned to defend his welterweight title against Barney Ross in New York. If Ross should win, there would be a return bout soon after. Naturally, every boxing fan had an opinion on the battle, including Tony Canzoneri. The former boxing champion had driven over to Grossinger's Country Club in Liberty, New York, to watch Barney Ross train. Canzoneri wisely wasn't going to take a firm position, but he let it be known that Ross had improved greatly since he faced him. McLarnin was like a miniature Dempsey, a hard hitter capable of ending a bout with one punch, while Ross was indefatigable. Because of this, Canzoneri had no intention of dropping a wager on the fight. Admitting McLarnin was dangerous and he admired the courage displayed by Ross to take the fight, Canzoneri avoided a prediction but confirmed both fighters would be prepared. For example, Ross had been training to counter McLarnin's left with a fabulous overhand right. Incidentally, Canzoneri was over to Grossinger's not merely to watch the training session but to accept *The Ring*'s popularity trophy along with Barney Ross—the two had tied in the voting.

Following a one-day postponement because of the weather, it was fight on. Canzoneri entered Ebbets Field a 6–5 favorite over Frankie Klick. Much of that favoritism had to do with Canzoneri's victory over Klick back on October 28, 1933, which some believed was questionable. Thus, once again Canzoneri had to pull out a decisive victory or risk being overlooked for a title shot, an opportunity he believed he was entitled to if he defeated Klick.

Scaling to a pound advantage, Tony Canzoneri defeated Frankie Klick, who tipped at 133, by way of a technical knockout. The end came at one minute and 42 seconds of the ninth round. With his face pummeled—right eye practically closed, bleeding and swollen the size of a golf ball—Frankie Klick endured an unforgiving left hook that forced referee Patsy Haley to step in and halt the fight. The game Westerner could take no more. Attracting 12,000 fight fans despite the initial postponement, the event created a $20,000 gate.

Critics had the fight two rounds for Klick, two even, and the remainder for Canzoneri. To the credit of the San Francisco pugilist, he started strong by sending a straight left to Canzoneri's chest. The punch set the stage for a remorseless confrontation. The sixth frame was responsible for the bulk of the damage, as Klick took a solid right to the chin, followed later by lefts targeted at his inflated optic. Despite the impairment, not only did Klick step out for the seventh round, but also he proceeded to win it. But the fuel tank was running low, and the eighth round was all Canzoneri. Three shattering lefts to the face, followed by a cruel right, nearly ended Klick's evening, but he fought back. Having seen enough, Canzoneri came out in the ninth round and fired heartless hooks from all directions. Accumulating damage at a record pace, a blinded Klick was helpless. Referee Patsy Haley had little choice but to stop the fight.

Not only was the main event impressive but so were the preliminaries: In the four-round opener, Caspar La Rosa outpointed Hoard Clark; Lou Ambers scored a TKO over Phil Rafferty; Harry Dublinsky decisioned Billy Hogan; and in the walkout bout (a fight scheduled after the main event), Mike Belloise decisioned Lew Feldman. It was an outstanding evening of boxing featuring names that would soon become very familiar.[6]

After the fight, Canzoneri cleaned up and headed over to Pat Rooney's Big Show at Beau Rivage on Emmons Avenue in Sheepshead Bay, a neighborhood in southern Brooklyn. The reason for Canzoneri's attendance was not a victory celebration, though that would have been appropriate, but to greet his cousin, George Canzoneri, who was part-owner of the waterfront resort. The pair had not seen each other since childhood and believed the visitation was long overdue. And it was.

Sammy Goldman, who could not persuade Sam Pian to alter his thinking, was pushing NYSAC hard to order Barney Ross to fight Canzoneri. Pian, who handled Ross, saw Jimmy McLarnin as the pot of gold at the end of the rainbow. A Ross versus Canzoneri bout, in Pian's mind, wouldn't draw anywhere near the gate of another Ross v. McLarnin bout. However, the roadblock on that path was Pop Foster, McLarnin's pilot. As fate had it, NYSAC sanctioned a return match between Barney Ross and Jimmy McLarnin for September. It would be the first welterweight championship defense for Barney Ross. Ironically, this was sanctioned after it had been stipulated that Ross defend his lightweight title against Tony Canzoneri.

Since the best Team Canzoneri could hope for was a possible date with Ross in December, it was time to get busy fighting. Al Weil, handling affairs at Ebbets Field, was talking about a welterweight skirmish between Tony Canzoneri and Harry Dublinsky. Eager to rumble at 147 pounds, Canzoneri was game. On short notice, Weill signed the ballpark bout for August 22. Tickets were scaled at $1, $2, and $3.

Although this fight would only be his fifth of the year, Canzoneri was in fine spirits. His success and notoriety fit him like his tailored suits. Even if he was a celebrity and extraordinarily popular, he didn't always enjoy seeing his name in social columns. One mention did arouse some interest: It appeared that Tony Canzoneri and entertainer Rita Roy were tying the knot.

Training at home or at the farm in Marlboro, Canzoneri was trying to keep things simple. Having worked with his fighter for six years, Lou Fink was with his boxer. Fink confirmed that Canzoneri didn't smoke (although his likeness was being used in cigarette ads), and when it came to alcohol, he turned only to beer. Fink, who also worked with Gene Tunney, did admit his fighter fancied his mother's home cooking—his favorites were always chicken and lamb. If Fink was surprised at any aspect of his fighter, it was his lack of concern. Canzoneri wasn't a guy who got caught up in hypotheticals or spent all night wondering what Harry Dublinsky was thinking. Calm and unpretentious, Canzy was Canzy. Yet he was a gracious competitor. He always acknowledged the elite opponents he had faced, Benny Bass, Sammy Mandell, and Barney Ross. In his opinion, Bass was the toughest hitter, Mandell the best boxer, and Ross a superb defenseman.

Suffering from an injured leg, Canzoneri asked for and received a postponement of his August 22 bout against Harry Dublinsky. The bout was rescheduled for August 29.

Harry Dublinsky

Born in Milwaukee, Wisconsin, on September 9, 1910, Harry Dublinsky turned to the fight game at age 16 in the perfect setting: Chicago. Fighting out of the typical haunts, White City Arena and Roosevelt Road Athletic Club, he displayed ability and strength but not much else. In his first 11 fights, he posted a record of 5–3–3. But he had a knack for being in the right place at the right time, and it paid off. For example, a mere 15 fights into his professional career found him on the undercard of the Cowboy Eddie Anderson versus Tony Canzoneri bout on September 2, 1927.

From June 7, 1927, until July 25, 1928, he fought 19 times and never lost a bout. At that point, a loss to Ignacio Fernandez sent the fighter into a tailspin; subsequently, he was victorious only four times in his next 11 contests. Considering his options, in August 1929, the economic conditions convinced the 19-year-old it was time to get serious about his boxing career. And boy, did he, as he fought 15 times in 1930 and posted a record of 12–2–1, with nine consecutive victories. While he lost decisions to Tony Herrera and Wesley Ramey, he managed to battle Barney Ross to a draw.

In 1931, after losing three of his first four fights, Dublinsky posted nine consecutive victories. The following year he was on the edge of contention, defeating Johnny

Jadick, Tommy Grogan, and Tracy Cox, but losing to Lew Massey, Benny Bass, and Tony Canzoneri. Fighting 17 times in 1933, Dublinsky added 12 wins and five losses to his resume. His victims included Eddie Cool, Young Joe Firpo, Battling Shaw, and Eddie Wolfe.

Even money was how the betting community saw it as Tony Canzoneri tackled Harry Dublinsky in a tournament of contenders at Ebbets Field in Brooklyn. As the first four rounds progressed, Canzoneri, who scaled at 134½, looked sound. Since he had suffered from a bad leg and a banged-up nose during training, it was a welcome sight to his corner. Pounding Dublinsky, who tipped at 139, relentlessly in the second round, Canzoneri nearly dropped him with a solid right cross to the jaw. Altering strategies in the third round, Dublinsky moved to his left hand to counter attacks and got the better of his adversary—he was particularly successful at close quarters. Annoyed by a hard right to the face at the beginning of the fourth round, Canzoneri instinctively responded with machine-gun combinations. Not surprisingly, the first of two backhanding warnings was issued by referee Billy Cavanaugh to a frustrated Harry Dublinsky.

Coming on strong in the sixth round, Dublinsky sent a damaging left to the face that caught Canzoneri's right eye. Stunned, the former champion looked bewildered. His punching accuracy diminished as he appeared to lose his range. With a minute left in the round, Dublinsky sent an unforgiving starboard blow to the face of his opposer. It shook Canzoneri. Taking the seventh frame, Dublinsky continued to pound the body and right eye of his rival. Canzoneri, who appeared fatigued, clinched and did his best to avoid contact in the eighth round. Cut on the mouth and under the right eye in the ninth, Canzoneri, covered in gore, was merely trying to make it through the round. To many, the final round looked even. More than 8,500 fans witnessed Harry Dublinsky take the 10-round decision, and not a soul objected to the verdict. Canzoneri's streak of eight consecutive victories had ended.

Before the second week of September ended, the pair signed for a rematch on the 26th. Additionally, Sammy Goldman deposited a $2,500 forfeit with the boxing commission to bind a challenge to Barney Ross. Whether it was prompted by confidence or concern, the commission took note and instructed Ross that he must meet the challenge within a 60-day window.

Another talented fighter on the fistic horizon was Luigi Giuseppe D'Ambrosio, aka Lou Ambers, from Upstate New York. The ambitious youngster from the village of Herkimer, near Utica, had appeared on some Canzoneri undercards and was making a name for himself at an impressive pace.

To make matters more interesting, on September 17, Jimmy McLarnin defeated Barney Ross to reclaim the welterweight championship of the world. Sammy Goldman was ecstatic, as the press had buried McLarnin in the same manner as they had Canzoneri when he lost to Ross. Why the media was never held responsible for their ridiculous views bewildered Sammy Goldman.

A band of boxing experts, along with media favorites, showed up at Tony Canzoneri's training camp in Marlboro on September 20. One of the individuals was Benny Leonard. The former lightweight legend thought Canzoneri looked great and was destined to reclaim the division title. With his rubber match against Dublinsky less than a week away, it was the shot in the arm Canzoneri needed.

Finding out he was a 6–5 favorite to whip Tony Canzoneri in the rubber match,

Harry Dublinsky wasn't surprised. That was because he honestly felt he was that good. As many recalled, Canzoneri won their first fight in 1932, and Dublinsky countered in August of this year. A repeat performance of the latter seemed only logical to the Chicago pugilist.

The crowd—estimated at nearly 17,000—began filing in early at Bedford Avenue and Sullivan Place in Brooklyn, eager for the 8:15 p.m. start. Canzoneri, scaling at 134½, looked like a man on a mission from the opening bell. A commanding left hand was the weapon of choice early, be it the extended range variety or a crushing hook. Dubinsky looked confused and could not find his target. The first four rounds were so one-sided that Canzoneri opted for some showboating. Moving to the right hand, Canzoneri landed damaging shots as he traversed the ring. His exuberance, particularly in the fifth round, mirrored that of his earlier days.

Dublinsky, slow out of the blocks, gradually found his stride. By the seventh session, Canzoneri's legs went on vacation; exhausted, the former champion was taking far more than he was giving. Two rounds later, Canzoneri, mouth swollen and bleeding, had cuts opening with nearly every blast to the face. One Dublinsky right hook struck Canzoneri's face with such force, it catapulted his mouthpiece across the ring. Drained of every ounce of energy at the final gong, both warriors slowly walked to their respective corners, unsure of the outcome. Defying the odds, the 10-round points victory belonged to Canzoneri.

As far back as 1928, Canzoneri's career had been over. But like a cat with nine lives, he always lived to see another day. Without question, he was the premier challenger for Barney Ross. But Ross obeyed his own drummer, whether anybody, be it Tony Canzoneri or even NYSAC, liked it or not. Of the latter, Commissioners Bill Brown, D. Walker Wear, and General John J. Phelan, were "in no mood to trifle with Ross."[7]

Sammy Goldman went right to work following his fighter's victory over Dublinsky. But after a few weeks it was clear that negotiations, with everyone involved in a potential battle against Ross, would not be easy. By the first week in December, talks between Sammy Goldman and prospective Chicago

In 1934, Tony Canzoneri was named *The Ring* "Fighter of the Year," along with Barney Ross (pictured here, ca. 1930s).

promoter Joe Foley broke off. In December, NYSAC declared Lou Ambers the out-standing boxing challenger for the lightweight title. That left Ross three weeks to fight Ambers or NYSAC would declare the 135-pound crown vacant and award the title to Ambers. For the record, Tony Canzoneri, Sammy Fuller, and Frankie Klick all refused to fight Lou Ambers. They weren't afraid of the upstate pugilist, only concerned that the kid from Herkimer lacked the drawing power of Barney Ross. It was all about the coin.

Fighting six bouts while posting a record of 5–1, Tony Canzoneri demonstrated once again his career was far from over. While more than one bout proved it, the September victory over Harry Dublinsky drove the point home. His smashing hooks to the body of his opponent were unstoppable, his indefatigability unquestionable. Having fought in a championship battle every year since 1927, Canzoneri was disappointed he could not land a battle against Barney Ross. But even Canzoneri understood "boxing, like life, was a long preparation for something that may never happen," to alter a line from W.B. Yeats.

Ten

Another Lightweight Championship, 1935

"No, that is the great fallacy: the wisdom of old men. They do not grow wise. They grow careful."—Ernest Hemingway, *A Farewell to Arms*

Wall Street's Dow Jones Industrial Average exhibited positive economic signs as it closed the year more than 40 points higher than the end of 1934, transatlantic travel continued to improve as the French liner SS *Normandie* took a mere four days, 11 hours, and 42 minutes to arrive in New York from Southampton, and former New York Yankees legend Babe Ruth appeared in his last game, playing for the Boston Braves in Philadelphia against the Phillies. Although many Americans believed the stock market would go higher and ships would go faster, it was hard to believe baseball could go on without "the Babe."

New York City, always the place to be for boxing, formally introduced pugilist Joseph Louis Barrow, an impressive heavyweight fighter who had been battling in the Midwest. On June 25, the 21-year-old pugilist entered Yankee Stadium and scored an impressive sixth-round technical knockout of colossus Primo Carnera. On September 24, Louis, once again in Yankee Stadium, knocked out the flamboyant Max Baer in the fourth round, and finally, on December 13 at Madison Square Garden, Louis floored the iron-jawed Paulino Uzcudon while driving the Spanish heavyweight's mouthpiece through his upper lip. Joe Louis, aka "the Brown Bomber," was on his way to becoming an American legend. As he once quipped, "If you gotta tell them who you are, you ain't nobody."[1]

The inability to land a rubber match, or big payday, against Barney Ross was an issue Tony Canzoneri needed to get over. Hence, he focused on a fourth title, the welterweight championship of the world. Pushing his manager for a title fight against division champion Jimmy McLarnin wasn't the issue; it was convincing Charles "Pop" Foster the match (McLarnin v. Canzoneri) would be as lucrative as any other option. Believing his fighter could defeat McLarnin, Goldman worked tirelessly to get Foster to the negotiation table.

Canzoneri opened the year on January 7 at Laurel Gardens in Newark. There he tackled veteran Eddie Ran, "the Polish Thunderbolt," in a scheduled 10-round contest. Canzoneri, scaling a robust 140¼, began his drive to the welterweight crown by knocking out Eddie Ran, who tipped at 143½, in the second round. Unaffected by the additional weight, Canzoneri moved swiftly about the ring. He stayed out of range of Ran's dangerous right as he measured his punches. Ran took the opening round by a slight edge and appeared comfortable. With Ran displaying the complacency Canzoneri had hoped to see, it was time to go to work. As Ran opened his stance, Canzoneri fired a left hook to the ribs followed by a volley of combinations that dropped the fighter. Desperately trying to reach his feet at the count of nine, Ran failed. Tumbling to the canvas, he needed to be carried to his corner. At the heaviest weight at which he ever fought, Canzoneri impressed the 1,800-plus fans in attendance and was satisfied with his performance.

Lou Who?

Lou Ambers, an Italian barnstorming lightweight out of Herkimer, appeared seemingly out of nowhere to capture the hearts of the Boxing Commission. Born Luigi d'Ambrosio, Lou Ambers grew up in the beautiful Mohawk Valley. During the Great Depression, he and his nine siblings watched their Italian-born father lose his business. Then they lost their father. Taking to the ring as a "bootleg" boxer, or a pugilist taking an unsanctioned fight for a payment, under the alias Otis Paradise, to support his family, he was successful at creating an intimidating persona.[2] As he improved, he began fighting under the name Lou Ambers and honed his skills to become a contender. Holding victories over Cocoa Kid, Johnny Jadick, Tony Herrera, and Pancho Villa, Ambers had lost one professional battle (to Steve Halaiko) entering 1935. A keen judge of distance with prodigious hand speed, he worked within punching range, busily slipping and feinting, then slashing in with hooks and uppercuts. Quiet, unassuming, and respectful, Ambers was in stark contrast to Jackie Kid Berg, and the Boxing Commission noticed. Embittered by the games being played by boxing managers like Sam Pian and Art Winch and fighters such as Barney Ross, NYSAC believed it was time for a change.

It happened on January 11: Lou Ambers defeated Harry Dublinsky in a 10-round unanimous decision at Madison Square Garden. Pounding Dublinsky into submission over the distance, Ambers gave the Midwesterner a drubbing he would never forget. It was the first nail in Dublinsky's coffin as he won only four of his next 18 professional bouts. The lightweight division had changed.

Speaking of Upstate New York, Tony Canzoneri was inked to meet Harold "Honeyboy" Hughes over eight rounds on January 21. The fight would take place at Convention Hall in Utica. It was an unusual signing, leading some to speculate that Sammy Goldman owed James "Red" Herring, matchmaker of the Midstate Athletic Club of Utica, a favor.[3] Hughes was a popular local lightweight whose claim to fame was two recent victories over Eddie Dempsey of Syracuse. Sammy Goldman also inked Canzoneri to a bout against Leo Rodak to take place at Chicago Stadium on January 31. This match had been in the works for weeks, but the pair couldn't agree on weight—Canzoneri wanted it at 135, while Rodak demanded 132. Finally, everyone agreed to 133½ pounds.

On January 15, NYSAC announced that lightweight champion Barney Ross couldn't fight in the state until he defended his title against Lou Ambers. The six-month grace period allowed every champion had come and gone. (Ross hadn't defended his lightweight crown in 16 months—not since he defeated Canzoneri back in September 1933.) However, Ross had fought for, and won, the welterweight championship of the world on May 28, 1934, then lost it in a title defense on September 17, 1934. Both bouts took place in New York. Later, Ross claimed he had no intention of fighting in New York State.[4] The entire situation was absurd and out of control.

Back to Canzoneri's battle in Upstate New York: It was a thrill for Utica fight fans to witness Tony Canzoneri battling inside a ring at a local venue. Elite fighters, unless they were from the area, like Lou Ambers, typically did not find themselves doing battle in the region. For many, including his popular opponent, Canzoneri looked like the photographs that appeared in newspapers, and his trademark smile was unmistakable. Nervous and starstruck, Honeyboy Hughes put on a respectable showing even though he was no match for the former champion. A targeted right cross caught Hughes in the third round, splitting his lip and sending him back on his heels. Canzoneri was scoring at close quarters, and his jabs began opening cuts on his opponent's face—Hughes had a small gash under his left eye. Halfway through the battle, Hughes looked confused by Canzoneri's dynamic style. In the sixth frame, Hughes switched tactics and went on the offensive—he even had the crowd on their feet as he tore into Canzoneri with straight right hands. But it was too little, too late. In the end, Tony Canzoneri, who scaled at 133½, outpointed Honeyboy Hughes, who scaled at 135. With the victory in his pocket, Canzoneri was off to Chicago. He wanted to work on some punches before his battle against the undefeated Leo Rodak. As for Honeyboy Hughes, he now had an unforgettable story to share with his grandchildren.

Staying in Contention

Born in South Chicago in 1913, Leo Rodak exhibited athletic prowess as a youth. Joining Chicago's Catholic Youth Organization as a teenager, he learned how to box. As his skills improved, Rodak wanted to take them to the next step. He entered the competitive Chicago Golden Gloves tournaments. From 1931 until 1933, he won three titles in three different weight division—flyweight (112 pounds), bantamweight (118 pounds) and featherweight (128 pounds).

Having turned a few heads with his boxing prowess, Rodak turned professional in 1933. By his fifth professional bout, he was at Comiskey Park on a boxing card that featured the wild-swinging King Levinsky against former heavyweight champion Jack Sharkey. When he greeted Tony Canzoneri, Rodak held victories over Dave Barry, Tommy Paul, and Georgie Hansford.

In front of an estimated 15,000 spectators in Chicago Stadium, Canzoneri, unimpressed by the winning ways of his opposition, gave Leo Rodak a 10-round boxing lesson. Taking command early, the former champion, with far more power behind his punches than anticipated, glided over his conservative opposition. Conducting a seminar on the art of the ring, Canzoneri was imposing. In both the second and sixth frames, Canzoneri rocked Rodak with razor-sharp right hands to the chin. While his opposer managed to right the ship on both occasions, he was forced to stay out of range from rounds seven through nine. Canzoneri, who tipped at 132¾, or to a two-pound advantage, took the unanimous 10-round decision. Critics saw it seven rounds for Canzoneri, one for Rodak, and two even—Rodak did manage to come on strong in the final round. For their trouble, Canzoneri took home about $8,000, while Rodak pocketed over $5,000. Promoters Jim Mullen and Nat Lewis were so impressed by the showing they were at Goldman's feet for a chance to match his fighter with Ross. Incidentally, not that superstition ever entered the mind of a pugilist, Canzoneri, an 8–5 favorite, took the northwest corner of the stadium ring against Rodak, which was Ross' corner when he lifted the Brooklynite's crown.[5]

The Fiasco—Ross v. Canzoneri III

The soap opera known as the rubber match between Barney Ross and Tony Canzoneri continued in February. Both fighters had signed with their choice to handle the promotion. Canzoneri had recently signed with promoters Nate Lewis and Jim Mullen to meet Ross at Chicago Stadium on April 12 or 26. Ross had signed with promoter Joe Foley the previous November. Which promoter would get the fight? It was anybody's guess. Certain—as if anything in the fight game was ever guaranteed—was that the location of choice was Chicago. The rub: Sammy Goldman refused to sign with Foley, and Sam Pian wouldn't allow anyone else to handle the promotion. Everyone involved appeared to be angry at someone. Thus, the match, destined to be an enormous gate, appeared only on paper. Meanwhile, Ross, under the gun to defend his title, had to fight or forfeit his crown. The logical contender remained Tony Canzoneri.

As the situation played out, Tony Canzoneri headed to Detroit to fight Chuck Woods at Olympic Stadium on February 26. Woods, a hometown fighter, had won four of his last six bouts. Yet not much was thought of the Detroit pugilist, who was a $5 a day laborer at the Ford factory and had mainly been fighting in clubs and smaller venues. The opposition Woods had faced had far less experience than Canzoneri. But as any former champion would tell you, these are often the bouts a fighter had to be concerned about—a situation where the opposition had nothing to lose. That was the case here.

Starting out strong—knowing he needed to win the early rounds before Canzoneri got his bearings—Chuck Woods won the first four rounds. He even managed to daze Canzoneri with a firm right hand in the second round, then outbox him in the third. The best round of the evening was the seventh, when both boxers slugged it out toe to toe. Woods caught Canzoneri with a left that sent him back, then followed with an overhand right that caught him on the jaw. Knowing he had to turn up the volume during the last few rounds, Canzoneri did. Late in the ninth, he caught Woods with a right hand that buckled his knees, but the boxer remained upright by falling into a clinch. That left the final round to make up the ground needed for a victory, so Canzoneri did his best. While it was enough to win the round, it fell short of garnering a decision. More than 3,500 elated patrons witnessed the upset victory by Chuck Woods, and not a soul complained about the verdict.

To little surprise, Tony Canzoneri was signed to a rematch against Chuck Woods—the bout to take place at Chicago Stadium on March 15. Canzoneri loved consolation bouts, precisely in this situation, where you could remove the hometown element. According to Sammy Goldman, Woods was one of three opponents in Canzoneri's entire career to offer him a rematch, the other two being Barney Ross and

Harry Dublinsky. Promoters Nate Lewis and Jim Mullen handled the event. Both Chuck Woods and Tony Canzoneri arrived in Chicago on March 9 and planned on finishing their training at Trafton's gymnasium. As usual, Canzoneri was accompanied by manager Sammy Goldman and trainer Lou Fink.

In a 10-round unanimous decision, Tony Canzoneri, who scaled at 134, defeated Chuck Woods, who tipped to a four-pound advantage. Switching styles and stepping up his game, Canzoneri won eight of 10 rounds (including the last six), with the other two even. Seeing the fire in Canzoneri's eyes, Woods allowed his opposer to lead; moreover, fighting a counter battle was the only way, he felt, he could make distance. When Canzoneri saw an opening, he took it, but even when he had his adversary in trouble, he could not deliver a fight-ending punch. Nevertheless, vindication tasted oh so sweet.

Matchmaker Jimmy Johnston, who always acted like he knew something that you didn't, was pushing hard for a Tony Canzoneri versus Lou Ambers date at Madison Square Garden, while promoters Nate Lewis and Jim Mullen wanted the pair for an April date at Chicago Stadium. Everyone had to sit and wait to see how the scenario played out. Meanwhile, Barney Ross was out in Hot Springs, Arkansas, recovering from neuritis (nerve inflammation) and complaining about his attempts at making the lightweight limit.

On April 1 came word that Barney Ross was thinking about giving up his lightweight title. Although nobody was certain if it was true, the fighter's frustration with losing weight was widely known. Later, he declared himself a welterweight, in pursuit of Jimmy McLarnin's 147-pound title—Ross won and lost McLarnin's crown the previous summer. Matching with McLarnin, Ross believed, had greater economic potential than Canzoneri and Ambers combined. Frankly speaking, Ross would rather quit than lose his title in the ring. But before the first two weeks of May ended, the fighter was planning to defend his lightweight crown against Lou Ambers at the Polo Grounds on May 29—prompting the change was Ross defeating Henry Woods in a junior welterweight contest. But would he do it?

In the middle of April, NYSAC accepted the resignation of Barney Ross as lightweight champion. Next, the commission decided to recognize the winner of the Canzoneri versus Ambers bout, scheduled for May 10 at Madison Square Garden, as the world lightweight champion. This was what matchmaker Jimmy Johnston had hoped for. Both fighters needed tune-up bouts and got right to work scheduling. Sammy Goldman signed Canzoneri to meet Eddie Zivic in Pittsburgh on April 25, while Al Weil, who looked after Lou Ambers, arranged for his fighter to meet Honeyboy Hughes in Providence. In addition to tune-up bouts, both participants needed to drop off a $2,000 check—to cover a weight and appearance forfeit—to the NYSAC office at 80 Center Street. These cash guarantees were now required before any ring engagement could be officially sanctioned.

It wasn't pretty when the fans stood on their seats screaming for referee Red Robinson to stop the beating being taken by Eddie Zivic in the seventh round. The Pittsburgh fighter had taken two counts of eight in the sixth frame and was hanging on to reality by a thin thread. Wisely, Robinson stepped in and halted the bout at the 1:41 mark of the session—the victory belonged to Tony Canzoneri. It was clear from the opening bell that Zivic, who scaled at 132½, was no match for Canzoneri, who tipped at 134. The former champion eased into the battle but throttled up after

Zivic snapped a solid right hand in the third. Pounding the local favorite for the remainder of the round and continuing the assault in the fourth and fifth rounds, Canzoneri was relentless. Saved by the bell in the sixth, Zivic miraculously walked to his execution the following round.[6]

Afterward, Canzoneri headed to Marlboro to begin training for Lou Ambers. Once he completed his workouts there, he would finish his last four days of training at Stillman's gym. Billy Gibson, who managed Benny Leonard and Gene Tunney, had witnessed boxing history; when the fight manager spoke, folks listened. Ranking Tony Canzoneri among the best, Gibson believed he would regain the 135-pound laurels by defeating Lou Ambers. It appeared that the veterans of the fight game, or old money, saw the contest in favor of the former champion. New money, such as the beat writers and novice fight fans,

One of the four fighting Zivic brothers, Eddie Zivic (shown here in the 1930s) began his professional career in 1932 and ended it in 1940.

favored Lou Ambers. Granted, Ambers was younger, but had Father Time taken his toll on Tony Canzoneri? After the Zivic bout, it didn't appear that way.

During the first week of May, the ever-confident Tony Canzoneri invited the press to his 144-acre farm to witness his training firsthand. After a lunch in the dining room of the old farmhouse, the former champion brought the herd over to the indoor gymnasium. It wasn't often that the press had the opportunity to view a fighter training in his own camp, so this was a treat. Both "Izzy the Painter" and Lou Fink were there to place gloves on both their fighter and his sparring mates. Not an eye moved away from the former champion as he climbed through the ropes. Canzoneri, trademark twinkle in full bloom, mesmerized his audience as he shadow-boxed and moved gracefully about the ring. Afterward, a few members of the media gathered around the fighter as he unwrapped his hands. It was time to discuss the contest, especially the age factor: On the day of his fight against Lou Ambers, Canzoneri reminded everyone, he would be 26 years, six months, and five days old. He was five years and three days older than his opposition. The fighter couldn't understand why so many members of the press continued to put him out to pasture. It must be to sell newspapers, he believed. Tony Canzoneri was ready for Lou Ambers; just ask Eddie Zivic.

Canzoneri showed the crew around the farm, pointing out the apple orchard that consisted of 2,500 trees, then over to the foothills covered with grape vines and tomato plants. He took them inside the new four-story, 55-room hotel, then back outside to the large swimming pool. During the visit, the press met the fighter's family, first his father, George, whom many had met ringside, and his mother, Josephine. Tony's three brothers, Joe, Si, and Jasper, along with his sisters, Lillian and Lena, were introduced next. The entire Canzoneri family called the farm home.

While it would be war in the ring, Canzoneri admitted, he and Ambers were friends. His opposer sought out his mentor—yep, the Herkimer youth idolized Canzoneri—when he first arrived in the city. Canzoneri hired Ambers at $5 a day to keep him in condition and even passed along a few pointers. The upstate youth admired Canzoneri so much, he hitchhiked from Herkimer to watch the fighter defend his title against Kid Chocolate in Madison Square Garden on November 20, 1931. Pride, which ran deep with both men, was tough to defeat. Constantly reminded if he won, Canzoneri would be the first ex-lightweight to regain the championship, the pugilist always smiled.

Tony Canzoneri v. Lou Ambers, Vacant World Lightweight Title

To the surprise of many, Tony Canzoneri dominated 15 rounds of boxing and defeated Lou Ambers by unanimous decision. With the victory, Tony Canzoneri became the first ex-lightweight to regain the world lightweight championship (title vacated by Barney Ross). Entertaining the 17,433 paying customers with a style all his own, Canzoneri dominated early. Flooring Ambers twice in the third round with an overwhelming right hand and again in the 15th term, the elder pugilist blew the dust off his resume. It was like watching a chess match, as Canzy followed every lead by Ambers with the perfect counter. The perpetual motion of Ambers—bobbing, feinting, weaving, and shuffling—had little impact on his antagonist, who had seen the play before. The flat-footed Canzoneri ignored it and led with that sliding left foot of his. Negating his opponent's reach advantage with his dominant left jab and targeted right hand, Canzoneri kept the clockwise-moving Ambers at a

Luigi Giuseppe D'Ambrosio, aka Lou Ambers (shown here in the 1930s), was defeated by Tony Canzoneri on May 10, 1935, to capture the world lightweight championship vacated by Barney Ross.

safe distance. When the final gong rang, there was no need to hear the ring decision. It was that definitive a performance.

It was the third round that took the wind out of Ambers' sails. The hesitation in his step was evident. Scaling at 133¾, Ambers had a fractional weight advantage. As destiny would have it, Canzoneri regained his lightweight title in the same boxing ring where he first won it, back in 1930.

Taking a closer look: Canzoneri won eight rounds, Ambers took five, and two rounds were even. One of the five rounds Ambers won was assisted by a low blow from Canzoneri. Critics felt Ambers was too cautious. He should have blazed a furious pace with hopes of wearing down his rival. Although he managed to cut Canzoneri's chin in the second round, it was not serious. The third round was the game changer, as the Herkimer Hurricane's bottom hit the canvas twice. Instead of remaining down for a full nine-count each time, the embarrassed pugilist arose after a two-count. Canzoneri's pre-fight prediction had his opponent lasting only four rounds, but he couldn't accomplish the task. Ambers had Canzoneri's knees weakened in the tenth frame but could not deliver him. A Canzoneri right hook dropped his antagonist in the 15th, but once again, the fighter bounded up with authority.[7] The referee was Arthur Donovan.

After the fight, in a sincere and sportsmanlike fashion, Ambers admitted Canzoneri earned the victory. While such a statement was rare, that was Lou Ambers being Lou Ambers. As for the sportswriters, Paul Gallico, who had Ambers winning the title, apologized like a champion. Barney Ross, who was afraid to defend his lightweight title, called Canzoneri washed up and Ambers a child—Ross was scheduled to meet McLarnin on May 28.

On May 16, syndicated columnist Ed Sullivan broke the news that Tony Canzoneri would wed Rita Roy—the pair were spotted at Belmont Park watching a race. As for the lightweight champion, he had no comment.

Busy sorting through offers to meet the champion, Sammy Goldman was elated by the renewed interest in his fighter. Scheduled to meet Frankie Klick in Washington, D.C., on June 10, Canzoneri intended to enjoy, at least for a few days, his second lightweight reign. Both Canzoneri and Ambers headed to the Polo Grounds in New York to witness Barney Ross take a unanimous 15-round decision over Jimmy McLarnin. More than 35,000 attended the battle on May 28 that was refereed by Jack Dempsey. With the result, the jinx of the welterweight champion losing his initial title defense continued—it was the 12th consecutive time. Tony Canzoneri, Lou Ambers, and Joe Louis were introduced prior to the main event, with each receiving a booming ovation.

It was off to Washington, D.C., for Tony Canzoneri as he met Frankie Klick over 12 rounds at Griffith Stadium. The non-title bout was the feature sporting event at the popular Shriners convention. Canzoneri, as most recalled, had met Klick twice and won both bouts by decision. Although experienced matchmaker Goldie Ahern handled the bout, it drew a disappointing 10,000 fight fans.

In fine shape, Frankie Klick took command of the bout early courtesy of an outstanding left jab. But the lack of power behind the punch hurt him. Canzoneri, who scaled at 134, didn't loosen up until the fourth round, when he began pushing Klick around the ring with solid combinations. In the sixth round, as Canzoneri began scoring with the right hand, it opened a bothersome cut over Klick's right eye.

During the next two rounds, both fatigued fighters grappled more than cuffed. This prompted a warning from referee Jack Dempsey to stop wrestling and start fighting. From the ninth round forward, both gladiators slugged it out. A Canzoneri rally in the final round made it a close fight. When the judges split their verdict, Dempsey became the deciding vote, and he ruled in favor of Canzoneri. The decision was met with little satisfaction from those in attendance—the heckling continued until spectators were commanded to leave. Later, it was claimed that 15 out of 18 sportswriters saw it for Klick.

Noting the local event, the *Evening Star* reported:

> That blatantly ballyhooed bout, that "battle of champions," proved no more interesting than a cuffing match between playful kittens. As it went along it was boresome and the decision given Canzoneri after the dozen drab rounds did not make the patrons think any better of the dreary affair.[8]

Canzoneri's most challenging adversaries continued to be newspaper reporters such as Jimmy Woods, who penned a column in the *Brooklyn Times-Union*. Woods

persistently had the pugilist one step from retirement. Canzoneri, despite his title, was amid a comeback campaign, and the writer compared to the pugilist to Mrs. Helen Wills Moody, who defeated Helen Jacobs in the prestigious finals at Wimbledon. The Brooklyn boxer had exactly enough fuel in the tank to beat Ambers and perhaps enough for a title defense or two, but that was it. While the observation was insulting, it was the tone of the article that was bothersome to Canzy. Yes, he regained the heights of his craft, but think of all those who never made it to the top of the mountain. Commitment, determination, and hard work separated champions from contenders. It was those qualities that Woods should have highlighted in his column.

This Clark Griffith Stadium ticket was for the Tony Canzoneri v. Frankie Klick bout. The event was conducted in Washington, D.C., on June 10, 1935.

Tony Canzoneri was matched for a 10-round non-title bout against Bobby Pacho of Los Angeles. The pair would square off at Mills Stadium, at 4700 West Lake Street in Chicago, on July 25. A sensational victory over lightweight Frankie Sagilio, whom he dropped four times, earned Pacho the bout. Speaking of outstanding battlers, Frankie Klick landed himself another 10-round bout with Canzoneri. The non-title confrontation was slated for the Civic Auditorium in San Francisco on August 19. Since the clock was ticking, Sammy Goldman was working through a list of possible opponents for a title defense. At this time, the two names that topped the list were Wesley Ramey and Al Roth.

Hype sells tickets, but it doesn't satisfy customers. Tony Canzoneri, tipping at 135, won a 10-round unanimous decision over Bobby Pacho, who scaled to a two-and-a-half-pound advantage. The first five rounds were so slow, referee Tommy Gilmore cautioned the fighters to pick up the pace or quit. The highlight of the evening came in the sixth frame, when Bobby Pacho fired a right hand to the chin of Canzoneri that sent him backward to his bottom. On his feet at the count of three, the champion was able to get his house in order before Pacho could capitalize on the situation.[9] Fortunately, Canzoneri was able to capture the final three rounds to clinch a victory.

Afterward, Sammy Goldman met with Jimmy Johnston to try to hammer out the terms of a lightweight defense at Madison Square Garden Bowl in late September or early October. The opponent of choice was Al Roth, who had posted recent victories over Leonard Del Genio and Davey Day. Dave Sonnenberg, Roth's manager, was eager as well to come to terms and land the lightweight championship bout.

Frankie Klick, never lost for words, was looking forward to meeting Tony Canzoneri on August 19. It wasn't for the money, he insisted, as he had plenty—a common and often facetious locution overused by active pugilists. Fighting in his hometown of San Francisco, Klick was in good spirits and excited. Naturally, he remained bitter about his loss against the lightweight champion last June. Klick was stunned when Jack Dempsey ruled in favor of Canzoneri; moreover, most spectators at ringside believed he won the fight. To be certain a similar circumstance wouldn't happen in his hometown, Klick promised to knock out Canzoneri. It was a big promise from a fighter who had yet to beat his opposer.

Canzoneri, traveling by train, arrived across the bay in Oakland on August 14. The lightweight champion had a full schedule. Accompanied by Sammy Goldman and Lou Fink, Canzoneri was greeted by the San Francisco Press Club. Four days before the contest, odds dropped from even money to 10–8 favoring Klick. Canzoneri, who enjoyed being the underdog, never gave it a thought.

Before a disappointing crowd estimated at 5,500, Tony Canzoneri, tipping at 135, shellacked Frankie Klick, who scaled a pound heavier. It marked the fourth time Frankie Klick, aka "Portola Pippin," had been licked by Canzoneri, and unlike their previous battle, there was no doubt. Ringside observers had it no fewer than eight rounds for Canzoneri. Klick's game plan was all defense and no offense. Despite damaging left hooks to the body, mixed with overhand rights to the stomach, Canzoneri couldn't get Klick to drop his force field. When Klick did decide to throw a punch, it was quick and painless. Even when Canzoneri stood flatfooted in the center of the ring and invited his opponent to engage, Klick declined. Apparently not realizing he was behind, the hometown pugilist decided to ignite in the eighth round. The misperception was an enormous mistake.

On August 22, NYSAC approved Tony Canzoneri's lightweight title defense against Al Roth on October 4 at Madison Square Garden. They insisted that the winner meet a NYSAC approved opponent within 60 days.

Al Roth

Born on September 22, 1913, in New York City, Abie Rothblut, aka Al Roth, learned early the value of self-defense—four siblings (three brothers and a sister) and living in the Bronx can have an impact on a kid. As a teenager, he found solace at the Unionport Athletic Club, and by 1931 he had won the *New York Daily News* Golden Gloves open championship at bantamweight. Turning professional in November 1931, Roth fought out of the Jamaica Arena, New Lenox Sporting Club, St. Nicholas Arena, and Starlight Park. It was in these venues that he established a strong fan base. Undefeated, with a record of 22–0–5, he took his first professional loss to Petey Hayes on May 13, 1933, at Ridgewood Grove. Heartbreaking, the event derailed his career. He won four of his next 15 bouts and injured his hand. One of those victories was against Nick Scalba on the undercard of Tony Canzoneri's loss to Barney Ross at the Polo Grounds on September 12, 1933. Three fights in 1935, and impressive victories over Leonard Del Genio and Davey Day, sent Roth on a course to meet Tony Canzoneri in a lightweight title defense.

Tony Canzoneri v. Al Roth, World Lightweight Title

While Sammy Goldman liked Canzoneri's match with Roth and was confident of his fighter being victorious, he requested a 90-day return bout clause. At this stage in the champion's career, he could never be sure. While Roth and Canzoneri were friends, they understood they had a job to do. The champion understood that Roth intended to give him a competitive battle. Roth, who lived with his mother and siblings in a small Bronx apartment, planned on buying his mother a house in the country should he win—Roth's father had died more than four years before, and times were tough. But he acknowledged the difficulty in defeating his friend inside the ring.[10]

Tony Canzoneri planned on fighting a warm-up bout on September 13 in St. Louis against Joe Ghnouly. More than a speed bump, Ghnouly, aka "St. Louis Bearcat," held recent victories over Battling Shaw, Roger Bernard, Tod Morgan, and Eddie Cool. His only loss of the year came at the hands of Cleto Locatelli. Since Ghnouly's 10-round draw against Davey Day back in July caught the eye of Sammy Goldman, he was deemed an excellent selection for the task.

Scaling at 137, Tony Canzoneri took a 10-round unanimous decision victory over Joe Ghnouly, who tipped at 135½. The bout was held inside the Arena in St. Louis. To his credit, Ghnouly took everything Canzoneri threw at him and made the distance. Nervous, the St. Louis fighter was nothing but a target for Canzoneri's left hand in the first frame. Gradually settling down, Ghnouly wisely began staying out of range. The second half of the unimaginative battle was essentially sparring for the champion, as he traded a variety of punches with his opposer. Although Canzoneri tried hard to put away his opponent in the final rounds, he failed. The champion couldn't muster the power needed. Despite the hometown favorite being on the back end of the verdict, the crowd of 6,700-plus fight fans appeared to enjoy the event. Ringside observers saw the bout as seven rounds for Canzoneri and three for Ghnouly.

The career of Tony Canzoneri had been written off more times than anyone could count, yet here he was again, defending another reign of the lightweight title. None of his predecessors had achieved that, not even Benny Leonard. Although older and wiser, he had slowed a bit. The punches, though debatable, didn't appear to have the power behind them they once had. Yet the legs that carried him to three titles— featherweight, lightweight, and junior welterweight—were once again being tested. At the age of 26, Tony Canzoneri was the same age as Jack Dempsey when the heavyweight defeated Georges Carpentier.[11]

Two years earlier, Al Roth had sparred with Tony Canzoneri, never dreaming he would be in a championship title fight against him, let alone at Madison Square Garden. But there he was, in front of more than 14,000 fight fans. As the opening bell sounded, Canzoneri began testing his arsenal by measuring range, a process that made every opponent nervous. A stiff right hand in the third frame dropped Roth for a count of nine. Once upright, the younger fighter stood humiliated as the champion made faces at him. Yep, instead of moving in for the kill, Canzoneri began showboating. It wouldn't last. Bleeding from his nose, Roth managed to outpunch the champion in the fourth round; moreover, a plethora of accurate right hands shook the champion. This round belonged to the challenger.

From this point forward, however, it was all Canzoneri until the 12th round. He had been warned twice (rounds six and nine) for low blows, and Roth's frustration had grown with each passing frame. Aware of this and leading in scoring, Canzoneri couldn't resist more showmanship. Having seen enough of the conceited behavior, Roth launched a starboard smash that struck Canzoneri in the face and opened a large and stomach-turning gouge on the champion's upper lip. Immediately, the blood began flowing over the torn flesh hanging over Canzoneri's lips. As his mouth filled with blood, the champion instinctively tried to wipe his face with his glove, but it made matters worse. Covered in gore, Canzoneri panicked and clung to Roth like a life preserver.

Joe Ghnouly, aka "St. Louis Bearcat" (shown here in the 1930s), was a popular boxer who was managed by August "Gus" Wilson, a prominent French American boxing manager and trainer.

As the fighter returned to his corner, Sammy Goldman and Dan Florio tried desperately to pluck, patch, and paste their fighter. It was of little use. Canzoneri returned to the ring looking as though he shaved blindfolded between rounds. Showing no mercy, Roth, still embarrassed, fired volleys, hoping to drop the champion. But Canzoneri clinched and stayed at close quarters—he had little choice. As the 14th and 15th rounds passed, Canzoneri's survival was owing to Roth's inability to deliver a fight-ending blow. Retaining his championship by taking a unanimous decision over Al Roth, the champion was exhausted. Both participants weighed 132½ pounds. Art Donovan was the referee, and the judges were Charley Lynch and Tommy Shortell. Ringside viewed the contest as nine rounds for Canzoneri, three rounds for Roth (12, 13, and 14), and the rest even.

Canzoneri was eager to return home and begin the healing process. By the end of the month, he was feeling good, attending banquets, and being seen regularly at his Manhattan haunts. For example, in Ed Sullivan's Broadway column, on November 1, Sullivan noted that Tony Canzoneri and Johnny Dundee turned up at Jimmy Kelly's place at 2:30 a.m. Frankly, who was going to argue with them?

Following Tony Canzoneri's successful lightweight title defense against Al Roth, those who saw him covered in gore, especially the media, felt obligated to assess his career. The *Evening Star* noted:

> What is driving Canzoneri on, when others who have tasted ring fame and fortune have retired to live on their earnings? Tony is not broke. He made a fortune, lost it, and gained another one. He has a large farm at Marlboro, N.Y. It is well stocked with fruit trees, cows, and chickens. He is devoted to his family. If he converts his farm into a summer resort, as he plans, there is no doubt he can make it a success.
>
> How long can Canzoneri continue the pace? Tony has been to the post too often, against the best fighters of his weight, to take such chances. Sooner or later one solid punch will land on a vital spot, and it will be all over. And those who have watched the gallant little battler these many years will be sorry they were in on the "kill" of one who has made fistic history.

In 1935, Canzoneri proved words were how others defined him and not the way he defined himself. As a three-division champion, Canzoneri was a novelty—only Robert Fitzsimmons had an equal claim. He had worked hard and enough to be given another championship opportunity and against the odds reclaim the former title he coveted most. He was now making history every time he stepped into the ring. Champions were champions for a reason: They don't let somebody else define their future by placing a label such as "washed up" on them. Posting a record of 11–1 for the year, he even managed to vindicate his only loss by defeating Chuck Woods. By the way, Canzoneri's opponents combined for a record of 582–135–94. Capturing the vacated lightweight championship by defeating a former sparring partner, then successfully defending it against another former sparring partner, was unique, as was Tony Canzoneri.

ELEVEN

In Defense of the Lightweight Championship, 1936

"A man is the sum of his misfortunes. One day you'd think misfortune would get tired but then time is your misfortune"—William Faulkner

President Roosevelt won reelection by a landslide as nearly three million voters in New York City cast their ballots, the city's electric streetcar system was converted to a system of buses manufactured by General Motors, and the Cotton Club, formerly of Harlem, reopened at 200 West 48th Street, off Times Square. It would remain at the location until 1942. Repetition, as even boxers understood, can be an act of confirmation.

On June 19, 1936, at Yankee Stadium in the Bronx, Joe Louis, the most significant Black athlete of his age and the most successful Black fighter since Jack Johnson, stepped into a boxing ring against Max Schmeling, a German heavyweight. Schmeling, an 8–1 underdog, dropped Louis in the fourth round, then knocked him out in the 12th. A stunned crowd of 42,000, many in tears, watched in amazement. Later, Schmeling, considered a representative of Nazi Germany, acknowledged the führer and his faithful people for thinking of him.

There was no need for Tony Canzoneri to think about what he had to do in 1936, because the promoters and newspaper writers did it for him. The Madison Square Garden show on January 3 put everything into perspective, or at least the writers thought it did. While Aldo Spoldi took an uninspiring points victory over Eddie Zivic, neither fighter had what it took to dethrone Canzoneri. Veteran Bobby Pacho gave a better performance in his decision victory over prospect Leonard Del Genio, but both fighters looked tired in the end. Lou Ambers, who gave the best performance of all, took a points victory over punching bag Frankie Klick. Al Weil, who managed Lou Ambers, believed his fighter had the best shot of the bunch to take down Canzoneri, but he would have to perform better than he had thus far. That was the idea behind the promotion: Who could end the second lightweight reign of Tony Canzoneri?

At the end of the first week in January, it was learned that Tony Canzoneri would meet Bricio Garcia, over 10 rounds, at Star Casino on January 22.

A Classic Club Fight

It was hard to believe, but this was Tony Canzoneri's first professional fight at Star Casino, aka Empire Athletic Club, aka Lenox, located at 105 East 107th Street in East Harlem. The tough neighborhood fight club was what every New York fight fan envisioned in their mind: a smoky, loud, musty environment where a patron was as happy tossing their chair as sitting on it. On January 22, 1936, 3,500 emotionally-charged fight fans jammed the club to watch lightweight champion Tony Canzoneri, who tipped at 138, or to a pound advantage, defeat Bricio Garcia, aka Midget Mexico, via a ninth-round technical knockout. Referee Billy Cavanaugh, having seen enough damage, waved it off at the 1:39 mark of the frame. The fight, as fights go, did not get much attention in the press. But it should have, as both fighters mixed it up as if their lives depended on it. When the non-title contest was over, not a soul in the club felt the battle wasn't worth every penny.

Garcia came out swinging at the opening bell and landed a couple of straight lefts early. Canzoneri countered with solid rights to the jaw before mixing it up enough with his opponent to gain a slight advantage. Turning on the jets in the third frame, Garcia forced Canzoneri to the ropes with stinging left hooks to the head. But Garcia slowed during the final minute, and Canzoneri evened the round with accurate right hands. Canzoneri rocketed a couple of hard right hands that buckled Garcia's knees in the sixth round. With little choice, Garcia fought back hard, as Canzoneri avoided his opposer's pesky straight lefts. Struggling, Garcia was dropped twice in the eighth round by combinations to the face. Each time he reached vertical, he reeled around the ring to avoid being hit. Walloped with a hard right to the head, Garcia hit the deck for a final time in the ninth.

Canzoneri and company headed to Philadelphia next for a bout against Fred "Tootsie" Bashara. The January 30 bout was held at the Olympia Athletic Club. Three days before the bout, Sammy Goldman and Madison Square Garden's Jimmy Johnston visited Convention Hall, where Barney Ross put away Lou Halper in eight rounds. The welterweight could have accomplished his task sooner had he worn regulation gloves rather than the eight-ounce variety. When Johnston offered Ross $35,000 to defend his crown against Canzoneri, Ross grinned, paused, and stated firmly $40,000. Ross was still bitter that Goldman made him pay plenty for his lightweight title shot. Art Winch, one of the fighter's handlers, laughed at what he termed matinee prices.

Back to the Bashara non-title bout. Tony Canzoneri, tipping at 139, or to a pound disadvantage, dropped Tootsie Bashara in the first round with a left hook before finally putting him away for good in the third round. The technical knockout victory came at the 0:42 mark of the frame. Because of the badly cut left eye of Bashara, referee Matt Adgie had little choice but to wave it off. Bashara, who had won three of his last 10 bouts, was clearly in over his head against the lightweight champion.

The McLarnin Factor

Always looking for the pot of gold at the end of the rainbow, Sammy Goldman had to concern himself with not only Barney Ross but also "the McLarnin Factor." Jimmy McLarnin fought twice in 1934, and both welterweight title contests were against Barney Ross at the Madison Square Garden Bowl for big money. He had been considering retirement since 1932, and McLarnin's decision was instantly altered by a large payday. In 1935, he was lured out of retirement only once: to take a rubber match against Barney Ross at the Polo Grounds. However, the loss and sizable paycheck sat him comfortably back into his rocking chair in Vancouver. To entice him to return to the ring wouldn't be easy, but Eighth Avenue matchmaker Jimmy Johnston felt confident that his pockets were deep enough.

On February 4, the press confirmed a match was made between Tony Canzoneri and Jimmy McLarnin. The fight would take place inside Madison Square Garden in the spring. Since Canzoneri's lightweight title would not be at stake, this led to considerable speculation—was there more to the agreement, such as a big money ballpark date? Speaking of the championship, five contenders were pushing hard for a title shot: Lou Ambers, Baby Arizmendi, Indian Hurtado, Pedro Montanez, and Wesley Ramey. Of the group, Ramey was the most dangerous, as he had soundly defeated Canzoneri back in 1933. As an artful boxing manager, Sammy Goldman would be certain to eliminate him from the scenario.[1]

Still making the rounds at the local fight clubs, Canzoneri was back at the Grove in Brooklyn on March 15.[2] Matchmaker Johnny Attell always had a soft spot for Canzoneri, so Sammy Goldman threw him a bone. Scheduled for 10 rounds against Irish Billy Hogan, the lightweight champion was looking forward to being back home and boxing against a familiar face: When Hogan was 17, he sparred with Canzoneri at Gus Wilson's old camp in Orangeburg, New York. To little surprise, an overflow crowd turned out to watch the non-title bout; at one point, the police had to be called for crowd control.

When Billy Hogan, aware of the talent possessed by Tony Canzoneri, encountered little opposition during the first round of their contest, it had a psychological impact on him. Canzoneri knew it. Questions raced through Hogan's mind: Was he sizing me up? Was he hurt? Did he want me to get overconfident? Knowing these concerns would be answered during the rounds ahead left him filled with apprehension. The feeling wouldn't last.

Before he knew what hit him, Billy Hogan, who had more than a two-pound weight advantage at 138¾, was draped over a lower rope. It was a tremendous Canzoneri right to the jaw that catapulted him across the ring during the second round. Managing to right the ship, Hogan turned to a left jab to sustain himself for another round. In the third, Canzoneri delivered another deleterious right that stupefied Hogan, but Irish Billy by some means remained upright. It was only a matter of time, and that moment came at 2:26 of the fourth round. Hogan, unable to regain his footing, was counted out on one knee. Invigorated, yet humbled by the experience, Canzoneri knew the bout was what he needed.

Steve Halaiko was a talented amateur boxer. As an AAU champion (135 pounds) and 1928 Olympic Games silver medalist, he appeared destined to become an elite boxer. Turning pro in the fall of 1929, he fought out of Buffalo and Rochester. He was undefeated in his first 13 bouts, and it took Sammy Dorfman, who beat him in two out of three fights in 1930, to test his skills. By the time Halaiko matched with Tony Canzoneri, he held impressive victories over Lou Ambers, Pete Nebo, Bobby Pacho and Wesley Ramey. Slipping of late, he had won four of his last 10 bouts. Nevertheless, Halaiko felt confident confronting Canzoneri at St. Nicholas Arena on March 2.

A seemingly endless flow of dedicated fight fans poured into the Arena, hungry to see the lightweight champion in a more intimate setting. It took only an instant to recognize the charismatic champion in the ring, as that trademark smirk of his confirmed his identity. As referee Johnny Marto gave his final instructions, you could sense the growing anticipation. Like a man on a mission or with a late dinner reservation, Canzoneri took immediate command with the left jab. While the short artillery was working, he was off his mark with his overhand rights. He did manage to catch Halaiko with a body punch that stunned the upstate fighter.

As the bell sounded for round two, Canzoneri stepped up his game. A crisp left hook at the midpoint of the round signaled rough waters ahead. Driving Halaiko hard into the ropes, the champion feinted an opening that cleared a path for a flush left hook to the chin. As Halaiko showed signs of capsizing, a right cross finished the job. Two minutes and 47 seconds into round two, the contest was over. Halaiko, who tipped at 138 ¾, a three-pound advantage, was Canzoneri's fourth straight knockout victim.

In the middle of March came word that Canzoneri would meet Johnny Jadick in an overweight match at St. Nicholas Arena on April 9. Unsure if he could schedule an additional bout during the month, Goldman informed Canzoneri that this could be his final bout before meeting McLarnin.

Days later came word that Tony Scarpati, the 1931 Golden Gloves featherweight champion, had died of an injury following a technical knockout by Lou Ambers. It happened in the seventh round of their battle at the Broadway Arena on March 17. The fight game has always revolved around violence and brought with it the risk of injury and even death. It was an element of the sport that was often forgotten until a tragedy occurred. Then it stared a fighter right in the eyes, waiting for him to blink—death a mere flicker from reality inside a boxing ring. Lou Ambers was shaken by the event but was able to console the Scarpati family. Deeply religious, Ambers turned to his spiritual advisor for assistance. Had he not, his boxing career might have ended.

Sammy Goldman, hoping to preserve the life of his meal ticket, found a "policeman" for the champion when he signed to handle the talented Leonard Del Genio. As a spoiler, or solution, if you will, Del Genio was perfect; moreover, he was always able to beat the odds. For example, he defeated Indian Hurtado as a 1–4 shot. Del Genio's job, as Goldman saw it, was to eliminate Wesley Ramey, who was on the verge of being named Canzoneri's number one challenger by NYSAC. The other contenders in the lightweight division didn't want to face Ramey, nor was the champion thrilled about a rematch.

Wesley Ramey, who through the media had applied pressure to match with Tony Canzoneri, was defeated by Del Genio on March 30. This left Lou Ambers to meet Pedro Montanez, with the winner taking on Canzoneri for the title. Goldman could rest assured a big money event was in his future. Mission accomplished.

Meanwhile, Canzoneri was preparing for the road ahead, or Jimmy McLarnin. To sustain his skills, he was meeting Johnny Jadick. It was Canzoneri's choice, as he wanted to settle the score. Feeling he hadn't been treated fairly in his previous two losing efforts against Jadick, it was time for a rubber match on *his* turf.

Johnny Jadick was plastered from pillar to post, as they used to say, and Tony Canzoneri was responsible. From the opening bell, Canzoneri valiantly tried to knock out Johnny Jadick while inflicting a tremendous amount of damage. While he failed at turning out the lights of his opposer, Canzoneri did manage to win seven of 10 rounds. Jadick, who ended up a bloody mess, was dropped in the eighth and 10th stanzas. Three right shots to the head, followed by a left to the stomach, dropped him the first time. In the 10th round, after Canzoneri's right eye was sliced, the champion delivered two targeted rights to the chin, followed by a sweeping left, that sent Jadick face-first to the canvas. Arising, a dazed Jadick fell again without being hit. Somehow, the Philadelphia fighter managed to make it to the bell. Tipping at 136½, Tony Canzoneri won a unanimous decision over Johnny Jadick, who scaled at 140¾. It was the most satisfying victory Canzoneri had since successfully defending his title.

Jimmy McLarnin

No sooner had the ink dried on Canzoneri's fight review than the press started riding him about McLarnin. On April 15, Canzoneri's opposer arrived by train from Los Angeles, with Lillian Cupit McLarnin, his beautiful wife, and Pop Foster, his cantankerous caretaker. The boxer trained at the Pioneer Gym in the heart of Manhattan. Soft-spoken, he sparred with Paris Apice and Dick Welsh.

Although McLarnin had slowed with age, he still possessed a solid punch. Yet the last time McLarnin fought a boxer other than Barney Ross was back on May 29, 1933. "The Belfast Spider" believed Canzoneri had grown too reliant on his right hand and was taking far too many punches. Canzoneri was ripe for the taking, McLarnin claimed.

While training, McLarnin had his picture taken on the lap of George Canzoneri, Tony's father. The publicity stunt worked, and the photograph was published in newspapers across the country.

Meanwhile, Tony Canzoneri was arduously training at his Marlboro farm. Sparring with Sammy Angott, Al Dunbar and Jerry Mazza, the lightweight champion looked and felt great. Even though this was a non-title fight, Canzoneri was totally committed to the task. Giving away 10 pounds to his opponent left him no other choice.

Granted, McLarnin fought far less frequently than his rival, but Canzoneri understood that this performance would be his self-portrait. McLarnin was the fight market's bellwether performer; every contender in the lower divisions had their skills compared to his. His fighting style was like that of Canzoneri. In his long and illustrious career, the Irish fisticuffer had beaten Young Corbett, Louis "Kid" Kaplan, Fidel La Barba, Benny Leonard, Sammy Mandell, Barney Ross, Al Singer, Bud Taylor, Jack Thompson, and Pancho Villa. Barney Ross (a boxer who had fought Canzoneri twice and McLarnin three times) didn't see how any boxer, past or present, had the capabilities to defeat Jimmy McLarnin, especially after spotting him a weight advantage.

Looking at the fight statistics: Jimmy McLarnin, a former welterweight champion, was older (28 years, four months, and 20 days) than Tony Canzoneri, the current lightweight champion (27 years, six months, and three days). The latter brought a record of 121–16–8 into the ring, while McLarnin's record stood at 53–10–3. Scaling at 145, a 6½-pounds advantage, McLarnin felt comfortable. Standing at 5'6", he had an inch in his favor when it came to height and a two-inch (67 inches) reach advantage. In a tale of the tape: McLarnin had a bigger chest, calves, wrists, ankles, and waist, while Canzoneri had a bigger neck, thighs, forearms, and biceps. At 11 inches, their fists were the same size. Both fighters utilized a low guard and wide stance. As newspapers compared the battle from every angle, they made their predictions. The results were about even.

Stunning! Tony Canzoneri, a 9–5 underdog, trounced Jimmy McLarnin over 10 rounds, as the *Daily News* said best, "from hell to breakfast all the rest of the way," in front of a capacity crowd at Madison Square Garden.[3] More than 16,000 fans watched as "the Belfast Spider" took the beating of his life on May 8, a day neither Canzoneri nor McLarnin fans would ever forget. The first was action-packed; ringside spectators spent the evening standing on their chairs, hoping for a glimpse at the fight. It was so loud, the ushers couldn't communicate or in certain instances see one another through the smoke-filled venue.

Everyone who was anyone in the fight game was there. From Jack Dempsey and Joe Louis to James J. Braddock and Barney Ross, the incredulity on their faces was tough to hide. As Joe Humphries raised the hand of a bloodied Tony Canzoneri, many found it hard to believe the Brooklyn fighter was still standing. Ironically, after round one, Barney Ross might have been the only person in the arena who believed Canzoneri had the fight won. He knew McLarnin had emptied the chambers, and Canzoneri remained vertical.

A Closer Look at a Classic—Canzoneri v. McLarnin I

After a slow start, with numerous misses, both fighters found their range. McLarnin's combinations began doing damage, and when they were combined with a left hook or right cross, he forced Canzoneri to retreat. McLarnin cut his opposer's nose with a left hook. Although he appeared dazed at times, Canzoneri was able to clinch while regaining his composure. The opening round belonged to Jimmy McLarnin. He would win only one other round, the eighth.

Looking refreshed, Canzoneri bounded out of his corner in the second term and looked like a different fighter. He even managed to send McLarnin to his knees briefly with a damaging right—the fighter was up without a count. While the Irishman had that deadly right of his loaded, he could not lock on his target. Canzoneri had begun accumulating rounds.

Canzoneri's ring generalship and superior movement became evident as the fight progressed—he won rounds three, four, five, six, seven, nine and 10. Although it was clear that he had to compensate for his reach, he did without leaving himself vulnerable. Halfway through the battle, McLarnin's timing and accuracy appeared off, and he couldn't make the proper adjustments. McLarin's frustration was evident by his actions: he delivered low blows in round three and hit on the break in round four. By the end of the fifth, blood could be seen from the noses of both fighters.

Canzoneri continued to bound from his corner and land the first punch of the round. McLarnin showed brief signs of brilliance by ducking a few punches; unfortunately, he needed more of an offense. By the seventh round, it was clear that McLarnin's nose, which had bled since round five, was bothering the fighter. Speaking of damage, Canzoneri's corner managed to patch a bothersome cut on the bridge of his nose. McLarnin did manage to take the eighth frame.

Canzoneri rocked McLarnin with combinations during the last minute of the ninth frame. Dazed, the Irishman fell backward against the ropes, then bounced forward. Canzoneri fired off another volley and hurt his rival. During the final 45 seconds of the round, McLarnin looked confused and was unable to protect himself.

Appearing unstoppable in the 10th round, Canzoneri continued to rock McLarnin with right hands.

Exhibiting dazzling foot speed and refined skills, Canzoneri was on his game. The lightweight champion kept on moving, and that was a key, as when he stood still, McLarnin got the best of him. Despite hitting the microphone with his head prior to the first round, Canzoneri knew he had fought one of his finest ring battles of his career.[4]

Afterward, McLarnin, exhibiting genuine sportsmanship, complimented Canzoneri on his boxing prowess while putting ice on his swollen jaw. He admitted that fighting once a year wasn't enough, and he should consider quitting. Cantankerous Pop Foster, never at a loss for words, was in one of those "I told you so" moods. He claimed his fighter should have quit after the last Ross bout and never should have taken this fight. He wasn't prepared for the beating he sustained. The comments contrasted with his pre-fight rhetoric. If Foster was so concerned, then why didn't he do anything about it?

Canzoneri admitted he was hurt in the first round and that McLarnin was a hard puncher. A quick glance at his countenance confirmed the observation—Canzoneri picked up two black eyes from the confrontation. Yet he believed he was ready to meet Lou Ambers in a title defense. However, Canzoneri's physicians nixed the idea following a post-fight examination; the fighter's proboscis required 48 stiches. The use of styptics on the fighter's cut nose caused an infection that would require two nasal operations and two months of healing. Thus, Canzoneri's ring commitments would be shuffled accordingly.

Taking advantage of the healing time, Canzoneri shifted his interests to his avocations. He had his booking agent arrange some Broadway nightclub dates, where he would act as a Master of Ceremonies. No stranger to city nightlife, the fighter continued to be drawn to the entertainment sector. Canzoneri also headed up to Lakewood, New Jersey, to pick up an award from *The Ring* and to join in the festivities surrounding the 22nd birthday of Joe Louis. "The Brown Bomber" was training for his rematch with Max Schmeling. On hand as well were James J. Braddock and Tommy Loughran.[5]

Wedding Bells

It was confirmed on May 24 that Tony Canzoneri had secretly married Rita (Goldberg) Roy, New York showgirl (Paradise Night Club chorus), the previous week in Jersey City. They were married by Mayor Murray Sheldon of Roselle Park. Rita was the daughter of Lester and Jennie Goldberg of 270 South 9th Street in Brooklyn. Formerly in the "Vanities" and featured in a Broadway cabaret, Roy was a few years younger than the lightweight champion. She resided in an apartment at 322 West 72nd Street (near Riverside Drive). The couple, who had been friends for three years, initially denied the rumor. Friends reported that a barrier to their marriage had been religion, as Canzoneri was Catholic and Roy was Jewish. On May 26, 1936, the *Daily News* published a seductive portrait of beautiful Rita Roy, on page 318, with a caption stating that Sammy Goldman, Tony Canzoneri's longtime manager, confirmed the marriage. On May 30, the couple boarded the Munson liner *Munargo* for a cruise to Nassau, Miami, and Havana.

Two photographs of the weigh-in for the Barney Ross (left) versus Phil Furr (right) bout held on July 22, 1936. Ross and Henry Armstrong were the only two fighters to hold three world titles simultaneously, although the junior welterweight title wasn't always recognized (Library of Congress).

The Ross Rub

The Canzoneris returned from their honeymoon on June 8. Tony Canzoneri planned to head north to Marlboro to begin training—naturally, with his doctor's approval—for his bout against Lou Ambers. The champion wasn't surprised to learn that Jimmy McLarnin confirmed he wasn't through with the ring and wouldn't mind another crack at Canzoneri. Meanwhile, a talented boxer from Cayey, Puerto Rico, Pedro Montañez, had emerged on the horizon and posed a threat to the lightweight division. By the middle of June, rumors flew that Tony Canzoneri wanted out of his bout against Lou Ambers to fight a big money bout against Barney Ross. But there was also talk that Sammy Goldman might have floated the hearsay to get Ross to bite—this was a common technique used by many early boxing managers.

By the end of June, Tony Canzoneri had traveled from his farm into the city to meet with NYSAC. He sought approval to fight Barney Ross without abdicating his 135-pound throne. The impediment: Canzoneri had signed to meet Lou Ambers on July

30. One suggestion was to have Lou Ambers fight Pedro Montañez for Canzoneri's vacated title on the same ticket—if Canzoneri decided to part with the lightweight crown.

Promoter Mike Jacobs of the Twentieth Century Sporting Club held the contract of Barney Ross and would direct the show. Canzoneri was signed to Jimmy Johnston, of Madison Square Garden. Sammy Goldman continued to tell anyone who would listen that, if necessary, Canzoneri would vacate his title to fight Ross.

Those who knew Canzoneri understood how much the lightweight title meant to him and found it hard to believe he would forsake it to battle Ross. Then word came that Goldman was holding up the Canzoneri-Ross agreement by demanding double the challenger's end to sign (25 percent of gate), plus compensation for vacating the lightweight championship ($10,000). When Jacobs finally agreed to terms,

This Madison Square Garden Bowl ticket was for the Tony Canzoneri v. Lou Ambers bout. The event was conducted in the famed Long Island City venue on July 30, 1936.

Sammy Goldman disappeared. When the fight manager reappeared, he had a new perspective: He demanded a $25,000 guarantee. The new figure was based on his concern that if all the terms and conditions were not met, it could leave Canzoneri without a bout against Ross and no title. Of course, the media coverage of negotiations hampered interest in the Canzoneri-Ambers bout. The entire affair was disconcerting and disrespectful to Lou Ambers and his entire team.

Sammy Goldman used superstition as an excuse to move the champion's title defense against Lou Ambers from the Long Island Bowl to Madison Square Garden on August 31; incidentally, it was common knowledge that every lightweight champion who fought in the bowl, since its construction four years ago, went home without the crown. There were times when even the fight game paid for its analytics.

Lou Ambers v. Tony Canzoneri II, World Lightweight Title

On August 4, NYSAC met and approved moving the Canzoneri-Ambers bout to Madison Square Garden on September 3. This postponement was owing to Canzoneri not being in proper condition, which puzzled many as NYSAC physicians could not find anything wrong with the champion. Most viewed NYSAC's claim as nothing more than a poor excuse. It was no secret that advance ticket sales for the bout were poor. Moving the bout inside, where spectators could be closer to the action, would help and would buy time to sell more tickets and hype the fight.[6]

Uncharacteristically vocal, or bored with all the postponements, Lou Ambers spent a great amount of time chatting with the media. Admitting he suffered from "buck fever," or nervousness, when greeting Canzoneri in their initial meeting, he claimed that was no longer the case. As he saw it, the lightweight champion was just another boxer, thus vulnerable to a contender such as himself. Confident, Ambers felt his speed and endurance would overwhelm his rival. In a stretch, Ambers felt he might knock him out.

Tony Canzoneri, who hadn't fought since May 8, when he defeated Jimmy McLarnin, was confident despite the layoff. His nose injury was healing, and he was working himself back into condition. The lightweight champion had fought six times this year, against outstanding competition, and had not lost a contest. Four of his six battles had ended in knockout victories. Frankly, Canzoneri's only concern regarding Ambers was his drawing power or ability to sell tickets. Lou Ambers wasn't Barney Ross or a big payday. Sammy Goldman, who shared in his fighter's view of his rival, believed his champion would deliver Ambers inside of six rounds.

On September 3, most of the nation's newspapers ran feature articles on the fight, with some noting that Canzoneri was an 11–5 favorite. Regardless of the odds, it was 15 championship rounds in Madison Square Garden between two outstanding lightweights: Tony Canzoneri, a multi-division conqueror and current lightweight champion, who was boxing professionally before his opponent was a teenager, and Lou Ambers, the nation's premier contender, whose ring education came courtesy of bootleg battles in local barrooms and halls. Canzoneri, his opponent's mentor, had given the Herkimer youth a decisive beating over 15 rounds at Madison Square Garden back on May 10, 1935. The unanimous decision handed the crafty veteran the world lightweight title vacated by Barney Ross.[7] And he intended on keeping it.

Still upset that he couldn't land a big-ticket fight against Barney Ross, a sulking Tony Canzoneri wanted to get this defense out of the way. At this stage of his career, the newlywed had become more concerned about retirement income than building another display case for a championship belt.

Ambers, in all honesty, kept his mouth shut after experiencing a ridiculous series of delays; furthermore, it was not his fault Canzoneri couldn't work out his business arrangements. It was unfair, and had it happened to any other fighter except for Barney Ross, NYSAC wouldn't have bought all the excuses.

After defeating Ambers the year before, Canzoneri won 11 consecutive battles over fighters such as Frankie Klick, Steve Halaiko, Johnny Jadick, and Jimmy McLarnin. Canzoneri still possessed that snappy, low-hanging left hand and powerful roundhouse right. But the champion's recent nose injury remained a concern— would it hold up to the blows from Ambers?

Since losing to Canzoneri, Ambers had won 14 consecutive bouts over fighters such as Fritzie Zivic, Frankie Klick, Tony Herrera, and Baby Arizmendi. As a contender, he remained as prolific as ever and capable of dancing around an opponent as if they were a statue. Having recovered from a broken jaw and the death of ring opponent Tony Scarpati, Ambers felt he was in top condition both mentally and physically.

The underlying current of the fight was youth versus maturity. Ambers, of great moral character, not to mention five years younger, would make an outstanding successor. Canzoneri, an aging popular champion and legendary pugilist, was a multiple division titleholder whose time had come and gone.

Madison Square Garden, despite many challenging factors, anticipated a large crowd (18,000) for the evening; Mike Belloise, NYSAC featherweight champion, was putting his title on the line against Dave Crowley, the English champion, in an outstanding undercard battle. Setting aside all the obstructions and preposterous predictions, it was fight time.

Using brilliant choreography, Lou Ambers waltzed around Canzoneri with such style that it appeared as if he had rehearsed all afternoon. Self-assured, regimented, and systematic, Ambers stayed away from Canzoneri's arsenal and countered every lead with precision. As fast as the first four rounds ticked off the clock, they were in Ambers' pocket. Watching Canzoneri's left eye swell, the Herkimer fighter locked on the target. In the fourth term, Canzoneri took significant damage: A solid left sent him back on his heels before a right to his mended muzzle started the blood flowing. His left eye was closing as his right eye began to swell.

But a champion was champion for a reason. Canzoneri came out strong in the fifth round. A flurry of combinations led to a close-quarters exchange won by Canzoneri. Ambers, sporting a fresh cut under his right eye, quickly realized the champion had awakened. Canzoneri gave a solid performance in both the sixth and seventh terms.

Blazing combinations to Canzoneri's jaw rocked the champion in round eight. An Ambers right to the jaw slowed Canzoneri early in round nine, before the challenger sent machine-gun combinations into the body of the champion.

Canzoneri's finest round was the 10th, when he outboxed Ambers. Encouraged, the champion went for broke in the 11th term and nearly dazed the challenger with a solid left to the head. But the energy expended wasn't worth the damage inflicted, and the champion appeared fatigued.

From this point forward, it was all Ambers. Opening a cut near the champion's left eye in the 13th round, Ambers attacked Canzoneri's left cheek until it was covered in crimson. In the end, it was a 15-round unanimous decision for Lou Ambers, who scaled at 134, or a pound below Canzoneri. The fight wasn't close: the judges saw it 9–5 and 10–5 in favor of Ambers, and referee Arthur Donovan had it 12–3.

As fights go, it wasn't invigorating, nor were spectators on the edge of their seats. It was simply a well-fought, systematic exchange of the lightweight title. Luigi d'Ambrosio, who would recall the event as the most memorable of his career, was now the lightweight champion of the world.[8]

Within hours, Canzoneri's professional obituary was written in dailies across the country. Transforming Canzoneri from champion to has-been, the same beat writers who stroked his ego and complimented his skills after the McLarnin fight buried him without a wake. The event lacked drama, as there was no crucifixion, no torn flesh oozing massive amounts of blood, no knockdowns, or even pugilists wandering aimlessly from corner to corner, only minor scars. It wasn't thrilling, nor did it have that one moment you could tell your grandchildren about decades later. It was a peaceful and decisive transfer of a boxing championship.

On September 5, to quell the criticism, it was announced that Tony Canzoneri would meet Jimmy McLarnin in Madison Square Garden on October 2. For many, it was a proper, if not fitting, goodbye. A ceremonial event, complete with a nemesis.

Since Canzoneri's loss followed on the heels of his marriage, sportswriters blamed Cupid for Canzoneri's diminished skills. After all, Jack Dempsey lost his crown after he wed Estelle Taylor, there was Schmeling's beating of Louis, and look what it did to McLarnin. It was a silly theory, but interesting. For now, Mr. and Mrs. Tony Canzoneri had been seen holding hands while walking in Times Square. The newlyweds also appeared on Kate Smith's *Bandwagon* radio show, along with Babe Ruth, on September 17.[9]

A St. Louis boxer named Henry Armstrong had appeared on the lightweight horizon. Popular crooner Al Jolson purchased the fighter's contract from Wirt Ross for the sum of $10,000. On August 22, Jolson traveled to New York to match Armstrong against Canzoneri with an offer of $25,000—which would be more than $500,000 today. When Sammy Goldman heard about the offer, he just smiled.

The incomparable Jimmy McLarnin, aka "Baby Face" (shown here in the 1920s), was born in Hillsborough, Northern Ireland. Winning five times as many bouts as he lost, McLarnin was considered one of the five greatest welterweights ever.

Nobody was certain as to what odds to take on which former champion. Do you take 6–5 on Canzoneri or opt for 5–7 on McLarnin? Both Tony Canzoneri, the former lightweight champion, and Jimmy McLarnin, the former welterweight titleholder, were working hard in preparation for their October battle. Canzoneri was at his home in Marlboro, while McLarnin was over at the Pioneer Gym. But as fate might have it, Canzoneri suffered a lip injury while sparring with Red Cochrane, so the bout was postponed until October 5. The injury, which could be traced back to Canzoneri's first bout with McLarnin, required numerous stitches and adequate healing time.

If ever there was a boxer who always wanted to set the record straight, it was Jimmy McLarnin. Nobody, with the exception of his manager, Pop Foster, got the best of him: When he drew Fidel LaBarba in their second match, McLarnin came back and defeated him; when he lost to Charles "Bud" Taylor, he defeated him in their second bout; when he lost to Sammy Mandell, he defeated him in a rematch; when he lost to Billy Petrolle, he defeated him in back-to-back contests; and when he lost to Barney Ross, he defeated him in a rematch. Now the name of Tony Canzoneri could be added to the list.

Jimmy McLarnin, who scaled at 145, captured a 10-round unanimous decision over Tony Canzoneri, who scaled at 137. In the final round, Canzoneri, butchered, beaten, and bloodied, somehow remained standing. When he focused downward, he could see portions of both his nose and lip, moving in unison. Gore flowed from his right eye, over his nose, and onto a portion of his lip, before landing on his chest. Both his trunks and gloves were coated with blood. The crowd of 11,000-plus patrons screamed at referee Billy Cavanaugh to stop the slaughter. As Canzoneri had never been knocked out in his career, the arbiter refused.

McLarnin skillfully won the bout, and as bad as it looked, it could have been worse. In his previous revenge fights, the Irishman would have willfully knocked out his opponent. But not in this fight; he let Canzoneri live. Taking no unnecessary chances, McLarnin carefully chipped away at Canzoneri's facade for the first five rounds. Periodically, the Irishman would deliver a power punch, like the right hook that dropped Canzoneri to a three-count in the second round. But they were precision punches to use only if needed. Canzoneri looked better in the fourth and fifth frames, but that was about the extent of his better rounds—he did manage signs of life in the tenth frame.

Afterward, the Canzoneris headed west to Hollywood, California, and pondered their future. Tony was talking about fight management but hadn't taken a firm stand yet. But by the first week of November, he was talking about a run at the welterweight crown. As the Canzoneris were anticipating a baby, putting more coin in the till could furnish an adorable nursery.

Somebody Pass Me an Apron

Outside the ring, every successful professional boxer believed they were automatically qualified for two occupations: restaurant owner and entertainer. Many pugilists did both. Jack Dempsey's first restaurant was on Eighth Avenue and 50th Street opposite Madison Square Garden. The restaurant, a two-and-a-half-story, red-brick building, had its grand opening on February 17, 1935. Fight fans loved it, and it was the place to be before and after a night of boxing. The Toy Bulldog Tavern, owned by Mickey Walker, was located at 813 Eighth Avenue, on the southwest corner of Eighth Avenue and 49th Street. It opened a year earlier and was an immediate success. Work began on Benny Leonard's Restaurant, opposite Dempsey's, at 174 West 72nd Street (at Broadway) in November 1936. If it was good enough for Jack, then it was good enough for Benny. Noting all the action, Canzoneri wanted to throw in his hat—which he no doubt bought at his own clothing store—into the mix. He started looking around the block. Columnist Ed Sullivan was calling this section of Eighth Avenue "Cauliflower Row".

Eight bouts, six victories, and two painful defeats marked the end of a memorable year for Tony Canzoneri. Although his second reign as lightweight champion ended, other aspects of his life were just beginning. He married Rita Roy, the love of his life, and the couple were anticipating their first child in May 1937.

TWELVE

Fatherhood, 1937–1938

"I guess it sounds sort of silly, but I really love fighting and I'm not going to quit until I stop loving it."—Tony Canzoneri[1]

Gradual economic recovery, having lasted four years, began to falter in 1937, and even though the Lincoln Tunnel between Manhattan and Weehawken, New Jersey, opened to automobile traffic, and *LOOK* magazine began publication, it was a time when many Americans weren't sure if they were coming or going. As George Bernard Shaw once quipped, "The reasonable man adapts himself to the world: the unreasonable one persists in trying to adapt the world to himself. Therefore, all progress depends on the unreasonable man."

New York City boxing observed Joe Louis, in his first title defense, going the distance to pick up a victory over Tommy Farr in August; Barney Ross, after waiting more than 300 days, finally defending and retaining his welterweight title against Ceferino Garcia in September; and knockout artist Henry Armstrong capturing the featherweight title by knocking out Petey Sarron in October, the first of three titles for the incomparable Armstrong.

Staying close to home, Tony Canzoneri was thinking more about fatherhood than the brotherhood of boxing. With a new addition expected in the spring, he was making appearances, working with young fighters, and talking about a possible European tour. The appearance of his name alongside the word "comeback" in newspaper articles irritated him. However, it was not enough to hinder his ring plans. Outside the ring, the pugilist hoped to open Canzoneri's restaurant, at 236 West 50th Street, behind Dempsey's, on February 11.[2]

It wasn't until February that there was talk of Tony Canzoneri reentering the ring, but it was hearsay—it still appeared as if his place was home with Mrs. Canzoneri until the birth of their child. The former champion continued to find solace at the Broadway Arena working with fighters such as Joe Fontana, aka the number one horse in his stable, and Tony Ciaccio.

Writer Paul Mickelson met with Tony Canzoneri at Sammy Goldman's men's clothing store on Seventh Avenue just off Broadway. Although he claimed he was there to discuss the former champion's schedule, there appeared to be much more behind his visit. Discovering a somewhat restless and apprehensive pugilist, Mickelson began jabbing and countering for information. Canzoneri wasn't convinced he was ready for retirement, not yet. At least that was what he claimed, even if a part of his soul was telling him something different. When Mickelson, armed with photographs, showed Canzoneri images of his deformed countenance after the last

McLarnin contest, it had no impact. The 28-year-old fighter had his eyes on reentering the ring. Sammy Goldman even asked him to quit (it was plausible that Goldman asked Mickelson to meet with his fighter). But the answer was no. Compromising, Canzoneri and Goldman agreed to a three-week training stint to evaluate his talent.

The media believed Lou Ambers hadn't improved since lifting the title from Canzoneri. They were convinced Tony Canzoneri, once great, was no longer. When the pair signed to meet again at Madison Square Garden, the journalists weren't surprised; they just didn't see the point. The pair would complete their trilogy on April 2. Later, NYSAC agreed to postpone this title contest in favor of a 10-round overweight scrap between Lou Ambers and rising star Pedro Montañez. The rubber match between Ambers and Canzoneri would take place in Madison Square Garden on May 7.

Lou Ambers (pictured here, ca. 1930s) defeated Tony Canzoneri on May 5, 1937, in Madison Square Garden, to complete their famed boxing trilogy. Canzoneri won only their initial battle.

It's a Girl

The Canzoneris, of 25 Central Park West, were proud parents of a six-pound baby girl. She was born on February 17, 1937, at Shore Road Hospital in Brooklyn. Dr. Philip Goldstein, the attending physician, said mother, Rita, and daughter, Denise, were fine and resting comfortably. That trademark smile of Tony Canzoneri appeared to double in size upon the birth of his daughter. Last seen handing out cigars at Stillman's gym, the former champion had never been happier.

In his first battle of 1937, Tony Canzoneri, tipping at 138, stepped into the ring at Laurel Garden and scored a technical knockout victory over veteran George Levy, who scaled at 136¾. This April 5 contest was the first of three tune-up bouts Canzoneri took in preparation for his approaching battle against Lou Ambers.

Levy, who won more than three times as many bouts as he lost, was dropped multiple times before referee Whitey Healy stepped in and stopped the bout. After being dropped three times in the opening round for counts of nine, Levy knew it was going to be a challenging evening. The bout, scheduled for 10 rounds, lasted only seven.

Afterward, Canzoneri commented to the press that he didn't understand why his friends wanted him to hang up the mitts. After all, Max Schmeling and James J. Braddock, who were older, continued to box. It was a valid point. While Canzoneri understood and appreciated that his friends didn't want to see him hurt, he confirmed his ability to defend himself. Though Canzoneri looked far from a broken-down old man against Levy, his antagonist wasn't Lou Ambers.

Canzoneri's next tune-up bout took him to the Broadway Arena, a venue that first hosted him in 1925 and hadn't seen him fight since 1930. It felt good to be back. His opponent on April 13 was Frankie Wallace. With one victory in his last 10 contests, Wallace was fighting for a paycheck. In other words, he understood his role and could make distance. A capacity crowd of 5,000-plus turned out to watch and welcome back Tony Canzoneri.[3]

Tipping at 139¾, Tony Canzoneri managed an eight-round decision over Frankie Wallace, who scaled at 138¼. It wasn't his best effort. Yes, he dropped Wallace in both the first and fifth rounds, but the Cleveland fighter was up without a count. Because Canzoneri didn't start the engines until the fourth round, the pace was slow and the fight tedious. As Canzoneri left the ring, the lifeless effort garnered boos from those in attendance.

One more bout remained before Tony Canzoneri climbed into the Madison Square Garden ring to reclaim the lightweight crown, or so he hoped. And boy, did the Ruthian-faced pugilist need it. Canzoneri, who was not himself against Frankie Wallace, needed to refine his skills to championship form. On April 24, he met Joey Zodda at Ridgewood Grove. Knowing that he couldn't outbox Canzoneri, who was a 3–1 favorite, Zodda concentrated on opening Canzoneri's scars in hope of a stoppage. The former champion, knowing Zodda's intent, planned otherwise.

Before 5,500 fight fans, Tony Canzoneri knocked out Joey Zodda. The end came at the 1:59 mark of the seventh round. Noting Canzoneri's slow start, his adversary took advantage by forcing the fighting. Zodda took round two, which was the only round he won, by hooking lefts to Canzoneri's face. Battling hard in the sixth round, Canzoneri, who tipped at 138, dropped Zodda, who scaled at 137¼, with an outstanding combination. But the fighter was able to regain his footing and last out the term.

Following the first minute of the seventh round, Canzoneri locked in on his target and dropped Zodda to a five-count. Once vertical, Canzoneri reloaded and locked on his target, firing a hard right to the body that put away his opponent for good.

Sammy Goldman had spent more time convincing folks Canzoneri wasn't retired than scheduling him to fight. That bothered him. He hoped the last three fights convinced folks that Canzoneri's tank wasn't empty and he was ready to face Lou Ambers once again. Setting aside the candor, he informed the press that he often told his fighter that he would know it was time to retire when he stopped lying about his age and started bragging about it!

Goldman reminded the press that Canzoneri was now a father and planned to bank the Ambers gate into a trust fund for his daughter. The pugilist admitted that if he failed to regain the title from Ambers, he might hang up the gloves. He wasn't sure. Since the Canzoneri family was growing out of their current residence, Tony was planning on building a home in the Bensonhurst section of Brooklyn. Naturally, that could alter his career plans.

Lou Ambers v. Tony Canzoneri III, World Lightweight Title

A crowd of 11,000 watched as Lou Ambers successfully boxed a 15-round title defense against Tony Canzoneri in Madison Square Garden. Both fighters scaled at 135 pounds. On May 1, the odds were 3–1 in favor of the champion to have his way once again with his mentor. The odds stayed that way when the fighters entered the ring on May 7. According to the judges, Eddie Forbes and Charlie Lynch, and referee Arthur Donovan, the fight wasn't even close. Aggressive, Ambers' offensive commitment upstaged his adversary's defensive tactics. Canzoneri appeared as if he only wanted to make the distance. There were no knockdowns in what turned out to be a lackluster event.

As Canzoneri's final championship bout, his third meeting with Lou Ambers deserves round-by-round scrutiny despite its lack of excitement.

Round One: Canzoneri surprisingly appeared nervous, while Ambers looked confident and prepared. Ambers had little success with his combinations early in the round. Canzy opted to go to the body and follow it with choice right uppercuts.

Round Two: Ambers worked the face—yes, testing the stability of Canzy's muzzle was an obvious and anticipated strategy—of his adversary with combinations and accurate left hands. Retaliating, Canzoneri strategically went to the body. A small cut on the right side of Canzoneri's nose was opened by a left hand. That same Ambers left hand sent Canzoneri's head back with a solid shot to the face.

Round Three: While Ambers moved efficiently around the ring, Canzoneri stood flat-footed. Advancing by sliding his left foot forward, Canzoneri, as usual, kept his left hand low. Combinations and solid lefts continued to work for the champion, while Canzoneri remained patient to score with rights to the body.

Round Four: Ambers left his corner and began circling to the left of his opponent. The hope was to land his left hand while staying out of range of Canzoneri's thunderbolt, or right hand. It worked briefly, but not long enough for Ambers to avoid two hard rights to the body and one to the head. When Canzoneri combined a swift left hook with a right cross, he was scoring.

Round Five: Ambers continued to try to negate Canzoneri's right hand by circling to his left. He was scoring better with his left hand. Stunned by a solid right to the jaw and a left hook to the stomach, Ambers struggled.

Round Six: Ambers landed three good lefts to the face, walked into a hard right to the chin, and delivered four sound lefts to the face. An unanswered left to the chin reminded his opponent that he was fighting the champion. Canzoneri continued the lefts to the stomach followed by rights to the face. He also continued to deliver solid rights to the body of the champion. It was a busy round by both parties.

Round Seven: Canzoneri would not relent with the body punches. Locking in with his left hand, he was scoring points. In a timely move, Canzoneri ducked four swift left hands before sending a powerful right uppercut to Ambers' chin. Tying up

Ambers in a clinch, Canzoneri shot a left to the face and a solid right on the break. For Canzoneri, it was his best defensive round.

Round Eight: Both fighters traded punches at the beginning of the round before Ambers began landing unanswered lefts. Canzoneri landed two inimical rights, one of which rocked Ambers by landing directly on his chin. Again, Ambers continued working the left to the face. Canzoneri finished the round strong by landing a right to the face, a left to the body, and a hard left to the face.

Round Nine: This was the first round where one of the fighters, in this case Canzoneri, looked noticeably fatigued. Lacking power behind his punches, Canzoneri did not answer many of Ambers' assaults. More than a half-dozen left hands reached Canzoneri's visage, and none were returned—his right eye was partly closed.

Round Ten: Relying on the left jab, Ambers was inflicting damage. A combination left hook and right cross woke up Canzoneri, who directed a fabulous right to Ambers' chin. Both fighters turned to combinations next to inflict facial damage, although Canzoneri couldn't resist adding another right to the body.

Round Eleven: Ambers worked combinations and left jabs to his opponent's face. Canzoneri was thinking about ending it with a single punch. He missed a right uppercut, landed a right to the face, and missed a right haymaker that would have catapulted Ambers out of the ring. The champion continued to answer with combinations and countered only when he was certain he was locked in.

Round Twelve: Ambers worked the left jab to Canzoneri's face and combinations in clinches. When the pair mixed it up in the center of the ring, Ambers delivered the greater damage. The frustration was beginning to take its toll on Canzoneri, who was casting wild rights at his rival.

Round Thirteen: The champion went to the head as Canzoneri continued his body assault. Ambers was dispatching many unanswered blows, and Canzoneri wasn't connecting.

Round Fourteen: Canzoneri came out strong with lefts to the face and stomach. He even drew Ambers in close but surprisingly was dominated by the champion. At this point, Ambers' left jab could not be contained and was slicing almost at will. Meanwhile, Canzoneri was missing his mark due to fatigue.

Round Fifteen: Combinations and left jabs by Ambers continued to score. Canzoneri was missing punches and again going to the body. It had been an ineffective strategy all along and should have been corrected. His gashed left eye lid excreted a steady stream of blood down his face. Canzoneri was taking two punches for each one delivered.[4]

Now What?

A title shot, in his farewell ring appearance, wasn't a bad way for Tony Canzoneri to exit the ring, presuming that was indeed the case. The observations made by fight fans and members of the media were not kind. Canzoneri was broke, spent, old, lethargic, worn, slow, weak, feeble ... you get the picture.

Judge Eddie Forbes awarded Lou Ambers all 15 rounds, Judge Charlie Lynch gave the champion 13 rounds and the challenger two, and referee Art Donovan saw it 12 rounds in favor of Ambers, two for Canzoneri, and one even. Ringside scored it like Donovan.

Canzoneri was unable to slow Ambers, and that was his only hope of landing a solid shot. Try as he did, he could not avoid the constant barrage of slicing jabs. The bobbing, weaving, and slipping that formerly defined the mentor now described the student.

The crowd, who did not want to see the former champion in such a condition, cheered his slightest rally or hard punch. Nearly 9, 500 fight fans hoped for a better performance, but they did not get it.[5]

Sitting on a green stool after the fight, Tony Canzoneri had his head down. The sweat and blood poured off his face and onto the floor, as a liquid pattern of clear crimson invited interpretation. With his right eye purple and swollen, Canzoneri could barely see. His left eye, badly sliced, continued to ooze gore. The flattened bridge of his nose was slashed in the usual troublesome spot that annoyed the fighter to no end. In a dejected tone of voice, he mumbled that he wasn't hurt and won the fight. He wanted a fourth battle against Lou Ambers. The horizontal head movement of those around him sent a clear message, even if no one attempted an elaboration. In his heart, Canzoneri believed his career wasn't over.

Reflection

The French novelist Albert Camus once quipped, "He knew now that it was his own will to happiness which must make the next move. But if he was to do so, he realized that he must come to terms with time, that to have time was at once the most magnificent and the most dangerous of experiments. Idleness is fatal only to the mediocre." It was a quote that applied perfectly to the enigma faced by this elite fighter.

While Tony Canzoneri contemplated his future, domestic vicissitudes dominated his life. While it was heartening to spend time home with the family, Canzoneri had always been a social butterfly. It was reported on June 1 that he had a falling out in his restaurant venture, and his name might be removed from the premises. Though he was spending time in the gym with the youngsters, he missed training. When he was seen out with friends such as Johnny Dundee, it was hard to take the fight out of the fighter.

Canzoneri, like many boxers, loved horse racing. Rita Canzoneri enjoyed it as well. When they could land a trustworthy babysitter, the pair were spotted at Aqueduct Racetrack in Queens. Opened in 1894, Aqueduct was the only racetrack located within the New York City limits. Tony also made it up to Saratoga Springs in August to watch the running of the Travers Stakes, a popular thoroughbred horse race. He was spotted trackside talking to Jack and Hannah (Williams) Dempsey; the group drew their share of attention.

As autumn approached, Canzoneri was struggling with his business enterprises. He tried making a "book." A bookmaker strives to accept bets on the outcome of an event in the right proportions to make a profit regardless of the outcome. When that enterprise was unsuccessful, he went back to being a player. But that failed as well, a couple of his hospitality hotspots folded, and then the men's clothing store closed.

His next venture was rumored to be as a ticket broker. If things didn't improve soon, he would have little choice but to reenter a boxing ring.

In October, Canzoneri was guest announcer at the reopening of the Westchester County Center in White Plains, New York. While he was tempted to make a statement regarding his ring future, he decided against it. Speaking of plans, Sammy Goldman was working hard with his stable of fighters and believed he had another champion in Leonard Del Genio. Canzoneri was always welcome to drop by the gym and work with Goldman's boys.

As the holidays approached, the Canzoneri family had much to be thankful for. Young Denise was healthy and growing faster than her parents imagined. Four fights—three wins and a loss—constituted the fewest fights Tony Canzoneri had ever had in a single year. While the highlight of the year was the birth of his daughter, the former champion wished it had ended with another boxing title in his hand. But it wasn't to be.

1938

The city and the nation were on edge as Germany's takeover of Austria in April sent shockwaves around the world, General Electric's introduction of fluorescent lighting began to revolutionize office-building construction, and *The Fifth Column and the First Forty-Nine Stories*, an anthology of writings by Ernest Hemingway, was published by Scribner's in October. Meanwhile, Everlast founder Jacob Golumb, noting increased interest in his products, moved his sports manufacturing company to 750 East 132nd Street in the South Bronx. As hard to believe as it sounds, all these events impacted professional boxing.

Four big fights entertained New York City fight fans: Max Baer avenged a previous loss by defeating Tommy Farr on March 11; featherweight champion Henry Armstrong trounced Barney Ross and took his welterweight title on May 31; in a bout with enormous international implications, Joe Louis floored Max Schmeling three times during a first-round knockout on June 22; and Henry Armstrong won the lightweight title—becoming the only boxer to hold three world titles at once—by defeating Lou Ambers on August 17.

In February, Art Donovan, who had been the third man in the ring during thousands of major bouts, commented about the subjectivity of boxing and the expertise needed to judge a ring battle. Noting that certain fighters were easier than others to handle, he confirmed the integrity of Tony Canzoneri. He never fouled, he never thumbed, back-handed, or elbowed an opponent, and he even refrained from rabbit-punching. As an easy fighter to handle, Tony Canzoneri was in sharp contrast to the toughest, which Donovan claimed was Max Baer.

In March, Tony Canzoneri made it official: He was seeking the welterweight title held by Barney Ross. Realizing it was going to take a few months to get into shape, he hoped for a series of tune-up fights to bring him back to competitive form. Wiser at age 29, Canzoneri understood his mistakes and had learned from them.

Criticized for being up at Saratoga Springs watching the ponies—along with every other horse racing fan in the country—Canzoneri confirmed that he was leaving soon for Bey's at Summit, New Jersey, to watch Lou Ambers train for his bout against Henry Armstrong. Canzoneri noted that Ambers should plan on exploiting his defensive skills—for example, his exceptional ring movement—to have any hopes of stopping Armstrong.

When It Rains, It Pours

Canzoneri's financial woes began hitting home in August, as a contractor—who enlarged Canzoneri's hotel on Lattintown Road in Marlboro and even installed a gymnasium—was granted a judgment of $4,211 and costs in an action brought for foreclosure of a mechanic's lien against George Canzoneri, Tony's father.[6] The work took place back in 1935. The judgment was against George Canzoneri, who owned the property.

The contractor also added a fourth story to the hotel. As only a verbal agreement had taken place, many elements of the argument were vague. The plaintiff believed that Tony Canzoneri had an interest in the property; however, the court held that the boxing champion had no interest, only his father. Unless the judgment was paid, the property would be sold. The Canzoneri family appealed the decision.

As fate had it, nearly 5,000 people attended the first day of a two-day, Italian American benefit affair held at Tony Canzoneri's country club in Marlboro. The event was a benefit for an orphanage. It included concerts and even exhibition bouts at Canzoneri's training camp. It shed a different light on the property, and one the Canzoneri family hoped wouldn't go unnoticed.

It was noted in November that 134 acres of the Canzoneri farm on Lattintown Road would be offered in a public sale on December 21 because of unpaid taxes. George Canzoneri was listed as the owner.

If any burden was placed on Tony Canzoneri owing to family financial obligations, it was not aired in public.

The Comeback Begins

Once Barney Ross lost his title to Henry Armstrong on May 31, he claimed he was never fighting again. He appeared to be telling the truth. Nevertheless, it wouldn't change Canzoneri's decision to reenter the ring. He would begin his comeback in Scranton, Pennsylvania, against Eddie Zivic. The bout was scheduled for October 17 at Convention Hall. Canzoneri was ready, as were Sammy Goldman and Nick Florio, who were right by his side.

A few devastating head shots rocked Zivic in the opening round. They were followed by a series of left hooks and powerful rights that catapulted the Pittsburgh pugilist across the ring. From an observer's perspective, it appeared it would be a short evening. Thinking otherwise, Zivic remained vertical and appeared complacent to plod around the ring. The second round was quiet, while the third saw Canzoneri, who tipped at 142, or a two-pound advantage, stun his adversary with a right. At that point, Canzoneri could have taken the fighter out, but he did not. Zivic tried to mix it up in the fourth round while cautiously staying out of range. Canzoneri went to the head and body in the fifth—a left hook and right cross to the head, followed by a left to the body staggered Zivic. Enraged by a hard right to the head, Canzoneri scored with combinations in the sixth round.

In the seventh and eighth rounds, Zivic ignited during exchanges and outscored his opponent. It was Canzoneri's turn in the ninth, as he unloaded the chambers. Yet by some means, Zivic remained upright. Exchanging left hooks with Zivic as the tenth round opened, Canzoneri spun off the ropes to pummel Zivic about the ring. Not one of the 1,378 customers left, as they appreciated Canzoneri allowing Zivic to stay the distance. When announcer Dr. Charles J. Feely announced a draw, people were stunned, but not half as much as when he changed his mind and gave Zivic the victory. Nobody could believe it. Canzoneri, with his mouth open, stood for two minutes in his corner. Referee Al Murphy gave the deciding vote after the judges disagreed. Judge Harry Levine saw it for Canzoneri, while Judge Joe Gaeton called it a draw. It was a pathetic injustice. Satirically grinning at ring officials, Sammy Goldman was dumbfounded by the verdict.

It was over to the Braddock Arena in Jersey City on October 26. Tony Canzoneri, scaling at 140, or a two-pound advantage, scored an eighth-round points victory over Howard "Cowboy" Scott of Washington, D.C. Canzoneri was slow out of the blocks over the first five rounds, and Scott took advantage of it. But in the sixth round, the former champion dropped Scott to a nine-count with an overhand right to the jaw. Of the 2,000 spectators in attendance, and unlike in Canzoneri's last fight, nobody felt cheated by the decision.

Both Goldman and Canzoneri believed two bouts a month was a proper comeback pace. Canzoneri was scheduled to meet Joey Greb, aka Joey Greco, from Herkimer, New York, at Convention Hall in Camden, New Jersey, on November 1. When Greb was unable to make the bout, Al Dunbar, of Jersey City, was chosen as a last-minute substitute.

It was clear from the start that Dunbar was on borrowed time against Tony Canzoneri. Of the 2,600 in attendance, not a soul was surprised when Dunbar was dropped by a volley of short rights to the head. It happened at 1:40 of the third frame.

It took Canzoneri a round to warm up and find his range, but when he launched a robust combination to the stomach of Dunbar in the second round, it was clear that the Jersey pug was pained. When he strolled out of his corner in the third round, Dunbar resembled a death row prisoner on the way to the electric chair. A short hard right to the chin, followed by a trio of rapid-fire rights, began Dunbar's descent to the canvas. The pugilist nearly made it to his feet at the count of 10, but referee Joe Mangold declared it a knockout victory for Canzoneri. Both fighters weighed a bit over 140 pounds.

Who Would Have Thought?

Too many dollars spent chasing too few (genuine) friends was an economic woe faced by many successful boxers. Even those familiar with the scenario who claimed it would never happen to them found themselves facing economic insecurity. Success came early to Tony Canzoneri, faster than he anticipated, and at a pace he found difficult to control. Glory has always been fleeting, and by the time he reached his 30s—young by most standards—Canzoneri's battle-scarred body began to ache in places he didn't even knew he had and at a pace he couldn't slow. The multi-divisional champion, who once basked in the celebrity spotlight, was now witnessing that light dim.

He had socked away some dough—a $75,000 annuity was the cornerstone of his life savings—but it disappeared courtesy of fast-talking salesmen, poor business decisions, gambling, and, frankly, overconfidence. A haberdashery, jewelry store and restaurant, not to mention some family enterprises, drained the cash quicker than the pug could make it. Recently, Barney Ross even offered the fighter a job with a chain of women's goods stores—he felt bad for his rival.

Canzoneri became addicted to the lifestyle, and who could blame him? How often in life do you share a dinner table with celebrities like Jack Dempsey, Joe DiMaggio, or Mae West? The champion didn't even have to recall where he was the night before because his every move landed in Ed Sullivan's syndicated column the next morning.

An economic recovery, disguised as a ring comeback to save face, was the only solution. His friends could look in opposite directions, but he needed to look forward. The name Canzoneri still carried weight. Enormously popular, he knew that nobody questioned his innate ability, and they were primarily concerned for his welfare.

On November 22, Tony Canzoneri faced Howard "Cowboy" Scott for the second time that year. This bout was held at New York Coliseum—the former champion's first bout in New York state after his loss to Ambers. Both fighters battled hammer and tongs over eight rounds, much to the delight of 10,000-plus fight fans. Scott's wild overhand rights kept his opponent in check all evening and even had Canzoneri dazed a couple of times.

Setting the tone in the opening round, Canzoneri dropped his opponent for the first time—Scott would also hit the canvas in rounds four and seven. Resetting the chess board, Scott fought hard over the next three rounds. Round four was action packed as both boxers traded punches. Seeing an opening, Canzoneri fired an unforgiving right hand behind Scott's left ear and dropped him to a nine-count. In the seventh round, Canzoneri's final knockdown of Scott was in retaliation for a shocking right hand.

At the final gong, both fighters were coated in crimson—Canzoneri from a cut over his left eye and Scott from a cut near his left ear. The eight-round majority decision went in favor of Canzoneri. Both boxers scaled at 142.

Tony Canzoneri's nostalgic return to the ring found him back at Ridgewood Grove on December 10 tackling local pug Jimmy Murray of Williamsburg. To little surprise, the eight-round contest drew more than 4,600 fans.

Tony Canzoneri, scaling at 143¼, won an eight-round points victory over Jimmy Murray, who tipped at 141. Murray, who had lost twice as many bouts as he won, was little more than a bullseye. Light jabs, mixed with an occasional uppercut, guided Canzoneri through the first two rounds. In the third, the former champion went to the right hand for the first time—had he needed the power punch, he would have gone to it sooner. Canzoneri won all eight rounds.

In his last fight of the year, Tony Canzoneri found himself in an unfamiliar venue, the Hippodrome, against a familiar opponent, Eddie Zivic. Scheduled for 10 rounds on Friday, December 30, it promised to be a donnybrook.

The Hippodrome Theatre (1905–1939), or the New York Hippodrome, shown here ca. 1905, was located on Sixth Avenue between West 43rd and West 44th streets in the Theater District of Midtown Manhattan (Library of Congress).

New York Hippodrome

The Hippodrome Theatre, also called the New York Hippodrome, was a popular playhouse in New York City from 1905 to 1939. It catered to the most successful theater productions and vaudeville artists of the day, including the 1920 Broadway musical extravaganza *Good Times* (1920) and illusionist Harry Houdini. Conveniently located on Sixth Avenue between West 43rd and West 44th streets, in the Theater District of midtown Manhattan, it was called the world's largest theatre by its builders. It had a seating capacity of 5,300 and a very large stage.

Recently, the Hippodrome had struggled—a series of late-run movies, boxing, wrestling, and jai alai games were a clear indication. Trying desperately to survive, it could not, and it was demolished in 1939.

Capturing a 10-round points victory over Eddie Zivic, Tony Canzoneri put to rest any doubts following the pair's last battle. Both boxers scaled at about 141. More than 4,600 spectators turned out to cheer on the former champion. He didn't disappoint as Canzoneri took nine of the available 10 rounds—the first round was even. Canzoneri mounted an immediate attack to the head and body, but as hard as Zivic was hit, he was never in danger of being knocked out. A ring battle with any of the Zivic brothers was never easy, so it wasn't a shock when Eddie pulled some tricks out of his bag. The endless lefts to Zivic's stomach annoyed the Pittsburgh pug, who

retaliated with questionable ordnance below the Mason-Dixon
line. Knowing Zivic would come
out strong in the final round, Canzoneri flew out of his corner, firing volleys of combinations. To
the astonishment of Zivic, his rival
maintained the pace for the entire
session. It was a great way to end
the year.

Over six bouts that added five
victories and one questionable loss
to his resume, Tony Canzoneri's
ring return appeared to be hitting
its stride. At the young age of 30, he
believed he was far from an old man
and even farther from the pasture.
The more he fought, the more bills
he could pay. While he hadn't sold
everybody on the validity of returning to the ring, he had sold some.
The question, and everyone knew it,
was how long it could last. Nobody
was certain, not even Tony.

This New York Hippodrome ticket was for the
Tony Canzoneri v. Eddie Zivic bout. The event
was conducted by the 20th Century Sporting
Club, Incorporated, in the famed New York City
venue on December 30, 1938.

THIRTEEN

The Final Rounds, 1939

"A story has no beginning or end: arbitrarily one chooses that moment
of experience from which to look back or from which to look ahead."—
Graham Greene

The world was on the brink of war as Nazi leader Adolf Hitler ordered his
troops and aircraft into Poland, Pan American Airways offered the first commercial transatlantic passenger air service, and traveling to the Midwest from New York
City was made easier as the Pacemaker went into service on the New York Central
and the Trail Blazer adorned the tracks of the Pennsylvania Railroad. Transportation improvements were altering the course of history, though few saw it from that
perspective.

New York City fight fans witnessed plenty of action during the year: In June,
Lou Nova cut the mouth of Max Baer, forcing an 11th-round stoppage; also in June,
Joe Louis successfully defended his title by knocking out "Two-Ton Tony" Galento in
the fourth frame; in July, Billy "the Pittsburgh Kid" Conn defeated Melio Bettina to
win the vacant light heavyweight title; and in August, low blows in multiple rounds
assisted Lou Ambers in regaining the lightweight title from Henry Armstrong.

The last time Tony Canzoneri fought in 17 bouts or more in a single year was
back in 1927. At the time, he was trying to sustain his contender status. Ironically,
more than a decade later, he was trying to accomplish the same—even if some didn't
view it that way. Critics were claiming he was only in the ring for the coin. It was
frustrating the former champion so much, he even threatened to sue a few of them.
Since Hollywood lightweight Wally Hally had been in town for a few weeks, his
management arranged for a meeting against Tony Canzoneri out in Denver on January 19.

Scaling at 139, Tony Canzoneri took a 10-round unanimous decision over Wally
Hally, who tipped at 136½, at the City Auditorium. "The Alhambra Assassin," who
had turned punching bag last February, had lost his last nine bouts. A heavy Canzoneri left jab in the third round started a flow of blood from the fighter's nose that
annoyed him the entire bout. Using his glove to wipe away the gore, Hally only made
matters worse. The following round didn't go much better for the Californian, as
Canzoneri opened a large cut under his left eye. Sensing he was getting the best of his
adversary, the former champion coasted in the fifth round. Hally rallied in the sixth
and seventh rounds to look as respectable as he could, but it wasn't that convincing.
The final three rounds of the battle were close.[1] It was a good start to the new year for
Tony Canzoneri.

Walter Halliwell (left), aka Wally Hally, was a popular pugilist battling out of Hollywood (Smithsonian American Art Museum). Eddie Brink (right), aka "Irish Eddie Brink," was born and raised in Scranton, Pennsylvania. Both are shown here in the 1930s.

Back in the Saddle Again

At the end of January, Tony Canzoneri was on the West Coast. He was scheduled for three battles: "Newsboy Joe" Gavras in San Francisco on January 27, Everett Simington in San Jose on January 31, and Bobby Pacho in Los Angeles on February 7. Entertaining the press, Canzoneri was forthcoming; he confirmed that he wanted to fight Henry Armstrong, even though it was improbable; mentioned he was still overweight by a few pounds—however, he was well below his high-water mark of 166; pushed off remarks about his economic condition and concern, which wasn't a secret; explained that his ring prowess spoke for itself, but he wasn't working for free; bragged about his two-year-old daughter, Denise, and his love of being a father; and noted that the California fruit trees and vineyards reminded him of home.

Newsboy Joe Gavras, hoping to garner a headline in the morning newspaper, bolted out of his corner in the opening round and unloaded the chambers. He targeted the jaw of Tony Canzoneri, and it was clear Gavras realized this was a rare opportunity to catch the former champion off guard. He was correct. A minute into the round, Canzoneri, having survived the initial assault, propelled his opponent to the canvas with a terrific right hand. To the fighter's credit, he got up and made it through the term.

Less than a minute into the second round, Canzoneri repeated the action. Gavras bounced off the canvas at the count of one. Sensing the fragility of his opposer, Canzoneri eased up, only to be driven into the ropes. Operating off the cords, Canzoneri caught the Newsboy on the jaw and sent him face-first to the canvas. When Gavras appeared unsteady during the count, referee Toby Irwin had little choice but to wave it off. Both fighters scaled at 139½ pounds.

Heading 50 miles south, Tony Canzoneri met lightweight Everett Simington at San Jose's Civic Auditorium. The bout was a favor to a young promoter named "Babe" Griffin, who was trying hard to reestablish the fight game in the Garden City. Simington, with combined losses and draws equal to his victory total, wasn't anticipated to give Canzoneri much of a workout, but it was a paycheck for both. Sure enough, Canzoneri dropped his opposer to a seven-count in the third round before sending him to dreamland with a right cross. Canzoneri scaled at 139½ to Simington's 145.

Bobby Pacho promised to be more than a sparring session for the former champion when they met in Los Angeles. Less than a month away from fighting Henry Armstrong for the welterweight crown in Havana, Pacho—though he hadn't received official word—needed a good 10-round workout, and Canzoneri was it. Many recalled the pair's previous battle during the summer of 1935. The Mexican fighter, in a losing effort, dropped Canzoneri to the canvas seconds before the gong ended round seven. Both Sammy Goldman and Nick Florio, who accompanied Canzoneri, knew the challenges they faced with Pacho.[2]

Tipping at 140, Tony Canzoneri took a hard-fought points victory over veteran Bobby Pacho, who scaled a robust 147½. More than 7,000 spectators jammed into Olympic Auditorium and witnessed an outstanding finish as Tony Canzoneri turned the engines on full during the final rounds to take the victory. There were no knockdowns. Pacho rocked Canzoneri twice in the fourth round, and it seemed only instinct saved him from disaster—Canzoneri's nose never stopped bleeding from this round forward. Getting the best of Pacho in the final round, thanks to a right hand that dazed the fighter, guaranteed Canzoneri a victory. Critics believed the match was even entering the final frame.

Canzoneri was back home the second week of February. The New York media continued to pound him regarding his financial position and questioned the validity of his comeback. True to form, Canzoneri made no excuses regarding his ring work. He confirmed that he had three annuities, two farms, a beautiful wife and daughter and was amid a successful comeback. What more could a man ask for?

Scheduled for what ended up being back-to-back bouts against Eddie Brink in March, Tony Canzoneri, along with Sammy Goldman, believed the Pennsylvania boxer was an excellent opponent because his style mimicked that of Henry Armstrong.[3]

On March 7, Tony Canzoneri, scaling at 140½, took an eight-round points victory over former sparring partner Eddie Brink, who tipped at 139½. The Coliseum crowd enjoyed the action, which was quick and aggressive. Canzoneri took control with a varying mix of combinations to the head. Brink missed far too many punches and was forced to retreat from Canzoneri's assaults. The boxers fought toe to toe in rounds two, four and eight, with Canzoneri delivering two punches for every one received. It was the type of contest Canzoneri needed to polish his skills.

Returning to Stillman's gym, Canzoneri began preparing for a battle against Norment Quarles at the Hippodrome on March 14. However, Quarles suffered a cut eye during training and had to call off the battle. With few options, the former champion prepared for a rematch against Eddie Brink. This bout would be held at the Hippodrome on March 28.

Hitting Bottom—Five Bouts Without a Victory

This was not the type of bout the former champion needed at this juncture. Had he forgotten it was a 10-round battle? More than 3,500 spectators watched as Eddie Brink finished strong and made Tony Canzoneri break ground with aggressive assaults. It was as if somebody pulled the plug at the end of the eighth frame. Canzoneri had Brink in trouble three times—in rounds one, six and eight—but could not muster enough strength to finish him off. Although the former champion's trademark defense, consisting of bobbing, weaving, and ducking, was clearly on display and effective, he was short on offense. It was a split decision in favor of Eddie Brink, who scaled at 139¾. Tony Canzoneri, who tipped two pounds heavier, faded during the final two rounds.

Shocked by the verdict, Canzoneri gave no excuses. Sammy Goldman, smart enough to realize that a proposed Garden match between Canzoneri and the red hot Al "Bummy" Davis had gone down the drain, was forced to reexamine his fighter's comeback. The fight manager, who was believed to be not much better off economically than Canzoneri, was counting on a big Garden payday. It would now have to wait if it happened at all. In March, Al "Bummy" Davis had an undefeated record of 30–0–2—the youngster was crushing opponents like apples at a cider mill. Even if Canzoneri had won this bout, he was not ready to greet Davis.

The loss, along with the humiliation it created, caused Tony Canzoneri to slip off the tracks. Once again, a chorus of "washed up" poured out of the mouths of critics. Canzoneri did admit to the media that while he had collected $50,000 from his comeback, he might hang up the mitts—the vague disclosure cast a shadow of doubt regarding the fighter's sincerity. The truth was Canzoneri wanted to continue boxing. His next battle was convincing Sammy Goldman that he could get back on track.

Drawing Jimmy Vaughn at the Coliseum on April 11 wasn't easy for Tony Canzoneri to swallow. Yet it was reality. His heart was in the bout, even if nothing else was—he was slow of foot in the ring and could not effectively counter. Frustration set in early for the former champion, as he fired a shot below the beltline in the second and it cost him the round—Vaughn had charged Canzoneri's midsection in the opening round. Vaughn also targeted Canzoneri's optics early, managing to damage both eyes during the early frames. Understanding he was losing rounds, Canzoneri tried to turn up the pressure in the fifth and sixth rounds, but it wasn't working. The former champion, who tipped at 140¾ or to a two-pound advantage, could garner nothing more than an even verdict. To Vaughn's credit, he fought an impressive contest.

A damage assessment following the bout confirmed that Tony Canzoneri's eyes required time to heal. Goldman immediately postponed the fighter's next bout.

Paul Cvecka (left), aka Jimmy Vaughn, battled out of Cleveland from 1931 until 1944. Nick Camarata (right) was born and raised in New Orleans and was managed by Chris Dundee, elite boxing manager and promoter. Both are shown here in the 1930s.

Canzoneri was to meet Jimmy Tygh on April 17. When Canzoneri's eyes didn't heal in time, the fight was postponed to April 24. The pair would finally meet on May 1. Looking ahead, the fight manager booked a May 15 bout for Canzoneri against Nick Camarata at the Municipal Auditorium in New Orleans.

The month did not open on a good note. A crowd of more than 3,000 turned out at the Arena in Philadelphia on May 1 to root for local pugilist Jimmy Tygh as he faced Tony Canzoneri. The former champion, who scaled at 141, had his adversary, who tipped at 134½, dazed in the opening round and in the sixth frame but could not capitalize in either instance. That hurt him more than he thought. As for Tygh, he tried to stay out of trouble as he chipped away at the scoring. In the end, both judges opted for Tygh, while referee Matt Adgie saw it for Canzoneri. It was an upset victory for Tygh—hey, it was Philadelphia. Many of those close to the action saw it 6–4 in favor of Canzoneri or, at worst, a draw. Honestly, Sammy Goldman should never have taken the bout.

In one of those out with the old and in with the new bouts, Tony Canzoneri, on a never-ending battle against Father Time, faced local rising star Nick Camarata.

The bout, predicted as a sell-out weeks before, took place at the Municipal Auditorium in New Orleans on May 15. Yes, the former champion was back home—his last ring visit was back in 1933—but things had changed. The ovation that once greeted the champion was no longer. Were spectators saving their cheers for Camarata? It appeared that way, as everyone stood and applauded when the youngster entered the arena. Sporting a long patch over his right eye, Canzoneri bounced around the ring like a buccaneer with water in his boots. Ring introductions included former bantamweight champion Pete Herman, now blind, who held the hand of Tony Canzoneri that greeted him ringside. With a tear in his eye, Sammy Goldman smiled, as both champions had played an enormous part in his life.

When the opening bell sounded, Camarata went right to work on Canzoneri's optics. It was as if he painted a target on his eye patch. Cuts opened within seconds of contact during round one. Canzoneri never found a rhythm. Searching for his target through a veil of blood the entire evening frustrated the former champion and slowed his reaction time. Perceived momentum changes were the only action that kept spectators awake during the lackluster battle. When the 10-round verdict was read, the crowd of nearly 6,500 booed. It was a draw. The post-fight chatter, often a time to reflect on highlights, was dominated by questions regarding Canzoneri's retirement. On a good note, it was one of the largest box offices—nearly $7,000—since 1933, when Tony Canzoneri fought Battling Shaw.

Pocketing the dough, the group headed north toward western New York. Tony Canzoneri was scheduled for a 10-round battle against novice Harris Blake. The Buffalo youngster was undefeated in five professional bouts and fresh out of the amateur ranks. While it was peculiar for a veteran such as Canzoneri to meet an inexperienced fighter like Blake, Goldman was hoping a victory might rekindle his fighter's confidence. He was wrong.

In nothing short of a humiliating affair, Harris Blake, scaling at 134, handed Tony Canzoneri, who tipped at 140½, a decisive 10-round beating. It wasn't even close, as the fast-moving Buffalo boxer fought a masterful bout at the Broadway Auditorium. Taking advantage of every opening, Blake sliced Canzoneri's countenance like a butcher over a side of beef. The former champion had no answer for his adversary's razor-sharp left jab or his powerful right hand. Ringside saw it seven rounds for Blake, two for Canzoneri, and one even.

There was only silence when Tony Canzoneri left the ring. Once he entered his dressing room, the atmosphere changed. Through with the speeches, Sammy Goldman wanted his fighter to quit. Looking Canzoneri straight in the eyes, the compassionate fight manager insisted it was over. Even Rita Canzoneri had tried to dissuade her husband from continuing his comeback. But the former champion, rocking his head back and forth, disagreed. In a scene that mimicked the careers of many boxers, the veteran boxer pleaded with his manager for one more noteworthy bout. Following additional discussion, parameters were set, and one final push toward a big money date was reluctantly agreed upon. Nobody was certain as to how many fights it would take to be considered for such a payday, but Goldman demanded that no bout exceed eight rounds.

The pugilistic boneyard, as some called it, included Max Baer, Kid Berg, James J. Braddock, Panama Al Brown, and Tony Canzoneri. And that was only the letters A through C. The economic conditions—many had lost a fortune in the stock market crash—left those in and around the fight game few options. Remember, it was rare for a boxer's skills set to go much beyond the ring. Too often, professional boxers invested in businesses without a clue as to their return on investment or even their financial obligations. Although not a single boxer would admit it, desperation often fueled comebacks.

The Home Stretch

It took six consecutive eight-round points victories to land Tony Canzoneri back in Madison Square Garden. Believing in his fighter, Sammy Goldman signed his fighter to the battles. Canzoneri, doing what champions do, delivered.

On July 6, Tony Canzoneri defeated Joe DeJesus in the first eight-round points victory. The bout was held at Woodcliff Park Arena—not exactly Madison Square Garden. To give you some perspective, tickets were scaled at $1.15 for ringside, 75 cents for reserve seats, and 40 cents for general admission. Canzoneri, who scaled at 140, started slowly but gradually built a decisive lead over DeJesus, who tipped at 139½. The former champion was bothered more by the swirling insects under the ring lights than his adversary. The conclusion was decisive: Canzoneri took five rounds, DeJesus won two, and one was even.

For the final bout of the month, Tony Canzoneri headed to the Coney Island Velodrome on July 17, where he met Irish Ambrose Logan. Logan was no tomato can, as the youngster held two recent upset victories, the first against Primo Flores, the second against by George Zengaras. More than 7,500 turned out to watch the entertaining clash. Both fighters traded vicious eye cuts that bothered them throughout the bout. Logan's left eye was cut in the second round, while Canzoneri's right eye was sliced in the fifth. Again, Canzoneri started slow and gradually accelerated his pace. He staggered his opposer in the seventh round and pounded him in the eighth but could not drop him. Canzoneri scaled at 142¼, while Logan came in two pounds lighter.

Three New York bouts were scheduled for Canzoneri in August: against the familiar face of Joe DeJesus in Brooklyn on the 3rd; against Frankie Wallace in Long Beach on the 18th; and against Gerald D'Elia in Staten Island on the 26th.

Before 7,000 enthusiastic fight fans at Fort Hamilton in Brooklyn, Tony Canzoneri, tipping at 141, took a commanding lead and rode it to victory over Joe DeJesus, who scaled four pounds lighter. Despite taking a slicing right hand to his left eye in the second frame, Canzoneri was able to stay strong and dominate the eight-round journey.

Cleveland boxer Frankie Wallace was always tough, even though he had turned punching bag a few years earlier. Tony Canzoneri, tipping at 141¾, got a workout from Wallace, who scaled at 140, but was never at risk of defeat. As the feature bout at Long Beach Stadium, it drew well, but honestly speaking, folks hoped for more action.

Gerald D'Elia was a streaky fighter, more than even Frankie Wallace, but he wasn't a threat—he lost three times as many bouts as he won. Never hitting his stride, Canzoneri was still able to make distance and gain a victory. Both fighters scaled at 142 pounds.[4] Again Canzoneri's eyes were sliced, treated, and pasted in what had become a common practice. Noticeable was the former champion's fatigue; moreover, the enervation worried Goldman. Because it was a concern, Canzoneri's scheduled bout against Johnny Horstman at Dexter Park on September 11 was cancelled.

Sammy Goldman, at Canzoneri's request, did schedule the former champion for a fight against Eddie Brink at the Broadway Arena on September 19. If his fighter performed well, he was hopeful of gaining a Garden date—he had offers to battle Henry Armstrong, Lou Ambers, and Al Davis. Canzoneri still wasn't over the perpetual thumbing he took from Brink the last time the pair met, which was in back-to-back bouts in March. This would be the rubber match and promised to be exciting—promoters Max Joss and Sammy Richman had an entertaining undercard in support.

Tony Canzoneri, tipping at 143¾, fought a shrewd, or what folks used to call scientific, battle over eight rounds to defeat Eddie Brink, who scaled at 144. To little surprise, Brink sliced Canzoneri's right eye in the opening round. Canzoneri happily reciprocated the following round. In an uncharacteristic move, at least lately, the former champion lured Brink to close quarters, then gave him a beating. Trading four punches to one, Canzoneri looked good—every round belonged to the former champion. There were times, and this was one, when the former champion managed to intensify his performance to ascertain victory.

On his way to becoming the most powerful figure in the sport of boxing, Michael Strauss Jacobs could turn a dime into a dollar before most people could count to 10. Much of this had to do with his discovery of heavyweight fighter Joe Louis—every bout Louis fought as a champion was promoted by Jacobs. Leveraging his success with Louis, Jacobs' organization began to assert its control over other divisions. In August 1937, the corporation MSG leased their premier facility, and the outdoor Madison Square Garden Bowl, to the Twentieth Century Sporting Club, aka Mike Jacobs. This arrangement put MSG out of the big-time boxing promotion business, which Jacobs would dominate in the years that followed.

It was announced during the first week of October that Tony Canzoneri had been signed to meet Al "Bummy" Davis of Brownsville over 10 rounds at Madison Square Garden on November 1.

Al "Bummy" Davis

Albert Abraham Davidoff, aka Al "Bummy" Davis, was born on January 26, 1920, in Brooklyn, New York. The crowded tenement flats, where his family lived, lent themselves to confrontation, so young Albert learned early the value of self-defense. Yeah, the Flatbush Jew was a bully, but this was New York, and if a punk was going to hang on your street corner, it was going to cost him, one way or another. Nobody in the neighborhood challenged Bummy—nobody. As the family struggled to make ends meet, the youngster was encouraged to work. It was while picking up odd jobs that he looked to boxing as an avocation.

Turning professional in 1937, battling out of Brooklyn haunts like Ridgewood Grove, Canarsie Stadium, and the Broadway Arena, to name a few, Davis was a natural. After 17 professional bouts in 1937, he remained undefeated. Granted, most of the men he fought were tomato cans with losing records, but a fight was a fight, and Davis needed to establish credibility. In 1938, the competition improved, and so did

Bummy. Posting a record of 10–0–2, he took victories over Jack Sharkey, Jr., Bernie Friedkin, and Jimmy Lancaster.

Davis' match against Friedkin, a neighborhood rival, became legendary. Both pugs detested each other. Originally scheduled to destroy one another at Dexter Park, they thought they could settle things once and for all. But each time it was scheduled, then rescheduled, it rained. When the story about the two neighborhood enemies reached Mike Jacobs, he couldn't resist transferring it to Madison Square Garden, a testament to the hatred the pair possessed and the interest level it created. Al "Bummy" Davis, who scaled at 135, sent Bernie Friedkin, who tipped at 131, to Neverland at the 1:09 mark of the fourth round. Friedkin had been a 2–1 favorite entering the July 21, 1938, contest. In the fourth term, Davis sent his trademark left hook to the jaw of his rival, and he dropped like an anvil for an eight-count. Fortunately, at

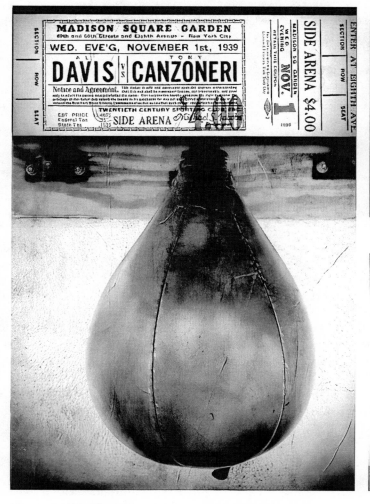

(Top left) This Madison Square Garden ticket was for the Al Davis v. Tony Canzoneri bout. (Top right) A poster for what would be the final professional boxing battle for Tony Canzoneri. (Bottom right) Albert Davidoff, aka Al "Bummy" Davis, was a popular and talented lightweight and welterweight boxer who fought from 1937 until 1945.

least for Friedkin, who was on his way up, he slipped back down. That was all it took to secure the Bummy Davis legacy.

In 1939, Davis began the year by defeating Wally Hally, Johnny Cabello, and Mickey Farber in back-to-back battles plus Eddie Brink. In his last fight, on July 21, he knocked out Gene Gregory and injured his hand.

Swollen hands kept the undefeated (33–0–2) Al "Bummy" Davis out of action for a few months. During that time, he added weight. Young and growing, the five-foot, five-inch scrapper would have to train hard, at Beecher's gymnasium in Brownsville, not only to test his mitts, but also to shed the pounds needed to make the 147-pound welterweight limit.

Meanwhile, Canzoneri had shifted his training from Stillman's Gym to his farm in Marlboro. Having exhibited splendid form and even impressed a few hungry beat writers at Stillman's, Canzoneri hoped to sustain his preparation upstate.

This was a decisive, make-or-break battle for both fighters. For Al Davis, an impressive victory over Tony Canzoneri would catapult him into the spotlight. For Tony Canzoneri, a solid victory over a rising and undefeated boxer like Al Davis, in Madison Square Garden, would finally put an end to the criticism that had marked his comeback. Granted, a loss by Davis would scar his undefeated record, but there was little downside for the young prospect, who already had the support of Mike Jacobs. A loss by the ever-popular Tony Canzoneri would finally halt his comeback and put an end to one of the finest careers in boxing history.

In 35 battles, southpaw Al Davis had knocked out 20 opponents. His portside wallop was one of the finest fight fans had seen in years. Armed with experience and heart, Canzoneri would need both, plus a bit of Lady Luck, to garner a victory.

The Crucible

As the bell sounded for round one, Al Davis, who scaled at 146¾, appeared apprehensive or perhaps a bit nervous. Canzoneri, who tipped at 143, appeared cautious yet confident. Getting their bearings, both pugilists went about finding their range. Tossing a flurry or two, Canzoneri won the first round by a shade.

Calmer in the second, Davis delivered a few misfires before driving his adversary to the ropes and unleashing a few head shots. Weakened by the exchange, Canzoneri countered with impressive overhand rights. Canzoneri was fighting flat-footed with his lips already crimson at the end of the second round, and his confidence faded.

Ringside spectators, on the edge of their seats, could sense that round three could be a turning point. Assured that Canzoneri's arsenal was not lethal, Davis quickly delivered his opponent into the ropes with a tremendous left hook to the stomach. Another smash to the chin, followed by a punch to the head, dropped Canzoneri to a four-count. Upright, Canzoneri was an instant target. Davis unleashed a volley of combinations that weakened Canzoneri's legs before crumpling him to the canvas. Miraculously, Canzoneri arose at the count of five. Referee Art Donovan, staring at the crimson-drenched former champion, looked for any sign of life. There was none. With a movement of his hand, Donovan did what no referee had ever done: Stopped a contest and awarded a technical knockout victory to an opponent of Tony Canzoneri.

The official end came at the 2:13 mark of the third round. Bleeding freely from nose and mouth and covered with gore, Canzoneri was led through the crowd to sympathetic cheers. It took every ounce of energy he had to muster a brief trademark smile. Still unable to catch his breath, Canzoneri immediately lay down on his dressing room table. Coughing because of the tremendous amount of blood in his throat, the former champion tried talking. Mumbling that Donovan should never have stopped the fight, he shook his sweat-drenched head from side to side. Everyone else in the chamber remained silent.

Promoter Mike Jacobs was thrilled by the performance. The card attracted nearly 13,000 fans and created a gate more than $30,000.

Whether or not Tony Canzoneri believed his career was over, the New York State Athletic Commission, having witnessed his crucifixion, announced on November 2 that they would no longer approve him for battle. The war was over. From his dressing room, Canzoneri seconded the motion because everyone else wanted him to do it, including his wife and manager.

Most professional boxers never *really* leave the fight game, as many assume roles as coaches, trainers, managers and even promoters. Canzoneri joined hands with Sammy Goldman to assist a stable of fighters which included Al Reid. But in case things don't work out, he also purchased a Brooklyn liquor store; Jack Dempsey, Gene Tunney and John Henry Lewis owned their own stores, so why not him? As usual, any extra moments would likely be filled with personal appearances.

In 1939, 17 bouts added 11 wins, four losses, and two draws to Tony Canzoneri's resume. His unpopular comeback managed to generate the income he was hoping for and landed him a big money bout in Madison Square Garden. However, the year ended on a sad note as he was knocked out for the first time in his career.

The Canzoneris, like any family with a toddler, were always busy. Rita wasn't initially thrilled by her husband's comeback but remained optimistic until the very end. Both parents faced their unfair share of bad luck this year, from Tony's Garden kayo to Rita's departure from the production of *Summer Night*, but in the end there was much to be grateful for.

FOURTEEN

Retirement, 1940–1949

"Life can only be understood backwards; but it must be lived forwards."—Søren Kierkegaard

Satisfaction, as Tony Canzoneri understood, had nothing to do with falling to the canvas, but rising once you fall. Hoping to apply that concept to his life outside the ring, he went to work choosing a direction. Knowing that replacing a career as an elite professional athlete was improbable, he would follow the path of those who had gone before him, like Jack Dempsey. The former heavyweight champion chose multiple sources (from referee to restaurateur), or occupations, if you will, to garner the satisfaction he had lost after leaving the ring. It appeared to be working.

Entering the Forties

The mortgage foreclosure sale, set for January 18, 1940, against George and Tony Canzoneri was postponed. The sale would take place on February 6. The property, located in the town of Marlboro, consisted of a farm and a large boarding house known as Homestead Farms. The action had been in the courts for four years. The Canzoneri family, with Tony as the financial pipeline, was still hoping to produce the sum of $5,271.36 to save their interest.

Wanting to stay close to the fight game, Tony Canzoneri offered his services as a referee. His personality was perfectly suited for the role, and nobody questioned his ring knowledge. It was a way to earn pocket cash while getting a break from child rearing. Like any job, it had both positive and negative elements. Every Italian society, in every town he visited, wanted to have a dinner in his honor. Although the former champion did his best to comply and appreciated the goodwill shown by fans, it ate away at his free time. On January 30, 1941, Canzoneri refereed a contest between Al Nettlow, who substituted for Lou Ambers, and Eddie Conolly in Barre, Vermont. The former champion was disappointed that Ambers had suffered a foot injury and was unable to box but did wish him well in his upcoming battle against Lew Jenkins.

When he wasn't in the gym working with another protégé, Tony Canzoneri could be found talking about his next business venture or visiting an ailing business he hoped to resurrect. By March 1941, he was looking for property in the Times Square district for another attempt at the restaurant business. By June, he

Dorothy Parker once quipped, "Yet, as only New Yorkers know, if you can get through the twilight, you'll live through the night." Canzoneri loved New York (pictured here in 1934) at night (Library of Congress).

was talking about buying a roller rink near Fort Bragg, North Carolina, while also thinking about opening a night club. The multiple business directions lent themselves to interpretation: Was he engaging in so many activities that he couldn't perform any of them well? Or was he looking for the pot of gold at the end of the rainbow?

In December of 1941, Tony Canzoneri signed for a theatrical role in a comedy called *They Should Have Stood in Bed*, which Sam H. Grisman was producing. The former champion played the role of pugilist Killer Kane. The production opened on February 13, 1942, and closed after 11 performances on February 21. Meanwhile, Mrs. Canzoneri had her heart set on becoming a nightclub singer.

On December 7, 1941, Japanese planes attacked the United States naval base at Pearl Harbor, Hawaii Territory, killing more than 2,300 Americans. A total of 12 ships sank or were beached in the attack, and nine additional vessels were damaged. The USS *Arizona* was destroyed, and the USS *Oklahoma* capsized. More than 150 aircraft were destroyed, and many were damaged. The event brought the United States into World War II.

Vaudeville—Joey Adams and Revue (1942–1950)

By the end of 1941, Tony Canzoneri—in a moment of introspection—believed that notoriety, income, and adulation were the three main elements that brought him satisfaction in his previous job. They needed to be replaced. Staying close to the ring, as a referee or manager, would provide the first element, and his business enterprises would provide the next, leaving the adulation to be satisfied through entertainment or his stage work.

Once the play closed, Tony Canzoneri couldn't get the acting bug out of his system. He began soliciting for acting roles. In preparation for the task, the former champion decided to have a face lift on March 3, 1942—having had his nose and eyelids pummeled during his career, it was time for some resurfacing. He was released from New Amsterdam Hospital following a short stay. Once out of the hospital, Canzoneri and his friend Joseph Abramowitz, aka Joey Adams, hit the subway circuit with a vaudeville act called *Joey Adams and Revue*. Vaudeville had been popular for decades and featured a mixture of specialty acts such as burlesque, comedy, and song and dance.

As 1943 began, Canzoneri's show with Joey Adams was going strong. There was a part in the floor show—featured at Leon & Eddie's over on 33 West 52nd Street—where the champ exchanged punches with Adams. Unfortunately, one night the champ forgot to pull a punch and nearly dropped Adams to a 10-count. Thankfully it brought a laugh, so Adams shook it off.

With the war raging, Tony Canzoneri was moved to 1-A status, aka qualified and available for military service. However, following a physical he was rated 4-F, not qualified for military service. Tony's brother, Corporal Joe Canzoneri, was serving as an interpreter in Italy.[1]

Still trying to stay in shape, Tony Canzoneri weighed about 155 pounds and felt comfortable—he avoided boxing as a form of physical fitness, in fear of resurrecting his urge to reenter the ring. Turned down by the army because of double vision in one eye, Canzoneri wanted to keep at least one eye healthy. Helping a friend train young boxing talent was extremely satisfying for

Comedian Joey Adams (left), serving as AGVA president, salutes jazz legend Louis "Satchmo" Armstrong in 1966. Adams, along with Tony Canzoneri and Mark Plant, had a successful run as vaudeville performers (Library of Congress).

the former champion, as was fatherhood. It was hard for him to believe his daughter was already eight years old.

Booked into the popular vaudeville scene of Miami Beach, Tony Canzoneri and Joey Adams were making the rounds. In April, they played the Olympia Theater, 172 East Flagler Street, and the Kitty Davis Theatre-Restaurant, 1610 Alton Road. The show at the latter venue was held over for weeks. In May, Canzoneri also appeared at the Monday night boxing show at Miami Field, along with Sergeant Barney Ross, Jack Britton, and the son of "Ruby Robert" Bob Fitzsimmons. Ross even made it over to Kitty Davis' restaurant to watch Canzoneri spar with Joey Adams. It was that level of camaraderie that Canzoneri missed about the sport.

Back home in June, Mr. and Mrs. Canzoneri never had a free moment. Mrs. Canzoneri, using the stage name Rita Angel, was signed to a production at the Essex Summer Playhouse in Essex, New York. Even more exciting, she passed her 20th Century–Fox screen test and would soon be heading to Hollywood.[2]

She admitted that she knew nothing about boxing when she first met Tony, then transitioned into a ringside wife. It was a learning process. When she got clamorous at boxing events, Tony would even yell to her from the ring to turn down the volume. Having been in the entertainment field since she was a teenager, Rita had taken a variety of roles from chorus girl to second lead in a play called *Summer Night*. Always tall for her age, her innocent beauty was attracting more offers now than ever before.

Tony Canzoneri and Joey Adams were back playing Leon and Eddie's at the end of July. It was their fifth engagement at the venue. The polished show had become so popular that they were contracted into the winter. The comedy team also did their part for the war effort by hosting many war bond campaign events. As time permitted, Canzoneri could be found refereeing bouts or even making an appearance at his liquor store at 594 Atlantic Avenue in Brooklyn.

The Postwar Years

The boys began revamping their vaudeville act in early 1945 and decided to add singer Mark Plant to the show. Plant had appeared in popular Broadway musicals including *Jubilee* and *Yokel Boy* and could add musical depth. Since Joey Adams was taking a screen test in March, nobody was sure how the act might be impacted. The comedian was being considered for a role in Bing Crosby's *Blue Skies*. The trio opened at the Kitty Davis Theater and Restaurant in Miami Beach on March 15 before moving to the Olympia Theater on April 11. By June, the trio was a hit working out of the Capitol Theater at 1639 Broadway in New York City.

Lou Fink, who trained fighters including Gene Tunney and Tony Canzoneri, died at his home on June 3, 1945. Louis Eberling, aka Louis "Dutch" Fink, was living with his sister at 3505 Broadway in Manhattan. The famous trainer was 54 years old.

In June 1945, the *New York Daily News* was running ads for the Tony Canzoneri Country Club, "A Champion Resort," in Marlboro, offering everything from excellent food to handball. Drop by and relax. Call Marlboro 3681 or 3481 for reservations. Word was, now that the war was over, that Tony Canzoneri hoped to turn the family farm into a posh resort like Grossinger's Catskill Resort Hotel.[3]

TONY
CANZONERI
invites you
to the...

CANZONERI
COUNTRY
CLUB

For a Wonderful Vacation!

70 Miles, N.Y.C.
Modern house and annex, hot and cold
water, many adjoining baths. Bounti-
ful country food. Children's activities
supervised.

BAR
CASINO
ENTERTAINMENT

Private Swimming
Tennis—Baseball—Ha
Boccie-Ping-Pon

A broadside for the Canzoneri Country Club in Marlboro, New York, ca. 1950s. The insert, featuring the image of Tony Canzoneri, was an image used for marketing purposes.

The Often-Redundant Art of Comparison

It has been anonymously said, "Don't compare your life with others. There's no comparison between the sun and the moon. They shine when it's their time." When a pugilist shone, he was often compared with the past: "He's the next Tony Canzoneri." At least, that was how one fighter was being heralded. His name was Anthony Gianiro, aka Tony Janiro, from Youngstown, Ohio.

Janiro received advice and assistance from fellow Youngstown native Lenny "Boom" Mancini (father of boxer Ray Mancini), who introduced Janiro to his manager, Frankie Jacobs, and boxing trainer Ray Arcel. In 1943, Janiro won the Chicago Golden Gloves Tournament of Champions by taking a decision over Jackie Graves and the Intercity Golden Gloves championship by defeating George Cooper, both in the featherweight division. In 1945, his trilogy against boxer Johnny Greco at Madison Square Garden thrust the boxer into the spotlight, though Janiro defeated Greco only once in the series. Although he was ranked in the 1940s among the top 10 middleweights, he could not live up to the skills of Tony Canzoneri, but who could?

Rita was signed to an important role in Milton Berle's production of *Spring in Brazil*. In addition to Berle, the cast included Rose Marie, Bernice Parks, and Joseph Macaulay. Rita was cast as a character named Divine Delight. Was this her big break?

Recently retired, Albert Abraham Davidoff, aka Al "Bummy" Davis, was shot and killed on November 21, 1945, during a robbery at a Brooklyn bar and grill. When Davis confronted one of four bandits during the hold-up, he was shot multiple times before the quartet fled by automobile. The proprietor of the tavern, Arthur Pulaski, was a friend of Davis. The bandits had held up multiple taverns during the early hours between 1:30 and 4:30 a.m.

Tony Canzoneri was back in a boxing ring in 1946, thankfully only as a second to boxer Gene Burton, who was battling Willie Russell in Cincinnati. The pugilist was managed by Ed "Pop" Miller, who worked with Canzoneri when he was the champion. Working with the young boxers was enjoyable for Canzoneri, a favor to Miller, and a thrill for the fans who attended the show. Fight managers loved to parade their talent in front of boxers like Canzoneri; not only was it encouragement for the youngsters, but it also made for good press. Canzoneri's troupe was touring the Midwest, so it wasn't a surprise when the situation presented itself.

The show headed south in February 1946, playing Miami Beach at venues like the Five O'clock Club. Once again, it was a huge hit and was held over. Miami in February was a pug paradise, as Canzoneri hooked up with old friends Max Baer, Melio Bettina, Maxie Rosenbloom, and Marty Servo.

The Death of George Canzoneri

It would be hard to find a father as proud of his sons and daughters as George Canzoneri. On March 27, 1946, the patriarch of the Canzoneri died at his home on Lattintown Road in Marlboro. He was 70 years old. Operating the family farm and summer hotel business for 17 years, he and his widow, Josephine, maintained the property along with their four sons, Joseph, Cyrus, Jasper, and Tony, and two daughters, Lena and Lily. George Canzoneri was buried at Cedar Hill Cemetery and Mausoleum in Newburgh, Orange County, New York.

In June, Tony Canzoneri was at Toots Shor's, at 51 West 51st Street, better known as the unofficial headquarters for sports celebrities. Getting a tap on the shoulder, he turned around and received a big hug from none other than Jimmy McLarnin. Naturally, Canzoneri recalled every detail of their Madison Square Garden battles. As interesting as eavesdropping on their conversation was watching the faces of those around them who gradually realized who these fashionably dressed gentlemen were.

The act played the Capitol Theater on Broadway at 51st Street in June. They teamed up with dancing star Hal LeRoy, along with George Paxton and his orchestra. The Capitol featured recent motion pictures, such as *Easy to Wed*, staring Van Johnson, Esther Williams, Lucille Ball, and Keenan Wynn. It wasn't unusual for a star of the featured movie to make a personal appearance, as Lucille Ball did for this picture. To get an essence of the act, all you had to remember was the North Jersey Mothers' Association awarded them the "funniest and cleanest comedy act of the year."

In August, after their show stopped playing in Cincinnati, Canzoneri entered a hospital to have more work done to repair his old fight injuries. Following the cosmetic work, the *New York Daily News* ran a photograph of the bandaged former champion in his hospital bed, being visited by Mrs. Canzoneri, aka Rita Angel. Speaking of Mrs. Canzoneri, the actress was signed by Universal and left for California in December.

George Dixon, the popular syndicated columnist, had lunch with Tony Canzoneri and asked the fighter about the spectators at his fights. Canzoneri admitted to being able to single out certain remarks, and even identify voices, during a bout. The regulars were always easy to recognize and, on occasion, if a remark was funny, Canzoneri would even chuckle. The former champion, known for his sarcasm, couldn't resist tossing one of his familiar lines to Dixon. Once, during a slow fight with little action, the silence was broken by a scream of "Hit him now! You've got the wind at your back."

By December, Tony Canzoneri was working at home with a small stable of boxers, including heavyweight Jack Bagby. Since he had extra time—his act was playing in town—he decided to take on the responsibility.

By mid–January 1947, the act was back on the road and heading to Miami to play Sam Barken's Five O'clock Club. It wasn't long before the popular troupe started breaking attendance records. Winter in Miami, as always, meant hooking up with the boys at various events. Canzoneri, along with Max Baer and Maxie Rosenbloom, was scheduled to referee at the American Legion boxing show held at the Orange Bowl, but it didn't happen. A miscommunication resulted in only Rosenbloom attending the event.

Mrs. Canzoneri, who had appeared in the Broadway shows *Spring in Brazil*, *Strip for Action*, and *Summer Night*, was also taking in the Miami fun. She was signed to do a movie in February.[4]

After refereeing the first six bouts of a boxing card at the St. Nicholas Arena in New York, Benny Leonard suffered a massive heart attack. It happened on April 18, 1947, during the first round of the bout between Mario Ramon and Bobby Williams. Leonard toppled to the canvas and died in the ring. The ringside physician, Dr. Vincent A. Nardiello, attempted to revive him but was unsuccessful. When Tony Canzoneri heard the news, he couldn't believe it. The "Ghetto Wizard" was 51 years old. Leonard was interred at Mount Carmel Cemetery in Glendale, New York.

Talking a quick break from the club circuit, Tony Canzoneri flew to Hollywood to be with his wife. His show was opening on June 25 at the El Rancho Vegas. The El Rancho Vegas was the first full-service resort built—at the southwest corner of Las Vegas Boulevard and Sahara Avenue—on the Las Vegas Strip. At the end of their Vegas stay, the group was off to the Golden Gate Theater in San Francisco. While sitting in his San Francisco dressing room, Canzoneri got a knock on the door. It was Frankie Klick, his four-time ring nemesis—the pair battled in 1933, 1934, and twice in 1935. Having left the ring in 1943, Klick looked great and couldn't resist an opportunity to drop by and visit with his rival.

Ed Sullivan wrote in one of his September 1947 columns that he heard that the Canzoneris were recently out for a rare evening together. Unfortunately, Rita was annoyed by a certain individual who refused to keep his distance—never a wise decision when a young lady happened to be married to a pugilist. This left Tony with little recourse but to deliver an overhand right. As expected, the punch hit the target but didn't drop him.

By October, the show was playing the Strand, on Broadway and 47th in Manhattan, before heading to Boston. As for Mrs. Canzoneri, now known as Rita Duncan, she was thrilled that Sol Wurtzel's melodrama *The Invisible Wall* was finally released and doing well at the box office. Told in flashback, the film recounts how gambler Harry Lane (played by Don Castle) ended up accused of murder. Cast in the 20th Century–Fox picture as Alice Jamison, Rita Duncan gave a solid performance. It wasn't a surprise that by December she was turning down substantial movie offers.

In January 1948, the trio of Joey Adams, Mark Plant, and Tony Canzoneri were back at the Olympia in Miami before heading to Pittsburgh to play Jackie Heller's Carousel over a two-week run. Their performance was so successful in Pittsburgh, they were booked for a return engagement.

Back at home in April, Tony Canzoneri attended the wedding of his younger brother, Jay. When the pugilist's mother invited Tony to see the bride's gown, he refused. The former boxer didn't think it was appropriate. That was when his mother reminded her son that the first pair of boxing gloves she ever slipped his hands into were made from her bridal gown.

Celebrating their fifth anniversary together, Joey Adams, Tony Canzoneri and Mark Plant drew up a new contract. Each would share—for life—in the others' earnings, be it night club and theatrical engagements, ancillary items, or other business ventures. It was clear to everyone that Tony Canzoneri had come a long way from his departure from the ring. The pugilist, who met Joey Adams while he was performing in a show called *They Shoulda Stood in Bed*, couldn't have met a finer partner.[5] Since that time, the former ring champion had worked on his stage presence and gradually developed into an outstanding thespian. The former champion was bringing home about $400 a week. Not bad for a second career.

The boys played the Steel Pier in Atlantic City in June before heading over to the Concord Hotel in Kiamesha, New York. They returned for a follow-up engagement at the Steel Pier in July. In August, it was out to St. Louis to play the Chase Hotel Starlight Roof. Even though the act was as polished as it could get, the nightclub circuit was noticeably slowing down.

The group found themselves in Minnesota in September. As always, Canzoneri was great about sending invitations to the local pugilists to attend as dinner guests. This meant Billy Petrolle, Mike O'Dowd, Johnny Ertle, Jonny Tillman, Augie Ratner, and the legendary Mike Gibbons would attend their gig at Club Carnival. Boxing fans flocked to the show, knowing they would encounter numerous former pugilists.

With the holiday season around the corner, the group finished playing Baltimore, packed their things, and headed to New York. They were scheduled to play the Capitol Theater during the middle of the month. Tony Canzoneri celebrated his 40th birthday on November 6, 1948, and congratulation notices appeared in the dailies across the country. Rumor had it that MGM was looking into a Tony Canzoneri biopic.

The talented act of Joey Adams, Mark Plant, and Tony Canzoneri was now commanding $2,500 a week, and many felt they were underpriced. For comparison purposes: Dean Martin and Jerry Lewis commanded $3,500; Sophie Tucker asked $6,500; Lena Horne charged $7,500; Milton Berle demanded $12,500; Abbott & Costello asked $15,000; and Danny Kaye received $20,000.

Although Joey Adams came down with bad case of laryngitis, the group took their sixth booking at the Capitol in less than 30 months. To say the boys entered the holiday season in good spirits would be an understatement.

In January 1949, columnist Earl Wilson, fascinated by the success of Tony and Rita Canzoneri, met up with the pair at a popular New York restaurant. Impressed by Tony's transition from the ring to the stage, he was struck immediately by the pair's wardrobe. Tony was decked out in a tailored suit, sporting a Homburg hat, while his beautiful wife was hard to miss in her new mink coat. During the second week of January 1949, the act played the Copacabana, the Madison Square Garden of night-clubs. Tony, rolling a fine cigar around in his mouth, reminded Wilson he was only 40, then asked the wordsmith if he liked Rita's coat. As an actor, Tony was bringing down about $25,000 (equivalent in today's money to about $300,000). Ever confident, he told Wilson what it was like being a straight man in a comedy group, then chatted about once leading a band. As Rita looked about the room—appearing as though she had heard the stories a thousand times, which she had—to see if anybody noticed her, Tony rambled on. Since he had been told he looked like Edward G. Robinson, Tony did some impressions for Wilson. They included not only Robinson but also Clark Gable and even Shirley Temple. Wilson had never heard any pug, from any genera-tion, attempt an impression of Shirley Temple—it was another first for Canzoneri.

On to Monte Proser's Copacabana, located at 10 East 60th Street, where din-ner remained priced at $2.50 and the minimum was $3.00. The boys were doing three shows a night, at 8, 10, and 2. Julie Podell, who inked the acts, was thrilled and signed the group to a long-term contract beginning on July 1.

In Buffalo in February, Canzoneri got roped into chatting about NYSAC. Far from an advocate of appointed positions, the former champion believed boxing should be governed by former fighters, say, Jack Dempsey, Gene Tunney, and even Billy Petrolle. Always asked about the present crop of fighters, Canzoneri believed Joe Louis, Willie Pep, Sugar Ray Robinson, and Ike Williams could have held their ground against numerous former ring legends. The boys were playing three shows nightly at Chez Ami at 311 Delaware Avenue in Buffalo, before they headed west—as far as Slapsie Maxie's in Los Angeles—in March.

Pass Me the Popcorn

In April, it was learned that Joey Adams, Tony Canzoneri and Mark Plant were appearing in a Hollywood motion picture called *Ringside*. The American film drama was directed by Frank McDonald for Lippert Pictures. The film starred Don "Red" Barry as Mike O'Hara, a pianist, who turned to boxing to avenge his broth-er's lost eyesight. Joey Adams played Duke Hensel, Tony Canzoneri played Swinger Markham, and Mark Plant played a gangster. The film was released on July 14, 1949, and all three of the boys got a noticeable blurb on the bottom of the movie poster.

The boys, aka "Sunday Revue," crossed the border into Canada in May to play the Elmwood in Windsor before heading back to New York. By the end of the month, the trio entertained at a professional baseball game at Ebbets Field, before Canzoneri opted for more plastic surgery to remove old scar tissue under his eyes in June. The following month, the act was playing again at the Copacabana.

With the release of *Ringside*, the incomparable comedy team started playing

George Burns once sarcastically quipped, "With the collapse of vaudeville new talent has no place to stink." Still, there was no place like the RKO Palace, shown here in 1953 (Library of Congress).

theaters in conjunction with the motion picture. Oddly, the performance by the comedy team in the movie bore little resemblance to their club act. Nevertheless, it was a great marketing ploy, and the fans loved it. As the holidays approached, the trio was back home in New York City, playing at Tom Ball's China Doll and later on the Capitol stage. It was hard to believe a decade had passed since Canzoneri was knocked out in the third round at Madison Square Garden.

In one of those interesting stories that surfaced years later, champion Tony Canzoneri was told by Lou Ambers, his sparring partner at the time, to stop smoking cigars as it was bad for his conditioning. Years later, Ambers fought Canzoneri for the title and won. Afterward, Ambers entered Canzoneri's dressing room and confirmed his old recommendation in one of those "I told you so" statements.

The boys finished their year at the RKO Boston. They were part of a show that opened with the movie *The Outlaw*. Introducing her motion picture, and naturally staying for the comedy act that followed, was none other than the curvaceous Jane Russell. As all three of the boys agreed, it was a fine way to end the year, and the decade, for that matter.

FIFTEEN

The Last Years, 1950–1959

"When he shall die, Take him and cut him out in little stars,
And he will make the face of heaven so fine, That all the world will be
in love with night
And pay no worship to the garish sun."—William Shakespeare

Most people can't imagine having one extraordinary professional career, let alone two. Even so, Tony Canzoneri, an elite athlete, had successfully transformed himself into an accomplished entertainer. Managing to transfer the satisfaction he realized from one occupation into another required dedication, hard work, and sacrifice. Like winning a boxing title, it wasn't as easy as Tony Canzoneri made it look.

The Fabulous Fifties

Having remained in Boston through the holidays, the comedy team was drawing well in January 1950, much of it to do with Jane Russell—no offense, gentlemen. The vivacious actress was promoting her film prior to the talented trio—Joey Adams, Tony Canzoneri and Mark Plant—hitting the stage. Off stage, Canzoneri was rumored to be thinking about entering the boxing promotion market in Cincinnati, partnered with Sam Feinberg. The comedy team finished the month in Baltimore.

Adams, Canzoneri and Plant appeared on Ed Sullivan's *Toast of the Town* television series during the first week of February. The exposure was wonderful for the successful act that had been playing mainly in major markets.

Mrs. Canzoneri, aka Rita Duncan, was cast in the play *The Bird Cage*, which opened on February 22, 1950. Rita played the character Renie Renay. Arthur Laurents' drama told of a man who gains control of a tawdry nightclub through nefarious means, abuses his power, and attempts to frame his partner when the club runs into financial problems. The play premiered at the Coronet Theatre at 230 West 49th Street in New York and closed on March 11, 1950.

In March, Earl Wilson, syndicated columnist of *It Happened Last Night*, ran a fascinating feature piece about the talented, attractive, and red-haired Mrs. Canzoneri. Rita Duncan (aka Rita Roy, Rita Rhoni, Rita Angel, etc.) continued to turn her share of heads on the Broadway stage. Married for 14 years, the Canzoneris shared a teenage daughter. Rita's promiscuous roles were part of being an actress and didn't bother her supportive husband. Tony Canzoneri was grateful that they both had successful entertainment careers.

The comedy team continued traveling around the country fulfilling bookings, many at old haunts, along with an occasional new one. They opened in March at the Elmwood in Windsor, Ontario. Since the successful act was drawing attention, other opportunities appeared on the horizon. Signed to emcee a quiz show for CBS television, Joey Adams was thrilled. Although there was no immediate word as to how the show might impact the comedy team, Adams hoped to keep the group intact. But that hope would soon fade.

On May 17, 1950, Tony Canzoneri was named as general manager of the Socko Athletic Club. His duties would include assisting in matchmaking and promoting contests in Cincinnati. Working with Harry Hartman, promoter, and Art Wieth, matchmaker, Canzoneri hoped to close an agreement with pugilist Rocky Graziano. Canzoneri would divide his time between Cincinnati and New York. From an outsider's perspective, it

Edward "Ed" Sullivan, shown here in 1955, was a television personality, impresario, sports and entertainment reporter, and syndicated columnist for the *New York Daily News* and the *Chicago Tribune* and *New York News* syndicate (Library of Congress).

wasn't clear how all this was going pan out, as Hartman had been on shaky ground with the Cincinnati Boxing Commission. When the foundation crumbled, Canzoneri resigned (June 20).

Back home, Tony Canzoneri began building a new boxing stable—whether it was in anticipation of the departure of Adams, he didn't say. His stable included middleweight prospect Jimmy Cerello. He still had the hotel and a farm—the latter was not the original, which was lost because of foreclosure. In September, Canzoneri did a radio show with *Daily News* sports editor Jimmy Powers. Appearing on the show with Canzoneri were Jack Skelly, Abe Attell, and Johnny Dundee. The five gentlemen chatted about everyone from John L. Sullivan and James J. Corbett to Willie Pep and Sandy Saddler. A key concern was the unauthorized broadcast of old fight films on television. While Canzoneri had filed a suit against telecasters, more needed to be done.

On a good note, Joey Adams and Tony Canzoneri teamed up once again in Binghamton, New York, on October 27, in a show to benefit the Damon Runyon Cancer Fund. The show staged at the Endicott-Johnson Recreation Hall drew about 700

A 1949 view of the corner of Broadway and West 49th Street in New York City (Library of Congress).

people. The pair would also team up for other charity events held during the holidays. Noting how much fun they were having, the pair contacted Mark Plant to reunite the triumvirate for selected appearances. The trio formally disbanded amicably on December 12, 1950. Canzoneri and Plant would continue, with Lou Nelson replacing Adams.[1]

Vaudeville—Tony Canzoneri, Mark Plant and Lou Nelson (1950–c. 1958)

As 1951 began, Tony Canzoneri was still working with the kids in the gym, like pugilist Jimmy Cerello, hoping to optimize their boxing talent. He typically found himself in the dailies for fight anniversaries, funny comments, or boxing criticism. Life appeared to be slowing down.

In March, Tony Canzoneri finally hit the road with Mark Plant and Lou Nelson. The trio played a two-week engagement at Jimmy Brink's Lookout House in Covington, Kentucky. Naturally, there was considerable pressure on Lou Nelson to fill the void left behind by the talented Joey Adams. Plant's baritone voice remained spot on, while Canzoneri continued to amuse patrons with his corny jokes, impressions, and slapstick comedy.

In May, the triad played the Sans Souci in Miami Beach. Initial reviews were good, and even Walter Winchell gave the boys a plug. The syndicated columnist especially enjoyed the work of Lou Nelson. The endorsement worked wonders to bolster the confidence of the group. By the end of June, they were playing Eddy's in Kansas City.

On July 26, 1951, Tony Canzoneri, Harry Greb and Tex Rickard were named to the Helms Athletic Foundation's Boxing Hall of Fame. The trio joined more than a dozen other boxing greats in the shrine. Founded by Paul Helms, the Helms Athletic Foundation was a Los Angeles organization that operated halls of fame for a variety of sports.

The comedy trio was working at Ben Maksik's Roadside on Flatbush Avenue in Brooklyn in September. They were on the bill with Columbia recording artist Tony Bennett, who had scored hits with "Because of You" and "I Won't Cry Anymore." The threesome finished up the year at the Enchanted Room in Yonkers and at the Chez Paree in Montreal. It was becoming increasingly clear that the act was getting stale. The departure of Adams left an enormous hole that was difficult to fill even by the talented Lou Nelson. Canadian critics pointed out the slow pace and lack of new material.

Legal Separation and Divorce

Returning home to New York, Mrs. Canzoneri underwent an appendectomy at Beth Israel Hospital. It came at a time when the couple were facing challenges to their marriage. Life wasn't easy with two successful careers that were in the public eye. Rita, still using her married name and frequently turning up in the newspapers, headed to Europe in June 1952. After the legal separation went public, even Earl

Wilson couldn't resist the opportunity to print hearsay regarding the couple. Ed Sullivan noted in his 1952 Christmas syndicated column *Little Old New York* that Mrs. Canzoneri had received her divorce decree.[2] Despite the couple's friendship with both columnists, there were times when both Rita and Tony believed their privacy and trust had been violated.

The comedy team of Tony Canzoneri and Lou Nelson was featured at the Monte Carlo Hotel's gala 1952 New Year's Eve party. Back in New York, the pair played places like the Casa Seville and The Breakers in Rochester the following month. Both Canzoneri and Nelson had reworked the act—which was often compared to Canzoneri's sketches with Joey Adams and Mark Plant—and could ad lib in an instant.

Opening night was thrilling, and the boys knew to front-load the better material, in case any members of the media had late-night deadlines. Before the show, Canzoneri fed the beat writers enough material to satisfy their needs: quotes about the fight game, a joke or two to preview the material, a funny story, and a fight prediction. The former champion used sarcasm to mask his genuine feelings and concerns. For example, in Upstate New York he joked about going back into the restaurant business if his act failed. And he was serious. Although Canzoneri and Nelson were treated like stars, especially in minor markets, their stars were dimming.

In June, the name Josephine Canzoneri, owner of a hotel and farm located on 134 acres on Lattintown Road in Marlboro, was noted for being in arrears for unpaid taxes to the amount of $953.51. If the debt was not satisfied, the land would be sold. Even though Tony Canzoneri didn't speak about it much, his Marlboro investments placed a large financial burden on his back. Ironically, he often countered a struggling investment with the creation of a new one. By the end of June, Tony Canzoneri was planning on opening a restaurant. It, he hoped, would be the gold mine—he needed more than a pot—at the end of the rainbow, at least for a period.

Trying to dismiss aspects of his personal life that appeared in the dailies, Tony Canzoneri was in New York, where he picked up his first dramatic television role with CBS in *Video Theater*. The piece was called "Face of Autumn," and he starred opposite Pat O'Brien. As the holidays approached, Canzoneri was putting the final touches on a new restaurant.

In January 1953, an interesting article about boxer "Irish" Eddie Brink appeared in a Binghamton, New York, newspaper. Brink, a resident at the time, was questioned regarding his life and career. As a competitive boxer, Brink never held a national title but fought the best, including Henry Armstrong and Tony Canzoneri. While Brink believed Armstrong was the most active fighter he ever fought, he believed Canzoneri was the best all-around boxer. Having fought Canzoneri three times—he won their first fight in 1939, then split the next two—he should know. Brink fought professionally from 1927 until 1940, entered the army in 1942, and started promoting fights in Massachusetts three years later.[3]

In January, Tony Canzoneri learned he would be one of the champions featured in a new television series called *Against the Ropes*. The program hoped to enlighten its audience on the trials and tribulations of being a professional boxer. The former fighter was trying to do as much television and radio as he could for marketing purposes. Earl Wilson, still noting the life and times of the Canzoneri clan, reported that the former pugilist was spending time with a model named Peggy Donnelly.

Countering, syndicated columnist Dorothy Kilgallen noted in March that Tony and Rita had been out and about together.

Picking up appearances while doing television and radio work, Canzoneri was complacent. He played a dramatic role in Rod Serling's *The Twilight Rounds* for the Kraft Television Theater in May. Although the story centered on an ex-lightweight boxing champion, Canzoneri played the role of a bartender. Not long after, Canzoneri was off to Marlboro, where his mother was recovering from surgery.

Death of Josephine Canzoneri

The matriarch of the Canzoneri clan, Josephine Canzoneri, died on August 21, 1953, in Newburgh, New York. She was interred at Cedar Hill Cemetery and Mausoleum, 5468 Route 9, Newburgh. Washington Irving once wrote, "A mother is the truest friend we have, when trials heavy and sudden fall upon us; when adversity takes the place of prosperity; when friends desert us; when trouble thickens around us, still will she cling to us, and endeavor by her kind precepts and counsels to dissipate the clouds of darkness, and cause peace to return to our hearts." The quote was an accurate assessment of how many in the family felt about Josephine Canzoneri.

Still appearing in the "Remember When..." and "Anniversary" columns, Tony Canzoneri never gave them much thought. However, on September 28, 1953, it was hard for the boxer to accept that 25 years had passed since he met French featherweight champion André Routis at Madison Square Garden. Where had the time gone? Moreover, since his retirement, "the next Tony Canzoneri," and there were many of them, had come and gone. Nevertheless, Sammy Goldman caught press when he compared rising star Lulu Perez, age 20, to Canzoneri. Such comparisons were silly, yet they sold newspapers. Perez would fight 56 bouts, winning 39 of them, and be out of boxing by 1958. If it hadn't been for a controversial victory over quintessential pugilist Willie Pep, he would have slipped into obscurity.[4]

The year 1954 began with indications that Tony Canzoneri and a partner were opening an exclusive club on East 69th Street in New York City. Initial reports claimed it would be called "The Tone." Along with other journalists, Ed Sullivan continued to reunite the Canzoneris. The former champion had mixed feelings about the comments. Meanwhile, he emceed a new show at Frank Russo's Top Hat at 407 Franklin Avenue in the Franklin Square section of Long Island. The weekend shows, as anticipated, drew plenty of athletes and sports fans.

Meanwhile, the former Mrs. Canzoneri was starring in a Puerto Rican television series called *Rita Mason, Girl Treasury Agent*. Earl Wilson noted that Denise Canzoneri, Tony and Rita's daughter, was rumored to be making a dancing appearance on Broadway—looked as if the family tree was an apple.

The Evolving Fight Game

It appeared that the days of fighting through the box office, or money pipeline, were gone. Television had changed everything—a $4,000 television paycheck became as common as a mugger in Central Park. In the old days, pugs were looking for $50,000 to $100,000 gates, and the reason was simple: They could get it. Tony Canzoneri, along with Sammy Goldman, would have laughed at the thought of entering the ring against Barney Ross or Jimmy McLarnin for anything less than a big payday.[5] Also, there was a time when it was assumed that any big championship fight was going to be held in New York City, but that too had changed. Of the big fights in 1955, only Rocky Marciano's knockout of Archie Moore landed in New York. Ralph "Tiger" Jones' upset of Ray Robinson took place in Chicago, as did Robinson's knockout of Bobo Olson. Pascual Perez knocked out Yoshio Shirai in Tokyo, Ike Williams knocked out Beau Jack in Augusta, and Carmen Basilio duplicated his knockout victory over Tony DeMarco in Boston.

Picking up an impressive watch at the annual dinner of the New York Boxing Writers Association, Tony Canzoneri couldn't resist thinking it was about time—the pun was intended. The special auxiliary awards, as they were called, were a welcome way to salute former champions, future champions, trainers, and contributors to the sport.

The former champion became part-owner of the Paddock Bar and Grill, at 1634 Broadway near 50th Street in the Winter Garden building. The official opening of the restaurant was on April 4, 1955. Fight fans now had six boxing-themed saloons they could visit in the city.[6]

In addition to Jacobs Beach, or West 49th Street between Broadway and Eighth Avenue—specifically, the front of Jacobs' ticket office at 225 West 49th Street—fight fans could also visit Cauliflower Alley. This location included Jack Dempsey's, on the west side of Broadway between 49th and 50th streets, and the Paddock Bar and Grill, and there was talk that Mickey Walker was going to take over House of Champs at 51st and Broadway. At the Paddock Bar and Grill, Tony Canzoneri greeted visitors and made them feel welcome. Naturally, all his friends dropped by, including Joe DiMaggio, the former Yankees legend. It was in San Francisco, while training for a fight inside Dolph Thomas' Gym, that former player and manager Lefty O'Doul introduced DiMaggio to Canzoneri. Although out of baseball, "Joltin' Joe" remained popular partly owing to his marriage to actress Marilyn Monroe—she had filed for divorce a year earlier.

In between his business exploits, Tony Canzoneri squeezed in some acting. He played the role of a boxing trainer in "Shadow of the Champ," a drama shown on *Television Playhouse*. Lee Grant, Robert Middleton, Eli Wallach, and Jack Warden were featured. While there were times when Canzoneri wanted to play more roles than those associated with boxing, he was grateful for the opportunity. He played a gangster on ABC-TV's program *Star Tonight* as well as other roles on the series. Canzoneri also appeared as a panelist on *Let's See*, the television quiz show. He was seen about town with a few ladies, including Susan Travis, who was rumored to be the next Mrs. Canzoneri. Speaking of the latter, Tony was rumored to be seen dining with his ex-wife Rita, aka Rita Ross, in his restaurant in July. The *Philadelphia Inquirer* even published a photograph of Rita Canzoneri, along with a column reporting a possible reconciliation.

On September 27, 1955, one of the best comical acts in show business history reunited at the Fox Theater in Hackensack, New Jersey. Tony Canzoneri and Joey Adams were one of the features of an all-star benefit stage show for the Boys Towns of Italy.

Hollywood caught the boxing bug in 1955, as they bought the rights to Vince and Joe Dundee's life story and already had transactions pending for biopics of Tony Canzoneri, Jack Dempsey, Barney Ross, and Mickey Walker. They also agreed to pay Rocky Graziano $210 a week, for 10 years, for the rights to his book *Someone Up There Likes Me*.[7]

Always willing to lend a hand, if there was time, Tony Canzoneri was a guest referee at a PAL (Police Athletic League) event held at Macy's in Herald Square— the event took place on April 2, 1956. Joining Canzoneri were James J. Braddock, Gus Lesnevich and Mickey Walker. It was Macy's Children's Week and one of 50 events.

Gossip columnist Dorothy Kilgallen, always keeping one eye on Tony Canzoneri and his ex-wife Rita, noted that the pair had been seen out almost every night and that they were still considering a reconciliation.[8] Still believing in the twentieth century mantra that bad publicity didn't exist, the pair were getting a thrill at the rumors.

The Ring Hall of Fame

Established in 1922, *The Ring* magazine quickly became the bible of boxing. In 1954, the magazine established its own boxing hall of fame and temporarily located it at the headquarters of the magazine in the *new* Madison Square Garden. Magazine editor and founder Nat Fleisher patterned the selection process after the Baseball Hall of Fame. It was an honor to be selected, as Tony Canzoneri was in 1956. He and six other inductees—Barney Ross, Jimmy McLarnin, Tommy Loughran, Jem Driscoll, George Dixon, and Peter Jackson—brought the total number to 41. As fate had it, the Hall of Fame inducted 155 members before it was abandoned after the 1987 inductions.

During the fall of 1956, Tony Canzoneri, who had been a greeter at his own restaurant, began exploring other opportunities, such as acting as an agent for fighters interested in the entertainment field. Many were fascinated by the transition. While the newspapers claimed his restaurant was doing a steady business, steady was not enough.

Banquets, banquets, banquets—as part of a retired professional fighter's life, they were as common as ticket scalpers outside a popular venue. The charismatic Tony Canzoneri was the perfect celebrity guest. He enjoyed the adulation and loved delivering his comedy shtick, and they were the perfect setting to polish new material for his stage act. It was also a great opportunity to establish new contacts in all aspects of life. Canzoneri, who understood notoriety had a short shelf-life, also used the dais as a marketing tool for many of his new ventures. That's why, nearly two decades after he last fought professionally, Tony Canzoneri couldn't walk down Broadway without getting stopped for an autograph.

Happily admitting that he must be growing old, as his daughter now got more space in the syndicated columns than he or his wife, Tony Canzoneri always had that proud smile possessed by a loving father. He truly wanted the very best for his daughter, not to mention his ex-wife.[9]

Trying to avoid one of the many excavations being conducted on Broadway, Tony

Canzoneri tripped and hurt his foot. The former champion, hobbling around with a cane, wondered where a good corner man was when you needed him. Lately, when he was standing or sitting, Canzoneri was recording his life story with hopes of landing a publishing agreement. He was also grabbing guest spots on television and radio programs—he was a *Red Barber's Corner* television guest in July.[10]

Everybody knew that if you couldn't catch Tony Canzoneri at The Paddock, then you could always try Lindy's, the original located on the east side of Broadway, between 49th and 50th streets or just a block south of the Winter Garden Theatre—it closed in July 1957. A second location was added in 1930 at 1655 Broadway, on the northwest corner of Broadway and 51st Street, a block north. Proprietor Leo Lindemann's all-night delicatessen gradually became a favorite haunt for the city night owls. Damon Runyon was not only a regular but also the restaurant's prime source of marketing; moreover, it (as Mindy's) regularly appeared in his syndicated column or in one of his short stories. Even if a visitor took their chances, they were likely to see a celebrity indulging on strawberry-topped cheesecake.[11]

The opening of *West Side Story*, in 1958, contributed an additional $1,500 a week to the cash registers at Tony Canzoneri's adjacent saloon—while the sign included the fighter's name, he had gradually left the business. This was the original Broadway production, directed and choreographed by Jerome Robbins, and it marked Stephen Sondheim's debut. It ran for 732 performances before going on tour. Talk about being at the right place, or selling the right place, at the right time; this was it. The former champion was now eyeing an establishment in Philadelphia.

Having worked up a new floor show, Tony Canzoneri was appearing on Friday and Saturday nights at Footies Melody Inn in Vineland, New Jersey. Later, he headed over to the Rainbow Inn in North Brunswick, New Jersey, to act as a host for their Saturday evening shows. Understanding the value of exposure, Canzoneri constantly tried to maintain his business contacts.[12]

The Canzoneri complex, aka Canzoneri Country Club and what little land remained, was sold and renamed San Catri (Lodge). It was purchased by a family friend who believed he could revitalize the resort. Without the Canzoneri name, much of the aura had changed. Not surprisingly, when the former champion retired, business gradually declined.

Tony Canzoneri turned 50 on November 6, 1958. Like novelist James Jones, baseball player Buddy Kerr, football player Lou Rymkus, and cartoon producer Stephen Bosustow, the former champion received syndicated birthday wishes in newspapers across the country. Unlike some at this age, Tony Canzoneri had exceeded his ring and entertainment goals, but he fell short of his economic needs. While freed of some family obligations, he was single and seeking gainful employment. Thankfully, he was Tony Canzoneri, whose image sat alongside the dictionary definition of charismatic.

As 1958 ended, Canzoneri was back at his Broadway restaurant. The transaction for his place in Philadelphia never came to fruition, so he returned home.[13]

The Broadway March of Dimes' Division "Man of the Year" award went to Joey Adams. A testimonial dinner was held in his honor at the Waldorf-Astoria in New York in April 1959. The dinner, attended by a boatload of celebrities, including Tony Canzoneri, raised more than $25,000 for the March of Dimes. As anticipated, Adams and Canzoneri shared a few jokes and memories.[14]

(Top) A guest room (Room 616) at the Hotel Bryant at Broadway and 54th Street in 1941 (Library of Congress). The exterior (bottom left) and interior (bottom right) of the popular Coffee Bar at the Hotel Bryant at Broadway and 54th Street (Library of Congress).

During the first week of December, Canzoneri was asked if he ever recalled his past. Reminded that two decades had passed since he left the ring, Canzoneri smiled. As he had done before, he didn't live in the past or for it. He earned his purses, spent them, and having reached the half-century mark in age, he was enjoying his current enterprises.

The Final Bell

"Did you see Tony today?" one of his business partners at the Paddock Bar and Grill yelled to one of his employees. "No," was the response. Sure, he had been late a few times in the past, but it was rare. And he always called if there was a problem.

Tony Canzoneri had been living at the Hotel Bryant, off Broadway at 54th Street. As the minutes passed, one of Tony's partners decided to contact the hotel. Late in the afternoon, on Thursday, December 10, 1959, bellboy Frank Medici, along with Canzoneri's friend Willie Lustig, used a pass key to open the door at 4:45 p.m.—this after repeated knocking and verbal commands to open the door. The bellhop entered the room at the request of Norman Schwartz, a friend of the former champion.

There they found the 51-year-old gladiator, clad in his underwear, unresponsive and lying across his bed. It was estimated he had been dead for two days.[15]

The boxer had hung a "Do Not Disturb" sign from his door, which prevented the hotel maids from entering his room. Police from the 18th Precinct answered the call and, following a cursory view, believed the pugilist died of natural causes. This observation was confirmed by medical examiner John Devlin from the coroner's office. Tony Canzoneri's body was removed to the Bellevue Hospital morgue to determine the precise cause of death. There was no confirmation whether an autopsy would be performed.

Canzoneri was last seen, by those who worked at the hotel, on Tuesday evening. He was in fine spirits with no sign of distress. The former champion, who had been living at the hotel for more than a year, had been hosting at his restaurant for the past three years. Canzoneri was paid for the use of his name that adorned the Broadway restaurant.

Much was made of Canzoneri living at the midtown hotel room at a rate of $21 per week (adjusted for inflation today, it would be $202.89). Granted, it wasn't a luxury hotel like the Waldorf-Astoria in midtown Manhattan, but it was convenient, and the hotel enjoyed the prestige associated with their guest.

Word quickly traveled the length of Broadway, and it wasn't long before patrons began showing up to the restaurant. Some stood outside and smoked a cigar in his honor, while others dropped off everything from flowers to newspaper clippings. When they chatted about the man with the trademark smile, they too had grins on their faces.

A hospital autopsy conducted on December 11, 1959, confirmed that Tony Canzoneri died of *natural* heart disease. The report was issued by Dr. Sidney Weinberg. The body was claimed by Jasper Canzoneri. Tony Canzoneri's body was in repose at the Frank E. Campbell funeral home at Madison Avenue and 81st Street. Funeral services were held on December 15, 1959, at 11 a.m., with burial in Mt. Olivet Cemetery, Maspeth, New York.

More than 400 mourners turned out to bid farewell to Tony Canzoneri at his funeral services. Although many had to be turned away, their presence was indicative of the popularity of the quintessential boxer and talented entertainer.

Dr. Norris Tibbets of Riverside Church conducted services. Appropriately, comedian Joey Adams gave a quiet eulogy filled with delightful, yet tearful, remembrances of his partner.

Abe Attell, Phil Kaplan, Jimmy McLarnin, and Barney Ross were honorary pallbearers, and of the many friends and acquaintances in attendance, noted were Paul Berlenbach, Teddy Brenner, Billy Brown, Joe Ferrera, Ruby Goldstein, Murray Goodman, Rocky Graziano, Lou Harper, Harvey Kelly, Emil Lence, Gus Lesnevich, Harry Markson, Toots Shor, Sam Taub, and Allie Tedesko.

Instant Memories

He was described as altruistic, charming, colorful, courageous, fashionable, friendly, funny, likeable, lively, popular, quick, smart, strong, talented, and witty. His disposition, anchored by his emblematic smile, made him approachable. Even though he was a celebrity and dressed like one, he wasn't conceited and he did not feel he was any different. Instantly recalled for his career record, title bouts—featherweight, lightweight, and junior lightweight—humble beginnings, longevity, earnings, comedy act with Joey Adams, and entrepreneurship, Tony Canzoneri was an incomparable boxer. People immediately recalled when his name was mentioned: Pete Herman, Sammy Goldman, Benny Bass, Andre Routis, Barney Ross, Jimmy McLarnin, and Al "Bummy" Davis.

The first-round knockout of Al Singer on November 14, 1930, the knockout loss to Al "Bummy" Davis, the second of his three scraps with Jackie "Kid" Berg, Lou Ambers pleading with him to stop smoking, and getting hit in the head by the microphone before the start of his battle against Jimmy McLarnin were the stories that immediately surfaced with his passing.

Of the men who likely knew Tony Canzoneri better than anyone, Joey Adams believed the boxer suffered from a broken heart because of his divorce from Rita Roy. The former champion was lonely and economically concerned. Although their successful comedy act had lasted for more than a decade—they pocketed as much as $30,000 a year—Canzoneri had trouble ignoring business opportunities and could never say no to a friend in need.

Sammy Goldman, confined to a wheelchair for the past five years, was heartbroken. Acknowledging Canzoneri's extraordinary ability, the talented manager believed his fighter's best battle—it occurred at the pinnacle of his career—was his first bout against Jimmy McLarnin. Pausing for a moment, Goldman smiled, then confirmed that Canzoneri was a simple guy: He once spent 20 minutes explaining to his fight manager how to milk a cow.

One of the greatest boxers ever, Tony Canzoneri (shown here in the 1920s) compiled a record of 137–24–10 (with four no-decisions and 44 knockouts). He was inducted into the International Boxing Hall of Fame in 1990 as part of its inaugural class.

"Hey, Tony, you ever play the stock market?"

"No, Joey."

"Well, do you ever play the horses?"

"Oh yeah, I love going to the track."

"You know the difference between playing the stock market and the horses is that one of the horses must win."

"Thanks, Joey, I'll remember that because the last horse I bet on was so slow, the jockey kept a diary of the trip."

Appendix A
Tony Canzoneri Fight Record

Born: November 6, 1908, in Slidell, Louisiana

Died: December 9, 1959, in New York City

Siblings: Brothers: Joseph, Cyrus, and Jasper; Sisters: Lena and Lilian

Alias: The Italian Terror, Williamsburgh Flash, the Italian Flash, Little Paisan, Little Babe Ruth, Canzi, Canzy

Stance: Orthodox

Measurements: In March 1927: Height: 5'4", Weight: 118 pounds, Neck: 15 inches, Reach: 62 inches, Chest Normal: 30 inches, Chest Expanded: 34½ inches, Forearm: 9¼ inches, Waist: 26 inches, Thigh: 16 inches, Calf: 9 inches, and Ankle: 7½ inches.

Fight managers: Sam Goldman, 133 West 38th Street, New York, NY

Sam Goldman fighters: Tony Canzoneri, Basil Galiano, Pete Herman, to name a few

Trainers/seconds: Izzy "the Painter" Faber (Isadore Faber), Sal Goldie, Dan Florio, Nick Florio, Al Ramo, Lou Fink, James Riccio

Career span: 1925–1939

Ranking span: 1927–1939

Championship span: five championship reigns—featherweight (1927–1928), lightweight (1930–1933, 1935–1936), junior welterweight (1931–1932, 1933)

Punch analysis: Fantastic right cross, great left jab, solid left hook to the body

Boxing inspirations: Joseph Canzoneri, Pete Herman, Basil Galiano, Benny Leonard

Boxing style: The jumping jack style, used by Pal Moore of Memphis, was adopted to some extent by Canzoneri; superb footwork, head movement (including backward), and defensive skills

Pre-fight meal: varied

Superstitions: Blessed himself before each round; always put his right glove on last

Hardest puncher: Benny Bass

Favorite colors: blue, gray, and violet

Favorite dish: Spaghetti

Favorite pastime: cards, movies, fashion (52 suits could attest to that), golf, and horse racing

First mention of being a potential three-division champion: *Brooklyn Daily Eagle,* January 22, 1926, page 22

Notes: As a youngster, Canzoneri wanted to be a cartoonist, and he was prone to doodling given pencil and paper. He enjoyed playing cards, games like pinochle and even bridge, as a form of relaxation. He also enjoyed bowling. Canzoneri was once fired as a sparring partner by Fidel La Barba's manager for working La Barba too hard.

Abbreviations: A.C. = Athletic Club; Aud = Auditorium; Bldg = Building; Can = Canceled; D = Draw; DV = Date of Fight Varies; E = Exhibition; KO = Knockout Victory; L = Lost; ME = Main Event; MSG = Madison Square Garden; ND = No Decision; NWD = Newspaper Decision; Post = Postponed; S.C. = Sporting Club; SP = Spelling Variations; Stad = Stadium; Sub = Substitute; TBD = To be Determined; TKO = Technical Knockout; W = Won

The Bouts

To better frame the career of Tony Canzoneri, assorted scheduled bouts that never took place are included. All fights have been confirmed by at least three sources. The names used to identify certain venues may vary.

Amateur (Selected)

At age eight, Tony Canzoneri received a (handmade) pair of boxing gloves for Christmas. The rest, as they say, was history.

1922

Fibbing about his age, Tony Canzoneri, 14, began his amateur career at the Gayoso Athletic Club, owned by ex-fighter Kid Gage, in New Orleans. A boxer named Mike Bernard, in the 100-pound division, was believed to be his first amateur opponent.

1924

Having arrived from Louisiana in the fall, Tony Canzoneri, with 17 amateur bouts under his belt, joined the National Athletic Club, where he participated in 84 amateur fights—a figure quoted often, but not confirmed—in less than one year. Canzoneri claimed 105 amateur bouts before the age of 16. Some of those were contest bouts, such as the St. John's College Tournament, while others were simply club bouts.

1925

New York State Amateur Boxing Tournament— 118-Pound Championship

Date	Opponent	Location	Result	Comments
Jan 8	Henry Usse	New York, NY	W 3	Madison Square Garden
Jan 8	Peter Burns	New York, NY	W 3	MSG

Date	Opponent	Location	Result	Comments
Jan 8	Joe Scalfaro	New York, NY	W 3	MSG, final
Feb 9	Jimmy Mendoza	New York, NY	W4	Unity Club
Mar 2	Frank Montana	New York, NY	—	Rink Arena; scheduled
Mar 2	Nick Del Genio	New York, NY	W3	Rink Arena
Mar 2	Jimmy McNamara	New York, NY	W4	Rink Arena

Amateur Athletic Union—
National Junior Boxing Championship

Date	Opponent	Location	Results	Comments
Mar 11	William Jones	Baltimore, MD	KO	104th Medical Reg. Armory
Mar 12	Sidney Lampe	Baltimore, MD	W3	Won bantam title

Metropolitan AAU Championship

Date	Opponent	Location	Results	Comments
Mar 18	Sammy Tisch	New York, NY	W3	MSG
Mar 19	Edward T. Healey	New York, NY	W3	MSG—semi-final
Mar 19	Tommy Lorenzo	New York, NY	L	MSG—defaulted
—	injured eye			
Mar 23	Jimmy Mendoza	New York, NY	—	Rink Arena; withdrew
Mar 23	Tommy Lorenzo	New York, NY	—	Rink Arena; withdrew

State Finals—National AAU Representative

Date	Opponent	Location	Results	Comments
Apr 6	Tom Donnelly	New York, NY	KO1	New York A.C.

National AAU Championship Tournament

Date	Opponent	Location	Results	Comments
Apr 13	Carl Kenney	Boston, MA	W3	
Apr 13	August Gotto	Boston, MA	L3	
Apr 27	Jimmy McNamara	New York, NY	W3	Rink Arena

Semi-Monthly Amateur Boxing Tournament

Date	Opponent	Location	Results	Comments
May 14	Louis McFarland	New York, NY	KO1	Crescent A.C.
May 14	Frank Neve	New York, NY	W3	Crescent A.C.

Semi-Monthly Amateur Boxing Tournament

Date	Opponent	Location	Results	Comments
May 28	James San Fillipo	New York, NY	KO1	Crescent A.C.
May 28	Abe Spinner	New York, NY	KO1	Crescent A.C.

Semi-Monthly Amateur Boxing Tournament

Date	Opponent	Location	Results	Comments
June 18	Vinny LaGuardia	New York, NY	W3	Crescent A.C.
June 18	Tommy Lorenzo	New York, NY	W3	Crescent A.C

Notes: *The February 9 bout was controversial owing to an extra round. Tony Canzoneri held three amateur titles—New York State, metropolitan and junior national. Fighting at 112 pounds, he was unmatched in his division. In June 1925, Canzoneri began sparring with Eddie Shea, who was training for a bantamweight title bout against Charlie Phil Rosenberg.*

Professional

1925

Date	Opponent	Location	Results	Comments
July 24	Jack Gardner	New York, NY	KO1	Pro debut, Rockaway Club
Aug 5	Ray Cummings	Bayonne, NJ	W4	Bayonne Stadium
Aug 8	Henry Usse	New York, NY	W4	Ridgewood Grove S.C.
Aug 22	Henry Usee	New York, NY	W6	Ridgewood Grove S.C.
Sep 12	Paulie Porter	New York, NY	TKO5	Ridgewood Grove S.C.
Sep 16	Lew Hurley	New York, NY	—	Scheduled
Oct 10	Johnny Huber	New York, NY	W6	Commonwealth S.C.
Nov 7	Pete Passafiume	New York, NY	—	Ridgewood Grove S.C.
Nov 7	Henry Molinari	New York, NY	KO1	Ridgewood Grove S.C.; sub
Nov 12	Harry Brandon	New York, NY	W4	Broadway Arena
Nov 26	Ralph Nischo	New York, NY	W4	Ridgewood Grove S.C.
Dec 7	Danny Terris	New York, NY	W6	Broadway Arena
Dec 23	Danny Terris	New York, NY	KO4	MSG debut as professional

Notes: *Years later, Jack Gardner (Grodner) would go into business with Tony Canzoneri. (See "A La Carte," News Journal, January 25, 1957, 22.) His professional debut was promoted by Bob Levy; Sammy*

Goldman paid Canzoneri $40, all in $1 bills, for his first bout; Tony Canzoneri claimed he fought 14 fights in 1925 without a defeat, winning most by knockout; Jack Gardner (Grodner) was Canzoneri's first knockout victim. Canzoneri referred to him as Jack Gardner. This bout was also quoted as taking place on July 17, 1925; Henry Usse was Canzoneri's first back-to-back opponent and his first six-round opponent; Canzoneri scored the first knockout in the new Madison Square Garden at the expense of Danny Terris. As a result, Tex Rickard gave him a watch. All professional title bouts appear above Championship subtitles.

1926

Date	Opponent	Location	Results	Comments
Jan 13	Georgie Nickfor	New York, NY	KO4	Manhattan Casino
Jan 21	Andy DeVodi	New York, NY	—	Scheduled
Jan 21	Kid Rash	New York, NY	W4	Broadway Arena
Jan 26	Mickey Lewis	New York, NY	W4	Pioneer S.C.
Feb 13	Romeo Vaughn	New York, NY	W6	Ridgewood Grove
Feb 18	Al Scorda	New York, NY	W4	Broadway Arena
Mar 6	Bobby Wolgast	New York, NY	W6	Ridgewood Grove
Mar 11	Jacinto Valdez	New York, NY	W4	Commonwealth S.C.
Mar 20	Tommy Milton	New York, NY	W6	Ridgewood Grove
Mar 25	Mike Esposito	New York, NY	D4	MSG-2
May 8	Benny Hall	New York, NY	D6	Ridgewood Grove
May 28	Sammy Nable	New York, NY	TKO6	Coney Island Stadium
June 16	Sonny Smith	New York, NY	W6	Golden City Arena
June 21	Willie Suess	New York, NY	W4	Dexter Park Arena
June 25	Archie Bell	New York, NY	TKO5	Coney Island Stadium
July 26	Manny Wexler	New York, NY	KO5	Dexter Park Arena
Aug 9	Young Montreal	New York, NY	W6	Dexter Park Arena
Aug 14	Bucky Josephs	New York, NY	W6	Ridgewood Grove
Aug 28	Georgie Mack	New York, NY	D6	Queensboro Stadium
—	injured eye			
Sep 3	Murray Layton	New York, NY	—	Scheduled
Sep 20	George Marks	New York, NY	W6	Dexter Park Arena
Oct 5	Benny Hall	New York, NY	W6	Pioneer S.C.
Nov 6	Davey Abad	New York, NY	L10	Ridgewood Grove
Nov 13	Georgie Mack	New York, NY	—	Scheduled
Nov 13	Monk Kelly	New York, NY	—	Scheduled
Nov 13	Enrique Savaardo	New York, NY	TKO5	Walker A.C.
Nov 22	André Routis	New York, NY	W12	Broadway Arena
Dec 10	Mike Esposito	Waterbury, CT	—	Withdrew
Dec 17	Bud Taylor	New York, NY	—	MSG; withdrew
Dec 17	Bushy Graham	New York, NY	W10	MSG-3

Notes: *Manhattan Casino was also known as the New Manhattan Sporting Club; Canzoneri's battle against Wolgast saw a double knockdown; Canzoneri suffered back-to-back draws for the first time (Esposito, Hall); some sources incorrectly note Nable bout as TKO5; first back-to-back knockouts (Bell, Wexler); the bout against Manny Wexler, promoted by Johnny Attell, was believed to be Canzoneri's first main event; during his fight with Young Montreal, his opposer burst out laughing as a result of Canzoneri's mimicking actions; Canzoneri took his first ring loss to Davey Abad, who also defeated him as an amateur, ending his consecutive streak of more than 30 bouts without a loss; Canzoneri's victory over Graham brought him into the forefront of the division; Canzoneri always considered his December 17 bout against Bushy Graham his first big break.*

1927

Date	Opponent	Location	Results	Comments
Jan 12	Joe Ryder	New York, NY	D10	Manhattan Casino
Jan 22	Vic Burrone	New York, NY	W10	Ridgewood Grove
Feb 4	Johnny Green	New York, NY	W8	MSG-4
Feb 10	Midget Smith	Chicago, IL	—	Scheduled; can
Feb 10	Bud Taylor	Chicago, IL	—	Scheduled; can

Canzoneri suffered a foot injury

Date	Opponent	Location	Results	Comments
Feb 24	Bud Taylor	Chicago, IL	—	Scheduled; can
Mar 7	Cal. Joe Lynch	New York, NY	W10	Broadway Arena
Mar 26	Bud Taylor	Chicago, IL	D10	Coliseum

Vacant NBA Bantamweight Title

Date	Opponent	Location	Results	Comments
Apr 18	Vic Burrone	New York, NY	D10	St. Nicholas Arena
Apr 25	Harold Smith	New York, NY	KO3	Broadway Arena
May 3	Ray Rychell	Chicago, IL	KO7	Coliseum
May 24	Eddie Anderson	New York, NY	—	Rained out
May 25	Eddie Anderson	New York, NY	—	Rained out
June 7	Eddie Anderson	New York, NY	—	Postponed
June 8	Vic Burrone	New York, NY	—	Ebbets Field
June 23	Bud Taylor	Chicago, IL	—	Scheduled; post
June 24	Bud Taylor	Chicago, IL	L10	Wrigley Field

Vacant NBA Bantamweight Title

Date	Opponent	Location	Results	Comments
July 27	Cal. Joe Lynch	Cleveland, OH	W10	Olympic Arena
Aug 9	Eddie Anderson	New York, NY	W10	Queensboro Stadium
Aug 17	Pete Sarmiento	Brooklyn, NY	KO1	Ebbets Field
Aug 25	Mexican Joe Rivers	Kansas City, MO	NWD10	Convention Hall
Sep 2	Eddie Anderson	Chicago, IL	LF2	Mills Stadium

license suspended 90 days by Illinois Commission

Date	Opponent	Location	Results	Comments
Sep 7	Red Chapman	Brooklyn, NY	—	Ebbets Field; can

reinstated for overweight suspension

Date	Opponent	Location	Results	Comments
Sep 28	Johnny Dundee	Brooklyn, NY	—	Ebbets Field; can
Oct 3	Tommy Ryan	New York, NY	W10	Broadway Arena
Oct 24	Johnny Dundee	New York, NY	W15	MSG-5; controversial
Nov 7	Billy Henry	Philadelphia, PA	KO2	Arena
Nov 22	Vincent DiLeo	New York, NY	TKO1	Olympia Boxing Club
Dec 1	Ignacio Fernandez	New York, NY	W10	MSG-6
Dec 1	Bud Taylor	New York, NY	—	Suspended
Dec 5	Bud Taylor	New York, NY	—	MSG; post
Dec 30	Bud Taylor	New York, NY	W10	MSG-7

NYSAC World Featherweight Title

Notes: Chick Suggs was the initial opponent signed to the May 3 bout; the September 7 battle, promoted by Humbert J. Fugazy, was scheduled; Dundee fought outside featherweight limit on October 24. This bout was viewed by some as being for the featherweight title (the title Dundee won from Eugene Criqui, acknowledged by many newspapers, including the Washington Times). Dundee was stripped of his title for not defending it on time. NYSAC did not recognize the October 24 bout as a title fight. On December 1, Ignacio Fernandez substituted for Bud Taylor. Also on December 1, Bud Taylor was suspended for an injury claim; On December 5, Canzoneri's bout against Bud Taylor was postponed because of injury.

1928

Date	Opponent	Location	Results	Comments
Jan 27	Benny Bass	New York, NY	—	MSG; post
Jan 30	Pete Nebo	Philadelphia, PA	D10	Arena
Feb 10	Benny Bass	New York, NY	W15	MSG-8

NBA World Featherweight Championship

Date	Opponent	Location	Results	Comments
Feb 17	Red Chapman	Boston, MA	—	Argonne Athletic Association
Feb 23	Pete Passafiume (Passifiume)	Brooklyn, NY	W4	Broadway Arena
Mar/Apr	tonsillitis/grippe			
Mar 23	André Routis	New York, NY	—	MSG; post
Apr 16	TBD	New Orleans, LA	—	TBD
May 17	Claude Wilson	New Orleans, LA	—	Postponed
May 28	Claude Wilson	New Orleans, LA	KO1	Coliseum Arena
June 13	Vic Foley	Montreal, Canada	W10	Baseball Stadium
June 21	Joey Sangor	Chicago, IL	—	Scheduled
June 27	Harry Blitman	Philadelphia, PA	L10	Baker Bowl
June 27	cracked ribs, followed by pneumonia			
Aug 28	Bobby Garcia	Newark, NJ	KO1	Newark Velodrome

Date	Opponent	Location	Results	Comments
Sep 28	André Routis	New York, NY	L15	MSG-9

World Featherweight Championship

injured right arm

Date	Opponent	Location	Results	Comments
Oct 29	Gaston Charles	New York, NY	W10	Broadway Arena
Dec 8	Chick Suggs	New York, NY	KO6	Olympia A.C.
Dec 14	Al Singer	New York, NY	D10	MSG-10
Dec 17	Phil McGraw	New York, NY	—	Broadway Arena

Notes: *In February 1928, it was stated in the* Bismarck Tribune *that Canzoneri had already earned $194,000 as a professional boxer; Canzoneri often called his battle against southpaw Harry Blitman, on June 27, one of his toughest bouts ever. Canzoneri, like many orthodox fighters, didn't favor a bout with a southpaw. Later, in 1955, Blitman claimed he was told to ease up on his rival. Following the fourth round, Blitman was rumored to have switched his style of fighting to carry Canzoneri over the distance. Canzoneri was so "busted up" after the fight it was rumored—a newspaper extra claimed he perished at age 20—that he died. Scoring for the battle against Routis, on September 28, varied considerably. For example, some scoring sheets had Canzoneri taking 11 of the 15 rounds. Canzoneri was suffering from a lingering illness when he fought Routis. He also had difficulty making weight and was two and a half pounds over featherweight limit at noon the day of the fight.*

1929

Date	Opponent	Location	Results	Comments
Jan 18	Armando Santiago	Chicago, IL	KO5	Coliseum
Feb 6	Joey Sangor	Chicago, IL	KO7	Coliseum
Feb 19	Bill Wallace	Cleveland, OH	—	Public hall; tentative
Feb 26	Ignacio Fernandez	Chicago, IL	W10	Coliseum
Mar 8	Cecil Payne	Detroit, MI	W10	Olympic Stadium
Mar 28	Ray Miller	Chicago, IL	—	Chicago Stadium
Mar 28	Honey Boy Finnegan	Chicago, IL	—	Chicago Stadium; sub
Apr 9	Eddie Anderson	Milwaukee, WI	NWD10	Auditorium
Apr 26	Sammy Dorfman	New York, NY	W10	MSG-11
May 10	André Routis	Chicago, IL	W10	Chicago Stadium
June 4	Ignacio Fernandez	New York, NY	W10	Queensboro Stadium
July 9	Dominick Petrone	New York, NY	—	Queensboro Stadium
July 9	Phil McGraw	New York, NY	W10	Queensboro Stadium
July 18	Sammy Mandell	Chicago, IL	—	Scheduled
Aug 2	Sammy Mandell	Chicago, IL	L10	Chicago Stadium

World Lightweight Championship

Date	Opponent	Location	Results	Comments
Sep 6	Tod Morgan	Chicago, IL	—	Chicago Stadium
Sep 20	Eddie Kid Wolfe	New Orleans, LA	W10	Heinemann Park
Sep 27	Eddie Mack	Chicago, IL	KO8	Chicago Stadium
Oct 18	Johnny Farr	New York, NY	W10	MSG-12
Oct 30	Stanislaus Loayza	Chicago, IL	W10	Coliseum

Date	Opponent	Location	Results	Comments
Nov 6	Jack Kid Berg	New York, NY	—	Postponed
Nov 15	Jack Kid Berg	New York, NY	—	Postponed

Notes: *On April 9, Canzoneri's victory over Anderson was a newspaper decision; the fight on May 10 set attendance records; Canzoneri claimed the August 2 title bout against Mandell was his top purse at $40,000; the bout with Stanley Loayza was promoted by Jack Dempsey.*

1930

Date	Opponent	Location	Results	Comments
Jan 17	Jack Kid Berg	New York, NY	L10	MSG-13
Jan 29	Steve Smith	Wilkes-Barre, PA	—	Did not appear
Feb 4	Suspended in PA and NY			
Feb 7	Goldie Hess	Chicago, IL	—	Canceled
Mar 4	Solly Ritz	New York, NY	KO1	Broadway Arena
Mar 14	Stanislaus Loayza	New York, NY	W10	MSG-14
Apr 1	Steve Smith	New Haven, CT	TKO7	Arena
Apr 8	Frankie LaFay	New York, NY	KO1	Broadway Arena
May 5	Harry Carlton	New York, NY	W10	St. Nicholas Arena
May 15	Johnny Farr	New Haven, CT	W10	Arena (date correct)
June 4	Joe Glick	New York, NY	W10	Ebbets Field
June 24	Tommy Grogan	New York, NY	W10	Queensboro Arena
July 21	Benny Bass	Philadelphia, PA	W10	Baker Bowl
July 25	—	Detroit, MI	—	—
July 28	Benny Bass	Philadelphia, PA	—	Moved up
Aug 26	Goldie Hess	New York, NY	W10	Queensboro Stadium
Sep 11	Billy Petrolle	Chicago, IL	L10	Chicago Stadium; benefit
Nov 14	Al Singer	New York, NY	KO1	MSG-15

World Lightweight Championship

Notes: *On July 21, Canzoneri warned Bass about hitting low in the first round. When Bass dropped another punch south of the border, a furious Canzoneri rushed to close quarters and sank his teeth into the right shoulder of his rival.*

1931

Date	Opponent	Location	Results	Comments
Jan 5	Pete Gulotta	New York, NY	EX	Paramount Gym
Jan 26	Johnny Farr	New Orleans, LA	ND10	Coliseum Arena
Feb 4	Goldie Hess	Chicago, IL	—	Canceled
Feb 4	withdrew because of a sinus infection			
Feb 25	Joey Kaufman	Jersey City, NJ	TKO1	Hollywood Arena

Date	Opponent	Location	Results	Comments
Mar 6	Sammy Fuller	Boston, MA	L10	Boston Garden
Mar 23	Tommy Grogan	Philadelphia, PA	W10	Arena
Mar 27	Billy Petrolle	New York, NY	—	MSG; can
Apr 24	Jack Kid Berg	Chicago, IL	KO3	Chicago Stadium

World Lightweight Championship

World Junior Welterweight Championship

Date	Opponent	Location	Results	Comments
June 25	Herman Perlick	New Haven, CT	W10	White City Stadium
July 8	Kid Chocolate	New York, NY	—	Ebbets Field; post
July 13	Cecil Payne	Los Angeles, CA	W10	Wrigley Field

World Junior Welterweight Championship

Date	Opponent	Location	Results	Comments
Aug 2	Ray Miller	Detroit, MI	—	Scheduled; Can
Aug 26	Herman Perlick	Bayonne, NJ	--	Postponed weather
Aug 27	Herman Perlick	Bayonne, NJ	--	Postponed weather
Sep 10	Jack Kid Berg	New York, NY	W15	Polo Grounds

World Lightweight Championship

Date	Opponent	Location	Results	Comments
Oct 29	Philly Griffin	Newark, NJ	W10	Armory

World Lightweight Championship

World Junior Welterweight Championship

Date	Opponent	Location	Results	Comments
Oct 30	Louis Kid Kaplan	Chicago, IL	—	Tentative; Can
Nov 10	Tommy Grogan	Milwaukee, WI	—	Tentative
Nov 20	Kid Chocolate	New York, NY	W15	MSG-16

World Lightweight Championship

World Junior Welterweight Championship

Date	Opponent	Location	Results	Comments
Nov 20	Stitches in eye			
Dec 3	TBD	Chicago, IL	—	Tentative

Notes: During the Kid Chocolate fight, Canzoneri was reported as showing off in the ring for a dame sitting ringside. The incident nearly got him knocked out in the fifth frame. Later, that beautiful woman became Mrs. Canzoneri; in late December, Canzoneri agreed to meet featherweight champion Bat Battalino. The agreement was cut by Nate Lewis of Chicago Stadium. The bout was to take place in January 1932.

1932

Date	Opponent	Location	Results	Comments
Jan 18	Johnny Jadick	Philadelphia, PA	L10	Arena

World Junior Welterweight Championship

Date	Opponent	Location	Results	Comments
Feb 15	Lew Massey	Philadelphia, PA	W10	Arena
Feb 26	Billy Petrolle	New York, NY	—	Offer rejected
Feb 26	Sammy Fuller	New York, NY	—	Declined offer
Mar 18	Sammy Fuller	New York, NY	—	Signed; declined

Date	Opponent	Location	Results	Comments
Mar 28	Harry Dublinsky	Philadelphia, PA	—	Signed; post
Apr 4	Ray Kiser	New Orleans, LA	W10	Coliseum Arena
Apr 18	Harry Dublinsky	Philadelphia, PA	—	Signed
May 9	Bat Battalino	New York, NY	—	Tentative; denied
May 23	Battling Gizzy	North Braddock, PA	KO5	Meyers Bowl
May 23	Injured shoulder			
June 6	Eddie Cool	Philadelphia, PA	—	Postponed; injury
June 16	Harry Dublinsky	Chicago, IL	W10	Sparta Stadium
July 11	Billy Petrolle	New York, NY	—	Tentative; MSG Bowl
July 18	Johnny Jadick	Philadelphia, PA	L10	Phillies Ballpark

World Junior Welterweight Championship

Date	Opponent	Location	Results	Comments
Aug 8	Billy Petrolle	New York, NY	—	MSG Bowl; can
Aug 29	Kid Chocolate	New York, NY	—	MSG; tentative
Sep 13	Lew Kirsch	New York, NY	—	Postponed
Sep 28	Ray Miller	New York, NY	—	Postponed
Sep 29	Lew Kirsch	New York, NY	TKO3	Queensboro Stadium
Oct 5	Ray Miller	New York, NY	—	Postponed
Oct 5	Frankie Petrolle	New York, NY	—	Postponed
Oct 12	Billy Petrolle	New York, NY	—	MSG; rescheduled
Oct 12	Frankie Petrolle	New York, NY	KO3	Ebbets Field; sub
Nov 4	Billy Petrolle	New York, NY	W15	MSG-17

World Lightweight Championship

Notes: *Canzoneri's opponent on April 4, was Ray "Kid" Kaiser, often spelled Ray Kiser; Canzoneri's match against Johnny Jadick on July 18 was likely a draw; Canzoneri's performance against Billy Petrolle, on November 4, 1932, has been mentioned as one of his finest. United Press International claimed he was "squarely at his peak."*

1933

Date	Opponent	Location	Results	Comments
Feb 3	Billy Townsend	New York, NY	KO1	MSG-18
Feb 23	Pete Nebo	Miami, FL	W10	MSG, Miami
Feb 23	Broken right thumb			
Mar 6	Steve Halaiko	Buffalo, NY	—	Auditorium; can
Apr 20	Wesley Ramey	Grand Rapids, MI	L10	Civic Auditorium
May 1	Steve Halaiko	Buffalo, NY	—	Auditorium; can
May 3	Wesley Ramey	Grand Rapids, MI	—	See above
May 18	Battling Shaw	New Orleans, LA	—	See below
May 21	Battling Shaw	New Orleans, LA	W10	Heinemann Park

World Junior Welterweight Championship

Date	Opponent	Location	Results	Comments
June 22	Barney Ross	Chicago, IL	—	Chicago Stad; changed
June 23	Barney Ross	Chicago, IL	L10	Chicago Stadium

World Lightweight Championship

World Junior Welterweight Championship

Date	Opponent	Location	Results	Comments
July 3	Barney Ross	Chicago, IL	—	See above
Sep 12	Barney Ross	New York, NY	L15	Polo Grounds

World Lightweight Championship

World Junior Welterweight Championship

Date	Opponent	Location	Results	Comments
Sep 14	Barney Ross	New York, NY	—	Polo Grounds; see above
Oct 28	Frankie Klick	Brooklyn, NY	W10	Ridgewood Grove
Nov 24	Kid Chocolate	New York, NY	KO2	MSG-19
Dec 4	Cecil Payne	Cleveland, OH	KO5	Public Hall
Dec 15	Cleto Locatelli	New York, NY	W10	MSG-20

Notes: The Chicago Stadium Operating Company, in receivership, presented the June 23 bout. The company's promotions had struggled; the September 14 bout against Barney Ross was promoted by Tim Mara, pro football pioneer; the December 15 bout was believed to be Tony Canzoneri's 100th career victory.

1934

Date	Opponent	Location	Results	Comments
Jan 12	Cleto Locatelli	New York, NY	—	MSG; post
Jan	Nose injury			
Jan 22	Eddie Cool	Philadelphia, PA	—	Postponed
Jan 26	Cleto Locatelli	New York, NY	—	MSG; Rescheduled
Feb 2	Cleto Locatelli	New York, NY	W12	MSG-21
Feb 19	Eddie Cool	Philadelphia, PA	—	Postponed
Mar 1	Pete Nebo	Kansas City, MO	W10	Convention Hall
Mar 13	Baby Arizmendi	Los Angeles, CA	W10	Olympic Auditorium
May 15	Roger Bernard	Detroit, MI	—	—
May 22	Roger Bernard	Detroit, MI	—	—
June 27	Frankie Klick	Brooklyn, NY	—	Ebbets Field; post
June 28	Frankie Klick	Brooklyn, NY	TKO10	Ebbets Field
Aug 22	Harry Dublinsky	Brooklyn, NY	—	Postponed
Aug 29	Harry Dublinsky	Brooklyn, NY	L10	Ebbets Field
Sep 26	Harry Dublinsky	Brooklyn, NY	W10	Ebbets Field

Notes: The February 2 bout, against Locatelli, was a reversed decision—originally a draw; the battle against Nebo completed a trilogy with the boxer.

1935

Date	Opponent	Location	Results	Comments
Jan 7	Eddie Ran	Newark, NJ	KO2	Laurel Garden
Jan 21	Harold Hughes	Utica, NY	W8	Convention Hall
Jan 31	Leo Rodak	Chicago, IL	W10	Chicago Stadium
Feb 26	Chuck Woods	Detroit, MI	L10	Olympia Stadium
Mar 15	Chuck Woods	Chicago, IL	W10	Chicago Stadium
Apr 25	Eddie Zivic	Pittsburgh, PA	TKO7	Motor Square Garden
May 10	Lou Ambers	New York, NY	W15	MSG-22; title vacant

World Lightweight Championship

Date	Opponent	Location	Results	Comments
June 10	Frankie Klick	Washington, D.C.	W12	Griffith Stadium
July 16	Bobby Pacho	New York, NY	—	L.I. Bowl
July 25	Bobby Pacho	Chicago, IL	W10	Mills Stadium
Aug 19	Frankie Klick	San Francisco, CA	W10	Exposition/Civic Auditorium
Sep 13	Joe Ghnouly	St. Louis, MO	W10	Arena
Oct 4	Al Roth	New York, NY	W15	MSG-23

World Lightweight Championship

1936

Date	Opponent	Location	Results	Comments
Jan 22	Brescia Garcia	New York, NY	KO9	Star Casino
Jan 30	Fred Bashara	Philadelphia, PA	TKO3	Olympic A.C.
Feb 15	Billy Hogan	Brooklyn, NY	KO4	Ridgewood Grove
Mar 2	Steve Halaiko	New York, NY	KO2	St. Nicholas Arena
Apr 9	Johnny Jadick	New York, NY	W10	St. Nicholas Arena
May 8	Jimmy McLarnin	New York, NY	W10	MSG-24
May 8	Nose injury			
July 16	Lou Ambers	New York, NY	—	Postponed; MSG Bowl
July 30	Lou Ambers	New York, NY	—	Postponed; MSG Bowl
Aug 6	Lou Ambers	New York, NY	—	Postponed; MSG Bowl
Aug 31	Lou Ambers	New York, NY	—	Postponed; MSG Bowl
Sep 3	Lou Ambers	New York, NY	L15	MSG-25

World Lightweight Championship

Date	Opponent	Location	Results	Comments
Aug 27	Jimmy McLarnin	New York, NY	—	MSG Bowl
Oct 2	Jimmy McLarnin	New York, NY	—	Postponed
Oct 5	Jimmy McLarnin	New York, NY	L10	MSG-26

Notes: *Brescia Garcia was also known as Midget Mexico.*

1937

Date	Opponent	Location	Results	Comments
Apr 2	Lou Ambers	New York, NY	—	MSG; Postponed
Apr 5	George Levy	Newark, NJ	TKO7	Laurel Garden
Apr 13	Frankie Wallace	Brooklyn, NY	W8	Broadway Arena
Apr 24	Joey Zodda	Brooklyn, NY	KO7	Ridgewood Grove
May 7	Lou Ambers	New York, NY	L15	MSG-27

World Lightweight Championship

1938

Date	Opponent	Location	Results	Comments
Oct 17	Eddie Zivic	Scranton, PA	L10	Town Hall
Oct 26	Howard Scott	Jersey City, NJ	W8	Braddock Arena
Nov 1	Joey Greb	Camden, NJ	—	Substituted by below
Nov 1	Al Dunbar	Camden, NJ	KO3	Convention Hall
Nov 22	Howard Scott	Bronx, NY	W8	New York Coliseum
Dec 10	Jimmy Murray	Brooklyn, NY	W8	Ridgewood Grove
Dec 30	Eddie Zivic	New York, NY	W10	Hippodrome

Notes: *Canzoneri's October 17 battle against Zivic was a draw at best.*

1939

Date	Opponent	Location	Results	Comments
Jan 19	Wally Hally	Denver, CO	W10	City Auditorium
Jan 27	Joe Gavras	San Francisco, CA	TKO2	Dreamland Auditorium
Jan 31	Everett Simington	San Jose, CA	KO3	Civic Auditorium
Feb 7	Bobby Pacho	Los Angeles, CA	W10	Olympic Auditorium
Mar 7	Eddie Brink	Bronx, NY	W8	New York Coliseum
Mar 14	Norment Quarles	New York, NY	—	Cancelled; injury
Mar 28	Eddie Brink	New York, NY	L10	Hippodrome
Apr 11	Jimmy Vaughn	Bronx, NY	D8	New York Coliseum
Apr 11	Eye injury			
Apr 17	Jimmy Tygh	Philadelphia, PA	—	Arena; post
Apr 24	Jimmy Tygh	Philadelphia, PA	—	Arena; post
May 1	Jimmy Tygh	Philadelphia, PA	L10	Arena
May 3	Al "Bummy" Davis	New York, NY	—	MSG; tentative
May 15	Nick Camarata	New Orleans, LA	D10	Municipal Auditorium
June 5	Harris Blake	Buffalo, NY	L10	Broadway Auditorium
July 6	Joe DeJesus	Poughkeepsie, NY	W8	Woodcliff Park Arena

Date	Opponent	Location	Results	Comments
July 17	Ambrose Logan	Brooklyn, NY	W8	Coney Island Velodrome
Aug 3	Joe DeJesus	Brooklyn, NY	W8	Fort Hamilton Arena
Aug 18	Frankie Wallace	Long Beach, NY	W8	Long Beach Stadium
Aug 26	Gerald D'Elia	Staten Island, NY	W8	Thompson's Stadium
Sep 11	Johnny Horstman	New York, NY	—	Dexter Park; can
Sep 19	Eddie Brink	Brooklyn, NY	W8	Broadway Arena
Nov 1	Al "Bummy" Davis	New York, NY	LKO3	MSG-28

Notes: The Philadelphia loss to Tygh was unjust. At worst it was a draw.

Appendix B

*Official Records of Associated Members
of the International Boxing Hall of Fame*

Inductee	*Year*	*Bouts*	*Won*	*Lost*	*Drew*	*KOs*	*ND*	*NC*
Lou Ambers	1992	104	90	8	6	30	—	—
Baby Arizmendi	2004	109	70	26	13	12	—	—
Benny Bass	2002	239	152	28	5	69	52	2
Tony Canzoneri	**1990**	**175**	**137**	**24**	**10**	**44**	**4**	—
Kid Chocolate	1991	146	131	9	6	50	—	—
Johnny Dundee	1991	335	90	31	19	22	194	1
Pete Herman	1997	144	67	12	8	21	57	—
Benny Leonard	1990	212	85	5	1	69	121	—
Jimmy McLarnin	1991	77	62	11	3	20	1	—
Sammy Mandell	2005	187	82	21	9	32	73	2
Tod Morgan	2022	220	143	44	33	30	—	—
Billy Petrolle	2000	160	83	21	10	62	45	1
Wesley Ramey	2013	195	158	26	11	9	—	—
Barney Ross	1990	81	72	4	3	22	2	—
Bud Taylor	2005	163	71	23	6	37	63	—

Chapter Notes

Preface

1. To provide a comparison: Tony Canzoneri received less than 1 percent of what a retired fighter like Jack Dempsey was able to sustain. Granted, Dempsey lived until 1983, but a figure of less than 1 percent is shocking.

Chapter One

1. "Sons of Sunny Italy," *New York Times-Democrat*, October 9, 1903, 11.
2. *Ibid.*
3. George Canzoneri's World War I Draft Registration states his DOB as December 21, 1875.
4. Tony Canzoneri stated that shortly after he was born the family moved briefly to Lumberton, Mississippi.
5. The rocket scientists came in the 1960s when NASA began doing assembly work in New Orleans.
6. In 1905, the Italian consul estimated that one-third to one-half of the Quarter's population were Italian-born or second-generation Italian Americans.
7. Pete Herman lived at 1131 Ursulines Avenue in New Orleans in 1917.
8. Herman professed the need for a fighter to battle quality opposition, and Tony Canzoneri heeded his advice.
9. Herman always denied that he intentionally lost to Lynch, but when he easily outpointed Lynch to regain the title on July 25, 1921, at Ebbets Field, few had their doubts.
10. Boxing historians, familiar with both fighters, still marvel at the conflict.
11. George Canzoneri's World War I Draft Registration #3936 (Order # 4566) claims a permanent address at 403 West Ninth Street, Johnston City, IL, in Williamson County. The address was also confirmed on multiple documents including the 1920 United States Federal Census.
12. Joey Scalfaro turned professional in 1926, and by the time he finished his career in 1932, he had won nearly three times as many fights as he lost. He took victories over Frankie Genaro, Jimmy Ireland, and Pete Sanstol. He also drew some good fighters including Pete Zivic, Johnny Vacca, and Kid Chocolate.
13. Gotto would enter the finals along with Tommy Graham, Tommy Lorenzo, and Mike Sansone.
14. Sources differ on Izzy "the Painter" surname. Some also claim Gastonfeld.
15. Some believed the fight was fixed.

Chapter Two

1. Years later, Canzoneri would learn that his opponent bet his entire purse on himself and lost it. The evening also saw Jack Grace defeat Harry Duer, Meyer "Cal" Cohen victorious over Vincent Forgione, Moe Ginsburg over Willie Kohler, and atop the ticket Babe Herman defeat Kid Henry.
2. The venue would have a storied past until 1956, when it was closed and replaced by a supermarket. An attempted revival began in 1982, thanks to Frank and Nancy Sciacca. The business struggled through the following decade and was eventually closed. A 1997 warehouse fire did considerable damage to the property.
3. "Canzoneri Takes Fast Four Rounder From Brandon at Broadway Arena," *Brooklyn Standard Union*, November 13, 1925, 14.
4. Watching certain fighters, like undefeated welterweight Harry Ebbets, was as enjoyable as it was inspirational for Tony Canzoneri.
5. William Lawrence "Kid" McPartland (1875–1953) was a former competitive lightweight boxer. He had a career that spanned from 1895 until 1905, that included bouts against George "Kid" Lavigne, "Barbados" Joe Walcott, and Joe Gans.
6. Canzoneri, unlike many boxers, mastered avoiding punches thanks to quick and exceptional upper-body movement that made it appear as if he was moving backward. He often accomplished the defense action without moving his feet.
7. "Canzoneri Wins Again as Revivalists Hold Sway at Broadway Club," *Brooklyn Daily Eagle*, January 22, 1926, 22.
8. Tony's mother thought her son looked like a movie star. Later, most saw him as a young Frank Sinatra.

9. Had it gone the distance, Canzoneri would have likely knocked out Suess.

10. A couple of reports claimed the fight was over six rounds.

11. Sources for this fighter's official record vary.

12. Reviews of this fight often varied from punching strategies to attendance.

13. Bantamweight Chick Suggs was also considered as a replacement for Taylor.

14. "Jimmy Delaney Blows as Fine Ring Prospect," *Washington Evening Star*, December 10, 1926, 50.

15. Some sources claimed Canzoneri took fewer rounds.

16. This was the first battle where Canzoneri's dazzling footwork was clearly on display.

Chapter Three

1. The fight caught the eye of Tex Rickard, who offered Mullen a $10,000 net profit for the Taylor-Canzoneri bout.

2. Actual measurements included in Appendix A.

3. "Bud Taylor and Tony Canzoneri Battle Ten Rounds," *Associated Press*, March 27, 1927. Article printed by numerous newspapers, including the *Douglas Dispatch*.

4. "Canzoneri Now Getting Ready for Smith Bout at the Broadway," *Brooklyn Citizen*, April 20, 1927, 10.

5. Tony's father arrived in Chicago on June 20 to attend his son's battle with Taylor. Tony was a 7–5 favorite four days before the bout.

6. Both Tony Canzoneri and Bud Taylor would defeat Fernandez during this stretch. Ignacio Fernandez would finish his career with a record of 64–54–20.

7. Kaplan could no longer make weight.

8. NYSAC slapped Canzoneri's hand with a short suspension for fighting overweight.

9. "A Tame Bout to Canzoneri," *Kansas City Times*, August 26, 1927, 10.

10. Weight reports varied.

11. Dundee lost his title for failure to defend it in time. Since he did not lose it in the ring, many, including Canzoneri, considered him champion.

12. Weights vary in some sources.

Chapter Four

1. Sources vary regarding his date of birth. The International Boxing Hall of Fame recognizes December 4, 1904, while other sources claim December 4, 1903.

2. "Victor Will Rule Featherweights," *Washington Evening Star*, February 8, 1928, 33.

3. For the record: The judges for the battle were George Kelly and George Patrick (both had the fight in favor of Canzoneri) and Art Donovan

(who had Bass the winner) was the third man in the ring.

4. Tony Canzoneri scaled at 128¾, while Claude Wilson tipped at 126¾ pounds.

5. James F. Dougherty, also known as the "Baron of Leiperville," was a charismatic sportsman whose hotel, bar, and fight arena in Leiperville, Pennsylvania, was a mecca for boxing from 1916 to 1947. During that time, he was the owner of one of the busiest fight camps in the country.

6. Despite promises, Canzoneri suffered cracked ribs, followed by pneumonia.

7. The referee was Eddie Forbes, and the judges were Charles F. Mathison and George Kelly; this was the first of seven planned world's championship fights scheduled for Madison Square Garden during the winter season.

8. On July 8, 1932, the Dow hit the lowest level of the 20th century, when it closed at 41.22.

9. This was the third Chicago Coliseum, located at 1513 South Wabash Avenue on the near south side. It was sold for redevelopment in 1982.

10. Canzoneri was an 8–5 favorite thanks to his left-hand jab and ability to protect himself in clinches.

11. Joey Sangor was so upset by his performance that he decided to quit the ring three fights later.

12. The number of knockdowns reported varied. In a fourth reported knockdown, in the fifth round, Payne did not reach the canvas; Payne was a prolific fighter out of Louisville who lacked the experience and skills of Canzoneri, yet managed to put together a solid career that allowed him to fight until 1937. A Chicago Stadium battle, at the end of March, never came to fruition. This gave Canzoneri a month worth of recovery time.

13. "Hot Bout Promised by Featherweights," *Washington Evening Star*, June 3, 1929, 31.

14. Canzoneri selected the Garden of Allah, near Evanston, as his training facility.

15. "M'Graw May Surprise 'Em," *Brooklyn Standard Union*, July 6, 1929, 43.

16. Scalpers were asking more than $100 per ticket.

17. Dempsey put together an entertaining card that also saw Louis Kid Kaplan victorious over Eddie Wolfe and Jackie Pilkington defeating Tony Herrera; Canzoneri was injured during the contest, and it forced the postponement of his bout against Jack Kid Berg.

Chapter Five

1. The venue, originally designated as the People's Arcade, was later renamed.

2. There was often hockey at the Garden on Sunday, Tuesday, and Thursday.

3. My apologies for the idiomatic expressions.

4. "Beating of Canzoneri Makes Invader

Lightweight Contender," *Brooklyn Standard Union*, January 18, 1930, 10.

5. Attendance figures differ source to source; Al Singer, the new world lightweight champion, was introduced to the crowd.

6. Al Singer would receive 37½ percent of the receipts. Many still recalled that Singer, having dropped to a nine-count earlier in round three, caught a targeted McLarnin right to the jaw that knocked him out at the 2:21 mark. Thankfully, his title wasn't on the line. It would be on the line against Canzoneri.

Chapter Six

1. Canzoneri, along with Jack Dempsey and Max Baer, enjoyed a Madison Square Garden introduction before the January 2 battle between Pierre Charles and Jack Renault.

2. Herman Perlick and Cecil Payne were two opponents under consideration as substitutes.

3. Reports vary about the number of times Kaufman hit the canvas. Sources believed he hit the canvas at least five or perhaps as many as seven times—somewhat difficult to squeeze into the timeframe.

4. Considerable holding added to a slow exhibition.

5. For the record: NYSAC believed Sammy Fuller or Jack Kid Berg would make a better defense. The commission also reminded Canzoneri that his six months of grace expired on April 14, so he had to accept a bout soon.

6. "Canzoneri Facing Ban in New York," *Washington Evening Star*, March 19, 1931, D-1.

7. Some sources claim less.

8. Phil Collins was the referee who counted out Berg.

9. Wrigley Field, owned by William Wrigley, Jr., broke ground in 1925 and was demolished in 1969.

10. Unlike some fight managers, Sammy Goldman did not get a large amount of press. There were no reporters hanging on to his every word.

11. Some sources claim Berg took two eight-counts.

12. This appeared to be a quid pro quo on behalf of Goldman.

13. His 100-fight amateur record was being quoted as 100–0 with 86 knockouts and 14 decision victories.

14. By the time both reached their 150th professional bout, Leonard had closed the gap. By their 175th battle, a much younger Leonard had more victories and fewer losses.

Chapter Seven

1. The candid editorial style of Husing, at least to some sports fans, was interpreted as too opinionated. No doubt Canzoneri's addition worked in favor of the broadcaster.

2. Speaking of Chocolate, the fighter hoped to tackle Canzoneri in March or early April at Madison Square Garden once again.

3. Joey Costa, a stablemate of Canzoneri, defeated Johnny Lucas in one of the undercard events.

4. He served as a guest referee at the Sunshine Gym in Brownsville—it was a favor for his friend, matchmaker Fritz Purvin. The champion was also assisting a few fighters, including Mike Esposito, a promising featherweight.

5. While the overflow crowd brought a $9,000 gate, dozens scaled the walls to avoid admission.

6. Meyers Bowl was a popular fight venue until the Depression finally sealed its fate in 1933.

7. Although it didn't matter, Pittsburgh fight fans were stunned by the media reports. Many believed Gizzy performed better than indicated—they believed he took at least three of the five rounds and was fouled twice for low blows. Following an exam and despite no external signs, Dr. John Farkas, commission physician, believed the fighter was injured. Some good did come out of the plunge and a subsequent examination, as Gizzy would undergo surgery for the removal of tonsils and adenoids.

8. The bout attracted about 4,000 fight fans; Canzoneri had closed Dublinsky's eye with sharp left hooks during the fourth and fifth rounds.

9. Later, after the postponement, Ray Miller wanted back on the card.

Chapter Eight

1. Canzoneri was also signed as a pitchman for Old Gold Cigarettes.

2. The Schuyler-Colfax House is located at 2343 Paterson Hamburg Turnpike, Wayne, New Jersey. Numerous locations served as headquarters for General George Washington during the American Revolutionary War.

3. Pete Nebo arrived in Key West during the third week in January and trained at the Athletic Club.

4. "New Price Scale Show Has Champ," *Washington Evening Star*, February 1, 1933, C-2.

5. And the Canzoneri charm and image could sell (see note 1).

6. In 1933, $5,000 was equivalent in purchasing power to about $110,600 in 2022.

7. Pete Gulotta, who outpointed Jack Rose in a six-round preliminary bout on the ticket, happened to be the second cousin of Pete Herman, the legendary bantamweight champion.

8. Canzoneri was believed to be the first current boxing champion to fight in Miami.

9. Pete Nebo would fight until 1936, posting a believed career record of 50–42–10. In January of 1940, Nebo, only 30, was committed to the Florida State Hospital, where he spent the rest of his life.

10. Canzoneri would later claim that some of the cuts were due to a head-butt.

11. Ramey fought Halaiko a second time to a draw. It was in his previous bout.

12. Today, the junior welterweight championship is also known as the world super lightweight or light welterweight championship.

13. The fight was scheduled to start at 3 p.m., with returning trains leaving New Orleans at 9 p.m.

14. A regulation of the Illinois State Athletic Commission made it obligatory to score prizefights by points, 10 to a round. The referee gave both fighters 50 points. One of the judges gave Ross 52, Canzoneri 48. The other judge gave Ross 53, Canzoneri 47. That made Ross the new champion.

15. For the record, the fighter listed first won the bout.

16. The movie rights for the bout were sold for $2,500.

17. Twenty-four years, 10 months and nine days, to be exact. He had already posted a career record of 96–13–8 entering the fight.

18. "Heavyweight Fights Top Week's Program," *Albany Times Union*, November 20, 1933, 12.

Chapter Nine

1. Sources vary regarding the fighter's weight.

2. Gabe Kaufman and Frank Gatto, who were behind the Convention Hall promotion, scaled tickets at $1.10, $2.20, and $3.30.

3. The pair would tangle in back-to-back battles (May 28 and September 17).

4. The weights of the fighters varied from source to source.

5. The former champion also continued to support his stablemates. For example, he attended the Charley Massera versus Yustin Sirutis heavyweight bout at Ridgewood Grove.

6. A certified check for $1,016.52 was delivered to the Mother Marianne Camp for crippled children in Nyack because of the evening's event. Too often forgotten has been the role the sport has played in funding charitable causes.

7. "Commish Threatens to Forfeit Ross' Title," *New York Daily News*, Dec 23, 1934, 53.

Chapter Ten

1. Speaking of legends, nobody will ever forget James J. Braddock, aka "Cinderella Man." On June 13, Braddock, considered washed up and 10–1 underdog, somehow managed to enter the Madison Square Garden Bowl and box exuberant Max Baer to a 15-round unanimous decision victory.

2. Mark Allen Baker, *Lou Ambers: A Biography of the World Lightweight Champion and Hall of Famer* (Jefferson, NC: McFarland, 2021).

3. Matchmaker James "Red" Herring, a former prolific pugilist, was well-connected to boxing in Central New York. He also had worked with Lou Ambers, aka Otis Paradise.

4. NYSAC also announced that Frankie Klick was suspended for fighting Ross in Miami on January 20. All Klick did was meet Ross in another state, and the lightweight champion wasn't under suspension at the time.

5. Some sources viewed the fight as Canzoneri's 100th professional victory.

6. The bout was handled by promoter Lew Raymond.

7. Baker, *Lou Ambers*, 78–79.

8. "Tame Scrap and Decision to Canzoneri Irk Crowd," *Washington Evening Star*, June 11, 1935, A-14.

9. Some reports, such as the United Press, claim Canzoneri was up before a count.

10. Roth conducted his fight preparation at Madame Bey's training camp in Summit, New Jersey.

11. To be exact: Canzoneri was 10 months and 18 days, including the end date, older than Dempsey; two days before the battle, Canzoneri was a 6–5 betting favorite.

Chapter Eleven

1. From Ramey's perspective, Canzoneri was a smart puncher who made the most of every advantage. If the champion sensed an opponent was vulnerable, he knew how to capitalize on the situation. The only criticism Ramey had was that Canzoneri was not a particularly good infighter.

2. Canzoneri was working the small clubs to expand his fan base and even repay some old favors.

3. "Tony Outpoints M'Larnin," *New York Daily News*, May 9, 1936, 34.

4. Boxing cartoonist Ted Carroll declared the bout the greatest fight he ever witnessed during a 50-year career. *The Ring*, April 1973.

5. Also at this time, Jasper Canzoneri, one of Tony's brothers, had the boxing bug. Witnessing firsthand his brother's accomplishments—not to mention picking up a few pointers from him—convinced the youngster to map out a career in the fight game.

6. Worth reiterating: Anticipation for the battle had been hampered by all the discussion around a possible Canzoneri-Ross bout.

7. Baker, *Lou Ambers*, 100.

8. *Ibid.*, 101.

9. I'll say it for you, "I bet that confused a few people, as Canzoneri was often called a miniature Babe Ruth."

Chapter Twelve

1. "In New York," *Dunkirk Evening Observer*, August 31, 1936, 4.

2. Canzoneri was part owner of the establishment. It was believed that he was backed by the same group that assisted Dempsey.

3. More than 2,000 fans were turned away as the venue reached capacity.

4. Baker, *Lou Ambers*, 119–121.

5. Some sources reported attendance of 11,000-plus.

6. A mechanic's lien is a security interest in the title to property for the benefit of those who have supplied labor or materials that improve the property.

Chapter Thirteen

1. Ringside saw Canzoneri taking the eighth, Hally the ninth, and the final round even. Promoter Jack Kenner was happy, but not satisfied, with the more than 4,000 fans who attended the event.

2. Lasting only four rounds against Henry Armstrong, Bobby Pacho lost via technical knockout on March 4, 1939.

3. I'll say it for you: Canzoneri was brazen to believe he would be matched with Armstrong.

4. Some sources varied.

Chapter Fourteen

1. Speaking of family, every action by either Rita or Tony Canzoneri was fuel for the gossip columns.

2. As a club singer at La Vie Parisienne, she also adorned some deceptive attire. The costume, combined with Mrs. Canzoneri's sensuous mannerisms—compelling eyelash-batting and alluring smile—caught the attention of every patron.

3. Grossinger's Catskill Resort Hotel was in the town of Liberty, New York. One of the largest Borscht Belt resorts, it was a kosher establishment that catered primarily to Jewish clients from New York City. After decades of activity and notable guests, it closed in 1986. The resort buildings were demolished in 2018.

4. Mrs. Canzoneri (aka Rita Angel, aka Rita Duncan) appeared in Sol Wurtzel's production of *The Invisible Wall*.

5. Adams and Canzoneri opened as a comedy team in 1940 at a theater in Astoria, Long Island. Their salary for four days was $50. The contrast from the end of Canzoneri's boxing career, when he was having trouble making ends meet, to now was an amazing transformation.

Chapter Fifteen

1. Actor Horace McMahon became Joey Adams' new fall guy.

2. The *Miami News*, on October 30, 1952, was the first newspaper to note the possibility of a split between Tony and Rita Canzoneri. When syndicated columnist Earl Wilson, who knew the couple, dropped it in his column, folks knew it was a reality. The legal separation, between the couple of 18 years, was noted the first week of November.

3. "Brink Rates Canzoneri Better Than Armstrong," *Binghamton Press and Sun-Bulletin*, January 4, 1953, 4-D.

4. In one of those lighter moments, Tony Canzoneri and Barney Ross faced each other once again—naturally, it had been 20 years—only this time they were battling for a pot of $1,600 on television's *Name That Tune*.

5. Jimmy McLarnin claimed his largest purse was $60,000. It came from his battle against Barney Ross on May 28, 1935.

6. Saloon owners included Abe Attell, Tony Canzoneri, Jack Dempsey, Bob Olin, Ray Robinson, and Mickey Walker.

7. Speaking of opportunities, the following year (1956) Tony Canzoneri was signed to play the role of a trainer in the movie *Shadow of a Champ*, starring Kirk Douglas. The movie would struggle to get financed. Always willing to lend a hand, if there was time, Tony Canzoneri was a guest referee at a PAL (Police Athletic League) event held at Macy's (Herald Square)—the event took place on April 2, 1956. Joining Canzoneri were James J. Braddock, Gus Lesnevich and Mickey Walker. It was Macy's Children's Week and one of 50 events.

8. No doubt Tony and Rita were discussing the success of their beautiful daughter, Denise, 18, who captured a role in the Broadway play *The Bells Are Ringing* and had even appeared in gossip columns regarding her dating. See Earl Wilson's columns in August 1956.

9. Earl Wilson noted in May 1957 that the former Mrs. Canzoneri would soon wed David Chandler, a writer at Columbia Pictures. She later did (1958).

10. Barber talked about himself more than Canzoneri during the lackluster interview.

11. Speaking of celebrity sightings, in August, Tony Canzoneri was spotted at Joe's Clam Bar in Asbury Park, New Jersey, having dinner with actress Sue Travers. The pair even managed to get their photo published in the *Asbury Park Evening News*. The lobster was always Tony's favorite.

12. By June 1958, columnist Earl Wilson was noting Canzoneri's interest in one Grace Levitt. Could matrimony be in the air? When asked about it, Canzoneri always took the same stance as Henny Youngman: The secret of a happy marriage remains a secret. By August, the marriage plans were canceled.

13. In 1959, the Louisiana Athletic Hall of Fame elected its first three members: Tony Canzoneri for boxing; Mel Ott for baseball; and Gaynell Tinsley for football. To be recognized in the state of his birth was a thrill for the former champion. On January 23, Canzoneri flew to Shreveport, Louisiana, to attend his induction.

14. From events like the March of Dimes dinner to the Wyoming Valley Old Time Boxers Association's annual "Main Event" at the American Legion Home in Wilkes-Barre, Pennsylvania, Canzoneri's calendar was always full. And he enjoyed the lifestyle. It gave him an opportunity to reconnect with his fans and even some old champions, like middleweight Billy Soose from Lake Wallenpaupack, Lakeville, Pennsylvania. Or even bigger opportunities: 11 of boxing's all-time greats made appearances at the 1959 New York State Fair in Syracuse, including Tony Canzoneri. They were part of Carmen Basilio's "Boxing Cavalcade," underwritten by promoter Norm Rothschild. Also accepting invitations were Rocky Marciano, Jack Dempsey, Barney Ross, Mickey Walker, Jersey Joe Walcott, Joe Louis, and Jack Sharkey.

15. According to reports, Canzoneri had less than $23 in cash in his room.

Bibliography

Books

Baker, Mark Allen. *Lou Ambers: A Biography of the World Lightweight Champion and Hall of Famer.* Jefferson: McFarland, 2021.

Goldman, Herbert G., ed. *Boxing: A Worldwide Record of Bouts and Boxers.* Jefferson: McFarland, 2012.

Sugar, Bert Randolph. *Boxing's Greatest Fighters.* Guilford: Lyons Press, 2006.

_____. *The Ring Record Book and Boxing Encyclopedia.* New York: Ring, 1985.

_____. *The Ultimate Book of Boxing Lists.* Philadelphia: Running Press, 2010.

Archival Sources

Library of Congress

Articles

Albertanti, Francis. "Tony Canzoneri Seeks to Emulate Teacher, Pete Herman, Former Champion." *Ring*, July 1927.

Borden, Eddie. "Broadcast from New York." *Ring*, October 1933.

_____. "Tony Canzoneri—A Gent of the Old School." *Ring*, April 1936.

Canzoneri, Tony. "This Is My Life, as Told to Stanley Weston." *Boxing and Wrestling*, Parts I and II, ca. 1950s.

Hill, Norman. "Can Canzoneri Win Another Crown?" *Arena*, July 10, 1929.

Lawrence, Jack. "Tony Canzoneri..." *Ring*, January 1930.

Maestro, Frank. "In and Near Chicago." *Ring*, July 1933.

Pardy, George T. "The Miracle Man..." *Ring*, August 1935.

Reynolds, Quentin. "Hand in Glove." *Collier's*, July 18, 1936.

Brochures and Programs

International Boxing Hall of Fame, Inaugural Induction, June 10, 1990

Internet Sites

ancestry.com
boxingtreasures.com
boxrec.com
britannica.com
chronicalingamerica.loc.gov
ctboxinghof.org
cyberboxingzone.com
espn.com
facebook.com
findagrave.com
ha.com
history.com
ibhof.com
josportsinc.com
newspapers.com
phillyjewishsports.org
wikipedia.org
worthpoint.com
youtube.com

Magazines

The Arena
Boxing
Boxing and Wrestling
Boxing Monthly
Boxing News
Boxing Scene
El Boxer
KO Magazine
Liberty
Pacific Stars and Stripes
Police Gazette
The Ring
Sporting News
Sports Illustrated
Weekly Boxing World

Newspapers

Bismarck Tribune
Brooklyn Citizen
Brooklyn Daily Eagle
Brooklyn Standard Union
Brooklyn Times Union

Brownsville Herald (TX)
Californian (Salinas, CA)
Carolina Watchman (Salisbury, NC)
Chat (Brooklyn, NY)
Daily Alaska Empire (Juneau, AK)
Daily Independent (Elizabeth City, NC)
Daily Messenger (Canandaigua, NY)
Daily Monitor Leader (Mount Clemens, MI)
Daily News (New York, NY)
Daily Worker (Chicago, IL)
Dayton Daily News
Democrat and Chronicle (Rochester, NY)
Detroit Evening Times
Douglas Dispatch (AZ)
Dunkirk Evening Observer (Dunkirk, NY)
Ely Miner (Ely, MN)
Evening Express (Los Angeles)
Evening News (Harrisburg, PA)
Evening Star (Washington, D.C.)
Fresno Bee
Hollywood Daily Citizen (CA)
Imperial Valley Press (El Centro, CA)
Indianapolis Times
Intelligencer Journal (Lancaster, PA)
Ithaca Journal (NY)
Kansas City Times (MO)
Key West Citizen (FL)
Kingston Daily Freeman (NY)
Las Vegas Age (NV)
Los Angeles Times
Middletown Times Herald (NY)
Midland Journal (Rising Sun, MD)
Modesto News-Herald
Montgomery County Sentinel (Rockville, MD)
Morning Call (Allentown, PA)
New Britain Herald (CT)
New Orleans Times-Picayune
Nogales International (AZ)
Nome Daily Nugget
Oakland Tribune
Omaha Guide

Philadelphia Inquirer
Pittsburgh Daily Post
Post-Star (Glens Falls, NY)
Press and Sun-Bulletin (Binghamton, NY)
Record (Los Angeles, CA)
Roanoke Rapids Herald (NC)
Sacramento Bee
San Francisco Examiner
Selma Times-Journal (AL)
Seward Daily Gateway (AK)
Standard Union (Brooklyn, NY)
Star-Gazette (Elmira, NY)
Tampa Tribune
Times Herald (Olean, NY)
Times Union (Albany, NY)
Times-Democrat (New York, NY)
Times-News (Hendersonville, NC)
Toledo Union Journal
Twin-City Herald (Minneapolis, MN)
Washington Times
Waterbury Democrat
White Bluffs Spokesman (WA)
Wilmington Morning Star (NC)
Wolf Point Herald (MT)
Wrangell Sentinel (AK)
York Dispatch (PA)

Organizations—Research

AAIB, Inc.
Associated Press
Bureau of Labor Statistics' Consumer Price Index (CPI)
Connecticut Boxing Hall of Fame
International Boxing Hall of Fame
International Boxing Research Organization: IBRO
The Smithsonian Institution
United Press International
United States Census Bureau

Index

Numbers in *bold italics* indicate pages with illustrations